CASEBOOK ON SHIPPING LAW

E. R. Hardy Ivamy, LL.B., Ph.D., LL.D.

Of the Middle Temple, Barrister
Emeritus Professor of Law in the University of London

FOURTH EDITION

LLP

LONDON NEW YORK HAMBURG HONG KONG
LLOYD'S OF LONDON PRESS LTD
1987

Lloyd's of London Press Ltd
Legal Publishing and Conference Division
26–30 Artillery Lane, London E1 7LX

USA AND CANADA
Lloyd's of London Press Inc
Suite 523, 611 Broadway
New York, NY 10012, USA

GERMANY
Lloyd's of London Press
PO Box 11 23 47
Deichstrasse 41, 2000 Hamburg 11
West Germany

SOUTH EAST ASIA
Lloyd's of London Press (Far East) Ltd
903 Chung Nam Building
1 Lockhart Road, Wanchai
Hong Kong

First published 1970
Second edition 1978 Third edition 1982
Fourth edition 1987

British Library Cataloguing in Publication Data

Ivamy, E.R. Hardy
Casebook on shipping law—4th ed.
1. Maritime law—Great Britain—Cases
I. Title
344.103'968 KD 1816.3

ISBN 1-85044-130-8

Text set in 9/11 pt Linotron 202 Times by
Wessex Typesetters, Frome, Somerset
Printed in Great Britain by
LR Printing Services Ltd
Crawley, West Sussex

PREFACE

The purpose of this new edition remains the same as that of earlier ones, i.e. to set out in a convenient form the leading and important cases relating to shipping law. At the head of each case there is a short statement of the principle involved. This is followed by a summary of the facts, the decision given, and extracts from one or more of the judgments delivered.

In Part II ("Carriage of Goods by Sea") *Kodros Shipping Corporation* v. *Empresa Cubana de Fletes: The "Evia" (No. 2)* [1982] 2 Lloyd's Rep. 307, H.L., decides that where a time charter-party requires the vessel to use safe ports only, the port, at the moment when the order to go there is given, must be prospectively safe. *Afovos Shipping Co. S.A.* v. *R. Pagnan and F. Lli: The "Afovos"* [1983] 1 Lloyd's Rep. 335, H.L. decides that the latest point of time which constitutes punctual payment of an instalment of hire is midnight of the day in question. It was emphasised in *Scandinavian Trading Tanker Co. AB* v. *Flota Petrolera Ecuatoriana: The "Scaptrade"* [1983] 2 Lloyd's Rep. 253, H.L., that the Court has no jurisdiction to grant relief to the charterer against the exercise by a shipowner of his contractual right under the withdrawal clause to withdraw the vessel where an instalment of hire is not paid by the due date. In *Mitsui O.S.K. Lines Ltd.* v. *Garnac Grian Co. Inc.: The "Myrtos"* [1984] 2 Lloyd's Rep. 449 it was held that a clause stating the estimated time of arrival of a vessel was a condition.

Also in Part II are some new cases on the Hague Rules. *Mayhew Foods Ltd.* v. *Overseas Containers Ltd.* [1984] 1 Lloyd's Rep. 317 indicates that the Rules do not apply to carriage or storage of goods before they are shipped. A clause enabling the carrier to limit his liability below the level permitted by the Rules where they apply is void: *The "Morviken"* [1983] 1 Lloyd's Rep. 1, H.L. *Empresa Cubana Importada de Alimentos "Alimport"* v. *Iasmos Shipping Co. S.A.: The "Good Friend"* [1984] 2 Lloyd's Rep. 566 is the latest authority on the burden of proof being on the carrier claiming exemption under Article IV, r. 1, to show that he had exercised due diligence to make the ship seaworthy. Under the Rules the ship is entitled to make any reasonable deviation: *Danae Shipping Corporation* v. *T.P.A.O. and Guven Turkish Insurance Co. Ltd.* [1983] 1 Lloyd's Rep. 498.

In Part III ("Collisions") all the decisions on limitation of liability hitherto included have been deleted in view of the changes in the law made by the

Merchant Shipping Act 1979, which has repealed the relevant sections of the Merchant Shipping Act 1894.

In Part V ("Marine Insurance") in the case of *Container Transport International Inc.* v. *Oceanus Mutual Underwriting Association (Bermuda) Ltd.* [1984] 1 Lloyd's Rep. 476, C.A., the word "judgment" in the Marine Insurance Act 1906, s. 18(2) (which states: "Every circumstance is material which would influence the judgment of a prudent insurer in fixing the premium or determining whether he will take the risk") is used in the sense of "the formation of an opinion". *Rhesa Shipping Co. S.A.* v. *Edmunds: The "Popi M"* [1985] 2 Lloyd's Rep. 1, H.L., is an illustration of the principle that the burden of proving a loss by a peril of the sea lies on the assured. *Athens Maritime Enterprises Corporation* v. *Hellenic Mutual War Risks Association (Bermuda) Ltd.: The "Andros Lemos"* [1983] 1 All E.R. 590 holds that "piracy" means "theft at sea involving force or threat of force", and that it may be committed inside territorial waters.

To Part VII ("Admiralty Jurisdiction and Practice") *The "Goring"* [1986] 1 Lloyd's Rep. 129 has been added. It was there laid down that the Court has jurisdiction under the Supreme Court Act 1981, s. 20(2)(*j*), even though a salvage operation takes place in non-tidal waters.

I am grateful to *Lloyd's Law Reports* and to Butterworth & Co. (Publishers) Ltd. (the publishers of *The All England Law Reports*) for giving me permission to use extracts from the judgments in the reports concerned.

I should like to thank Mr E. Martin and Miss Catherine Anderson, both of the Legal Publishing and Conference Division of Lloyd's of London Press Ltd., for seeing the book through the press.

May 1987 E. R. HARDY IVAMY

TABLE OF CONTENTS

PAGE

PART II—CARRIAGE OF GOODS BY SEA

TABLE OF CASES

Cases which are set out in this book are indicated by page numbers in bold type

TABLE OF STATUTES

PART I

SALE, MORTGAGE AND LIEN

A. SALE OF A SHIP[1]

McDougall *v.* Aeromarine of Emsworth Ltd.

[1958] 3 All E.R. 431

By s. 10(1) of the Sale of Goods Act 1979: "Unless a different intention appears from the terms of the contract, stipulations as to time of payment are not of the essence of a contract of sale." Section 10(2) states: "Whether any other stipulation as to time is or is not of the essence of the contract depends on the terms of the contract."

A firm of yacht builders agreed to supply a pleasure yacht according to a certain specification. Delivery was to be made on May 1, 1957, but cl. 3 in the contract stated that "owing to the effect of delays and shortages such delivery date cannot be guaranteed". The yacht was not delivered on that date, and on Sept. 19, 1957, the buyer repudiated the contract since delivery had still not been made, and four-fifths of the yachting season was over by the beginning of September.

Held, by the Queen's Bench Division, that he was entitled to do so, for the time of delivery was of the essence of the contract, and the sellers had not delivered within a reasonable time after May 1, which, in the circumstances, had expired by the beginning of September.

DIPLOCK, J. (at page 438)

In my opinion, in the circumstances of the present case, which relates to the sale of a pleasure yacht built in accordance with the buyer's special requirements, for use by him in the 1957 yachting season, and where delays in completion after June 3, 1957, were due solely to the prior bad workmanship or the prior incorporation of defective materials by the [sellers], a reasonable time had certainly expired by the beginning of September, 1957, that is three months after June 3, and at a time when four-fifths of the 1957 yachting season had passed. Whether this stipulation as to time of delivery is a condition or a warranty depends, under s. 10 of the Sale of Goods Act . . . , on the terms of

---

[1] The cases in this Section were decided under the Sale of Goods Act 1893, which has now been replaced by the Sale of Goods Act 1979.

the contract. In my view, the obligation to deliver within a reasonable time of May 1, 1957, is a condition. It was conceded by Counsel for the [sellers] that this was so as a general rule in mercantile transactions, but he contended that it did not apply to the sale of a vessel for use by the purchaser solely for his own pleasure, not for commercial use or for re-sale. I am not impressed by this argument. Where a purchaser buys a yacht for use for his own pleasure from the beginning of a particular yachting season, I think that it must, as a matter of common sense, be of the essence of the contract that he should receive delivery in time to make substantial use of it during that season. It may be that he expects to use it also in subsequent seasons, but he cannot foretell whether he will be able to do so, and in any event it will have deteriorated in some degree by the time the next season comes round.

Sir James Laing & Sons Ltd. *v.* Barclay, Curle & Co. Ltd.

(1908) 97 L.T. 816

By s. 17(1) of the Sale of Goods Act 1979: "Where there is a contract for the sale of specific or ascertained goods, the property in them is transferred to the buyer at such time as the parties to the contract intend it to be transferred."

B. Ltd. were owed money by an Italian company for whom L. Ltd. were building a ship. By the terms of the contract between L. Ltd. and the Italian company it was provided that (i) she should be ready completed by a certain date; (ii) on completion of the vessel L. Ltd. were to hand to the Italian company certain certificates; and (iii) the price of the vessel was payable in cash instalments at various stages of construction, i.e., when plated, when launched, when handed over after trials and six months after delivery. B. Ltd. arrested the vessel while she was on the stocks in L. Ltd's yard, and a question arose as to whether the property in her had passed to the Italian company.

Held, by the House of Lords, that the contract was for a completed ship and that the parties did not intend that the property in her should pass until she was completed and delivered.

THE EARL OF HALSBURY (at page 818)

A contract might no doubt have been framed which would have given to the purchasers the property in the parts of the ship as they were successively finished; but that is not the case here. I also have misgivings with respect to the use of the word "presumption" in connection with a contract the language of which has to be construed. What your Lordships have to do is to interpret the contract as it is brought before you, and it appears to me to be a contract for a completed ship.

LORD ROBERTSON (at page 818)

The question in the present appeal seems to me to be governed by the Sale of Goods Act . . . , and by that statute to be determinable by the intention of the instrument under which the ship was built. In aid and supplement of construction the statute supplies certain rules, but these rules may or may not come into operation according as the contract requires it. In the present case I find the contract to require no aid or supplement from the statutory rules, for it seems to me to provide from the beginning for the completion of this ship by the shipbuilders with their materials, and transfers it to the purchasers only as a finished ship, and at a stage not yet reached.

Re Blyth Shipbuilding and Dry Dock Co. Ltd.: Forster *v.* Blyth Shipbuilding and Dry Dock Co. Ltd.

[1926] All E.R. Rep. 373

By s. 18, r. 5(1) of the Sale of Goods Act 1979: "Where there is a contract for the sale of unascertained or future goods by description, and goods of that description and in a deliverable state are unconditionally appropriated to the contract, either by the seller with the assent of the buyer, or by the buyer with the assent of the seller, the property in the goods then passes to the buyer . . ." Whether there has been such an unconditional appropriation depends on the circumstances.

In 1924 the Blyth Shipbuilding and Dry Dock Co. Ltd. agreed to build a vessel for an Italian company. Clause 6 of the contract stated that:— "From and after the payment to the builders of the first instalment on account of the purchase price the vessel and all materials and things appropriated to her shall . . . become . . . the absolute property of the purchasers". Construction continued until debenture holders appointed a receiver of the undertaking of the builders. At that date the vessel had been partly constructed and two instalments of the purchase price had been paid. Certain worked material, which was ready to be incorporated into the hull of the vessel, had been brought into the builders' yard. This material had been approved by the buyers' surveyor. There was also unworked material in the yard which he had not approved. A question as to whether the worked and/or the unworked material was the property of the buyers.

Held, by the Court of Appeal, that the property in neither type of material had passed to the buyers, for neither had become so inextricably a part of the vessel as to be "appropriated to her" within the clause set out above.

POLLOCK, M.R. (at page 377)

I do not desire to go over the same ground again, but it is pointed out that in s. 18, r. 5(1), for the purpose of ascertaining when the property passes the goods must be "unconditionally appropriated to the contract". If any test is to be derived from the Sale of Goods Act, I do not think that that word "unconditionally" ought to be overlooked. What is meant by "appropriated" in this connection? Does it mean that once some goods have been brought on the site definitely to be used in the vessel, no others can be substituted for them—that if those particular goods were damaged or injured or found for some other reason unsuitable, no change could be made except at increased cost to the purchaser of the vessel? Does it mean that those goods and those goods only are to be used, and in respect of them, if any misfortune happens, it falls upon the shoulders of the purchaser? Unless such is found to be the case, it does not appear that it would be right to say that the materials and things had been unconditionally appropriated. More than that, it would appear from an examination of the Sale of Goods Act that there must be an assent to the appropriation. The appropriation offered by the builder must be assented to for or on behalf of the purchaser of the vessel, and it appears to me that you cannot accept the passing of these materials and things by the surveyor appointed by the purchaser of the vessel as being an acceptance of the appropriation for the purposes of this contract. It seems to me that the materials and things must be appropriated in a much closer and more complete sense than by mere acceptance by the surveyor or by having been made in such a manner as that they could be fitted upon the vessel. I come ultimately to the conclusion after examining the cases that the words in question mean materials which have been fitted into the vessel, or, if they have not been completely fixed in the vessel, are substantially *in situ*, so that the removal of them would involve a going back upon the work to be done upon the vessel. It seems to me that we are to read the word "appropriated" in that sense. I have, therefore, come to the conclusion that these worked materials, although worked up and suitable for placing into the vessel at the appropriate time, and accepted, it may be, by the surveyor, have not yet taken their place and become so inextricably a part of the vessel as to have satisfied the meaning of the word "appropriated".

The "Bineta"

[1966] 2 Lloyd's Rep. 419

By s. 48(2) of the Sale of Goods Act 1979: "Where an unpaid seller who has exercised his right of lien . . . re-sells the goods, the buyer acquires a good title to them as against the original buyer."

A yacht was sold by a Miss Simmonds to a Mr Garthwaite in June, 1963, and the vessel was registered in his name. He defaulted in the payment of the purchase price, and she retained possession of the yacht in exercise of her unpaid seller's lien. In March, 1965, she sold her to a Mr Dalby. Mr Dalby sought a declaration that he was the owner of the yacht and was entitled to be registered as such in place of Mr Garthwaite under the Merchant Shipping Act 1894 because Miss Simmonds could vest a good title in him under s. 48(2) of the Sale of Goods Act.

Held, by the Probate, Divorce and Admiralty Division, that the declaration would be made accordingly.

BRANDON, J. (at page 420)

I consider that Miss Simmonds had power to re-sell the ship under the Sale of Goods Act. . . . The plaintiff acquired a good title from the bill of sale which she gave him. He is, therefore, the owner of the ship and is entitled to be registered as such under the Merchant Shipping Act 1894.

Behnke *v.* Bede Shipping Co. Ltd.

[1927] All E.R. Rep. 689

By s. 52 of the Sale of Goods Act 1979: "In any action for breach of contract to deliver specific or ascertained goods the Court may, if it thinks fit, on the plaintiff's application, by its judgment direct . . . that the contract shall be performed specifically, without giving the defendant the option of retaining the goods on payment of damages."

The seller had agreed to sell the *City*, which was of peculiar and practically unique value to the buyer. The seller refused to deliver her, so the buyer applied to the Court for a decree of specific performance of the contract.

Held, by the King's Bench Division, that damages were an inadequate remedy and a decree of specific performance would be ordered.

WRIGHT, J. (at page 690)

The plaintiff claims a decree of specific performance; this claim is strongly contested on behalf of the defendants. It is curious how little guidance there is on the question whether specific performance should be granted of a contract for the sale of a ship. Section 52 of the Sale of Goods Act gives the Court a discretion, if it thinks fit, in any action for breach of contract to deliver specific or ascertained goods, to direct that the contract shall be performed specifically. I think a ship is a specific chattel within the Act. . . . In the present case there is evidence that the *City* was of peculiar and practically unique value to the plaintiff. She was a cheap vessel, being old, built in 1892, but her engines and boilers were practically new, and such as to satisfy the German regulation, and hence the plaintiff could, as a German shipowner, have her at once put on the German register. A very experienced ship valuer has said that he knew of only one other comparable ship, but that may now be sold. The plaintiff wants the ship for immediate use, and I do not think damages would be an adequate compensation. I think he is entitled to the ship and a decree of specific performance in order that justice may be done.

Kelman *v.* Livanos

[1955] 2 All E.R. 236

A clause stating that a vessel is to be delivered "free from average" means "free from claims against her".

A vessel was sold under a contract which stated in cl. 4 that she should be delivered "free from average". Clause 6 in the contract provided that the sellers agreed to place her in dry dock for inspection by Lloyd's surveyors and "in the event of the bottom or any outside part of her below the water line being found broken or damaged, and [buyer] decline to accept her in such state, it shall be repaired and put in good and seaworthy condition to the satisfaction of the surveyor . . . at the [sellers'] expense". The surveyor found that there were indents in the keel and shell plates, but that the ship could maintain her classification even though they were not repaired. The buyer refused to accept the vessel until they had been repaired on the ground that delivery "free from average" meant "free from damage".

Held, by the Queen's Bench Division, that the words meant "free from claims against the vessel".

McNair, J. (at page 240)

I would prefer to take the view that, inasmuch as cl. 6 deals with the bottom damage and underwater damage, and inasmuch as another clause of the contract gives the purchaser a right to inspect, the words "free from average", in cl. 4, relate not to physical damage at all but to the freedom from claims against the ship, of whatsoever nature.

It is clearly of importance to the prospective purchaser that he should know (whether under English law or under some foreign system of law) whether there may be claims against a ship, or extra charges, which Sir Mackenzie Chalmers says, in the passage I have read, is the meaning of these words in ordinary shipping law. If I give that construction, it seems to me that I avoid any conflict at all between cl. 1, which contains the obligation that the vessel shall be seaworthy, and cl. 6, which deals with damage to the bottom. If, on the other hand, one takes the view that "free from average", in cl. 4, means "free from physical damage to the ship", one gets a most awkward conflict between cl. 1 and cl. 6 in relation to cl. 4. Applying what I conceive to be the right method of construction, namely, to adopt a construction which does not involve conflict with other provisions of the document, and taking the view that there is a reasonable and accepted meaning of the phrase "free from average" which does not connote damage, I take the view, as a matter of construction, that, in this context, "free from average" does not mean "free from damage to the ship", but does mean "free from claims against the ship".

It is quite true that that view involves, or may in certain circumstances involve, some surplusage in the contract, because there is, in cl. 13, a provision, "The [sellers] agree to deliver the steamer to the [buyer] free from all debts and encumbrances", but there may well be claims against a ship, either in

English law or in foreign law, which are not debts or encumbrances, from which a prospective purchaser would wish to be guaranteed that the ship is free.

Piccinini *v*. Partrederiet Trigon II: The "Alfred Trigon"

[1981] 2 Lloyd's Rep. 333

Where a vessel is sold "free of average damage affecting class", this means "free of damage occasioned by a peril ordinarily covered by insurance as opposed to defects through wear and tear or general old age".

The vessel *Alfred Trigon* was sold under a contract stating in cl. 21: "The vessel to be delivered with class maintained free of recommendations and free of average damage affecting class". On delivery of the vessel it was found that there were certain leakages from the tank tops. The buyers claimed damages from the sellers on the ground that they were in breach of cl. 21.

Held, by the Queen's Bench Division (Commercial Court), that the words "average damage affecting class" meant damage occasioned by a peril ordinarily covered by insurance as opposed to defects arising through wear and tear or general old age. The case would be remitted to the arbitrators for them to find the cause of the defects in the tank tops.

ROBERT GOFF, J. (at page 336)

Once the conclusion is reached that the clause concerns the words "The vessel to be delivered free of average damage affecting class", then it is necessary to face up to the question: what is meant by the words "average damage"? There is, I think, no doubt what is meant by the words "affecting class". Those are words which reflect other provisions in the contract, (in particular cll. 6 and 17, which I have already referred to) and really mean, quite simply, damage of such a character as either to prevent the vessel being in class or to result in the surveyor, on his becoming aware of the damage, imposing some qualification on class in the way of a recommendation. In that sense the damage would, of course, affect the vessel's class. But the question arises: what is meant by "average damage"? The two rival contentions were these. [Counsel for the sellers] said that effect must be given to the word "average". You cannot just treat it as meaning, as the arbitrators have done, "any damage" because to do so would be really to put a line through the word "average" and treat it as surplusage in this case. Therefore, he said, meaning must be given to the word "average" on the basis really of the general presumption against surplusage. [Counsel for the sellers] referred me to *Compania de Navegacion Pohing S.A.* v. *Sea Tanker Shipping (Pte.) Ltd.: The "Buena Trader"*,[2] which was concerned with a similar but not identical clause in a sale contract, including the words

[2] [1978] 2 Lloyd's Rep. 325, C.A.

"free of recommendation/average damage affecting class". He adopted the concession that was made by the buyers in that case to the effect that, in the context of that particular case, the words "average damage" meant: ". . . damage occasioned by a peril covered by insurance as opposed to defects arising through wear and tear or general old age."[3]

[Counsel for the buyers], on the other hand, sought to support the conclusion of the arbitrators in this case and he said that really one was driven to conclude that either the words "average" and "damage" meant the same thing, in which case they are repetitious, or, alternatively, in truth, the word "average" really only meant "damage" on the ordinary meaning of that word and in the circumstances it was surplusage and added nothing to the word damage. He said that that is because the buyer is only concerned with the question whether or not the damage does affect class; and so the words "affecting class" are the governing words and the whole purpose of cl. 21 is to ensure that the buyer shall receive a ship which not only is in class but suffers from no damage which, if discovered, could affect her class. That was the criterion, and in those circumstances to cut down the words "damage affecting class", in the manner suggested by [Counsel for the sellers], would go against the purpose of the clause and undermine the protection which the clause was intended to give to the buyer.

[Counsel for the buyers] said that that is all very well in the context of marine insurance; but here we are concerned with a sale contract for a ship, and why, he asked, should one import a meaning which is used in the context of marine insurance when one is concerned with the sale of a ship? To my mind, the answer to that question is, that the effect of limiting the responsibility of the seller, after an inspection (both superficial and detailed underwater inspection) has taken place and after delivery, to cases of average damage affecting class is that at least in those cases the seller has given the buyer the opportunity of inspection, and having done so then restricts his responsibility for defects to those defects in respect of which, in ordinary circumstances, he would have a claim on his own insurers. Now if that is right, it certainly makes sound sense of the qualification placed on the word "damage" by the word "average". So having reached the point that *prima facie*, on the ordinary rules of construction, some force should be given to the word "average", so that it should not be treated as surplusage, I find that there is a rational meaning which can be given to that word in accordance with the concession made by Counsel in *The Buena Trader* case. I think that when [Counsel] in that case referred to "average damage" as meaning "damage occasioned by a peril covered by insurance", he was not concentrating on any particular policy of insurance, but, as [Counsel for the sellers] put it, was referring to damage ordinarily covered by insurance. Defects arising through wear and tear or

---

[3] *Ibid.*, at p. 329.

general old age are, by virtue of s. 55 of the [Marine Insurance Act 1906], not ordinarily covered by a policy of insurance.

So I come to the conclusion that on the principles of construction the meaning of "average damage affecting class" is not just any damage affecting class. It is damage affecting class of a certain kind, and means damage occasioned by a peril ordinarily covered by insurance as opposed to defects arising through wear and tear or general old age.

It is right to say that had it been intended that the seller should remain responsible for *any* damage affecting class at time of delivery, that result could have been achieved in many other ways by very simple words, for example "free of any defect affecting class". Of course, if such a word as "defect" was used instead of "damage", then it would be made plain that what was being legislated for was not damage in the sense of physical damage but a defect in the wider sense, including deterioration. It may be that the word "damage" is not, in the ordinary sense of the word, apt to include deterioration; but I do not myself rely upon that fact because I observe that in, for example, cl. 17 the word "damage" is being used in a context which may well have been intended to include deterioration. I rely simply upon the fact that I consider that, *prima facie*, a meaning ought to be given to the word "average", and I am satisfied that a sensible meaning can be given to it by adopting the concession in *The Buena Trader* case.

Diamante Sociedad de Transportes S.A. *v.* Todd Oil Burners Ltd.: The "Diamantis Pateras"

[1966] 1 Lloyd's Rep. 179

A manufacturer of ship's equipment supplied to a vessel may be held guilty of the tort of negligence if the equipment is defective and causes damage.

The plaintiffs ordered a vessel from a firm of shipbuilders, and specified that certain oil burning equipment manufactured by the defendants should be installed in her. After she had been at sea for about a year fractures in the furnaces of her boilers were discovered. The plaintiffs claimed damages from the defendants on the ground that the damage was caused by the faulty design of the equipment.

Held, by the Queen's Bench Division, that the defendants owed a duty of care to the plaintiffs, but the action failed because the damage was due to the bad operation of the boilers by the engine-room staff.

LAWRENCE, J. (at page 187)

Plainly in this present case the plaintiffs must have been reasonably in the contemplation of the defendants when the defendants were complying with the order from the shipbuilders; and, indeed, this fact was admitted by the managing director of the defendants when he gave his evidence.

It was, however, contended by [Counsel], for the defendants, that there was in this case an escape for the defendants offered by the decision in *Donoghue* v. *Stevenson*,[4] on the ground of "reasonable opportunity of intermediate examination". I do not find myself able to uphold this contention in the light of modern authorities of which the case of *Clay* v. *A. J. Crump & Sons Ltd.*[5] is one, a case to which I was referred by [Counsel] for the plaintiffs. A consideration of modern authorities leads me to the conclusion that the opportunity of intermediate examination is a matter which goes now rather to the question of causation than to the issue of whether or not a duty of care is imposed on the defendants. In any event, on the facts of this case, it was the defendants who had an opportunity for such examination and adjustment of burners; and although the plaintiffs also may be said to have had an equal opportunity thereafter, I think it is reasonable that the plaintiffs' superintendent, Mr Robertson, and the chief engineer should have relied on the adjustments and assurances of the representatives of the defendants. In short, I hold that the defendants did in the circumstances of this case owe a duty of care to the plaintiffs, and, subject to the facts, the action is well founded.

They had not altered their equipment for years; they had experience of it over and over again, and by 1953 they received a specific order for specific equipment. It is not suggested that there was anything wrong in the particular set of apparatus which they supplied, but that its design was defective. Was it doing something which a reasonable prudent man would not have done for these defendants to supply their standard equipment and design in those circumstances? To put the matter in another way, ought they reasonably to have foreseen the degree of slackness and mismanagement that I have found to exist on this ship? Ought they reasonably to have foreseen that the boilers would be allowed to get dirty, and oil scale, and so on, to be allowed to form?

I do not think so. I think they were entitled to assume that the certificated chief engineer would be an expert and would not allow slackness to approach anything like the danger limit.

B. MORTGAGE OF A SHIP

Fletcher and Campbell *v*. City Marine Finance Ltd.

[1968] 2 Lloyd's Rep. 520

Where a mortgagor of a vessel is wrongfully prevented by the mortgagee from exercising his right to redeem the morgage, the mortgagor is entitled to claim damages.

---

[4] [1932] All E.R. Rep. 1.
[5] [1964] 1 Q.B. 533.

On May 12, 1966, Fletcher mortgaged a vessel, of which Campbell was the owner, to a finance company as security for a loan. Monthly instalments of the sums due under the mortgage were punctually repaid until April, 1967, when Fletcher defaulted. On Apr. 25 the company wrote to him stating that they were taking possession of the vessel, and that she would only be released on payment of the outstanding balance. On May 1, Campbell, acting as Fletcher's agent, tendered to the company sufficient money to pay off the debt. The company refused to accept the tender, and sold the vessel to a third party. Fletcher claimed damages from the company on the ground that it was an implied term of the mortgage that the company would permit him to pay off any sums due in order to redeem it.

Held, by the Queen's Bench Division, that the claim succeeded, for the mortgagor had a right to recover damages from the mortgagee, since his right to redeem was prevented by the wrongful action of the mortgagee.

ROSKILL, J. (at page 538)

There is, as a matter of English law, a right in the mortgagor of a ship to recover damages against his mortgagee, if his right to redeem is prevented by the wrongful act of the mortgagee. I do not think it matters whether one makes the necessary implication into the collateral deed as a matter of law or whether one makes the implication therein as arising from the other express terms of the deed or whether one arrives at the same result by the application of basic principles of equity. Basically, as I have already said, the ordinary principles of the law relating to mortgages and their redemption apply and, as I read the cases, have always been applied to mortgages of ships during the 19th century. It is true that the right to damages in the case of a comparable breach in relation to the mortgages of land is now statutory but that, with all respect to [Counsel's] argument to the contrary, does not seem to me to advance the matter further. It would be strange if a mortgagor's only remedy in these circumstances were to bring a redemption action if he could do so timeously, particularly having regard to the system of registration of title now prescribed for ships by statute. It would obviously be difficult to deprive a *bona fide* purchaser for value of his title to a ship which he had already registered, even though he had acquired that title through default on the part of the mortgagee in the manner in which the latter had exercised his power of sale.

It seems to me, therefore, right, in these circumstances, to make the implication sought by the plaintiffs, and I hold that the defendants wrongly prevented the plaintiffs from exercising their right to redeem and must answer for that in damages.

The "Basildon"

[1967] 2 Lloyd's Rep. 134

Where a mortgagee does not take possession of a mortgaged vessel and insures her, he is not entitled to add the insurance premium to the mortgage debt unless there is an express clause in the mortgage deed empowering him to do so.

The plaintiffs were mortgagees of the *Basildon* under two mortgages, and commenced an action against her in respect of money due under them. The first mortgage did not empower them to pay insurance premiums and add them to the mortgage debt. But the second mortgage expressly gave them such a power. A question arose as to whether they had an implied right under the first mortgage to do so.

Held, by the Probate, Divorce and Admiralty Division, that they had no such right, and that, where a mortgagee did not take possession, he was not entitled to pay the insurance premiums and add them to the mortgage debt.

BRANDON, J. (at page 136)

It seems to me that if a mortgagee did take possession in such circumstances, and properly took possession, he could then insure the ship and charge the insurance together with other outgoings against any freight which he received. But I am not satisfied that where the mortgagee does not take possession, he is entitled to pay insurance premiums and add them to the mortgage debt. That is sufficient to decide the point of principle raised. I think I ought to add this. If I had taken a different view, that there was an implied right under the first mortgage to make insurance payments and add them to the mortgage debt as well as an express right under the second mortgage, I should not be satisfied on the evidence that the payment had been made under the powers conferred by the first rather than the powers conferred by the second mortgage. There is no evidence in the affidavits before me to prove this. [Counsel] relied on the fact that in the statement of claim there is a claim that the plaintiffs are entitled to recover these payments under the first mortgage and he argues that I ought, therefore, to infer that any payments made after the statement of claim were made under the first mortgage. I am not satisfied that that would be a reasonable inference. In any case, no such inference is capable of being drawn in regard to the bulk of the payments which were made earlier.

For these reasons I decide that the insurance payments are in principle recoverable under the second mortgage and not under the first.

C. LIEN

The "Ripon City"

(1897) 77 L.T. 98

A maritime lien is a privileged claim upon a thing in respect of service done to it or injury caused by it.

BARNES, J. (at page 104)

That maritime liens arise in certain well-known classes of claims is now firmly established. The principles of maritime law in relation thereto have been developed to a large extent from certain principles of the civil law (see the learned judgment of CURTIS, J., in *The Young Mechanic*, 2 Curtis, Reports of Cases in the Circuit Courts of the United States, p. 404). So far as I can trace the origin of the modern doctrines on the subject of maritime liens, it is not difficult to follow this development in cases arising out of contractual relations between the parties. But it is otherwise in cases of injuries done by vessels and there is a diversity of opinion as to the source from which the notion of a lien for the amount of damage done is derived. In his interesting and excellent work on the Common Law, O. W. HOLMES, J., of Boston, finds this source in the ancient law of deodand, and considers that it is only by supposing the ship to have been treated as if endowed with personality that the seeming arbitrary peculiarities of the maritime law can be made intelligible (see pp. 25–27, Edn. of 1882). Mr Marsden, in his recent work on "Collisions at Sea", on the other hand, prefers the theory that the present law of maritime lien for damage has sprung from the Admiralty practice of arrest to compel appearance and security (see p. 76, 3rd Edn.). This practice was similar to that which appears to have prevailed on the Continent of Europe (*Ib.*, p. 79), and may have been deduced from, or suggested by, Roman procedure (see Ortolan's *Institutes of Justinian*, 8th Edn., 1870, p. 586, s. 2034; 12th Edn., 1883, p. 586). If the former view be correct, it would seem to be immaterial in a case of collision caused by the negligence of persons on board a vessel to inquire whether or not they were the servants of the owners or of persons in possession; but if the other theory is adopted, the position is not quite the same. The exhaustive judgment of the President, Sir FRANCIS JEUNE, in *The Dictator*[6] favours the latter view. He investigates the Admiralty rules on this subject, as it had been treated for the last two centuries. He states that the Admiralty Court did not in early times treat the action *in rem* as a specific and distinct form of action, and explains how the process of the Court was carried into effect by the arrest of the person or any property of the defendant to compel him to appear and put in bail; how actions beginning with arrest of the person became obsolete in the last century, and arrest of property to enforce appearance and security became rare and obsolete; how, in later times, the arrest of property over which a lien could be enforced became more common as the idea of a pre-existing maritime lien developed, and arrest of property in order to assert for the creditor a legal *nexus* over the proprietary interest of his debtor; and how, if the owners do not appear, the judgment should be limited to the *res* in the hands of the Court, but if they appear, they are in the same position as if they had been brought before the Court by personal notice. In that case he allowed execution to issue against owners who had appeared in an action *in rem* to recover the amount by which a decree exceeded the amount of the bail in the case. Again, Lord ESHER, in that part of his judgment in the case of *The Parlement Belge*[7] from which the passage above quoted is taken, also expounds the nature of the

[6] [1892] P. 304.
[7] [1874–80] All E.R. Rep. 104, C.A.

process and how the owners are indirectly impleaded to answer the judgment of the Court. But whatever may have been the origin and process of development of a maritime lien for damage, there is no doubt that the doctrine of such a lien is now established, and the right to enforce it is different from the ancient right of arrest to compel appearance and security in this, that it is confined to the property by means of which the damage is caused, and may be enforced against the property in the hands of an innocent purchaser. I believe that the earliest English authority which distinctly establishes this doctrine is *The Bold Buccleugh*,[8] where it was held by the Privy Council that in cases of collision a maritime lien for damage arises and may be enforced against the vessel which was in fault, and that such lien travels with the vessel into whosoever possession she may come, and when carried into effect by a proceeding *in rem*, relates back to the period when it first attached. *The Bold Buccleugh* was approved by the House of Lords in *Currie* v. *McKnight*[9] where the learned Lords considered the judgment of the Judicial Committee satisfactory in its reasoning, and that it was not only consistent with the principles of general maritime law, but rested upon plain considerations of commercial expediency (see *per* LORD WATSON). The definition of a maritime lien as recognised by the law maritime given by LORD TENTERDEN has thus been adopted. It is a privileged claim upon a thing in respect of service done to it or injury caused by it, to be carried into effect by legal process.

The "Stream Fisher"

(1926) 26 Ll.L.Rep. 4

Where there are several claimants in respect of maritime liens arising "ex delicto" (i.e., as a result of damage done by the vessel), they rank pari passu *with each other unless one of the claimants gets judgment in respect of a claim. In this case he will have priority.*

The *Stream Fisher* collided in succession with the *Squawk*, the *Criterion*, the *Enable*, and the *Rio Leopold*, and damaged them. The *Stream Fisher* was sold but the proceeds of sale were insufficient to meet the claims of the four damaged vessels.

Held, by the Probate, Divorce and Admiralty Division, that since none of the claimants had obtained judgment in respect of the collision, all the claimants ranked *pari passu*.

BATESON, J. (at page 8)

The result as to priority of lien seems to be this. First of all you could get priority if you obtained judgment first. Secondly, you could get priority by

---

[8] (1852) 7 Moo. P.C.C. 267.
[9] [1897] A.C. 97.

later lien, as in salvage and bottomry; and thirdly, there were the cases where they rank *pari passu*.

Now the first of those is not contended for here at all, probably because all judgments are now given subject to the question of priority being determined hereafter. In the second case of priority in inverse order—that is, by the later lien—I see no reason to apply this except possibly as to the *Squawk* case, owing to the delay; because the master of the *Squawk* could quite well have put forward his case at the same time as his owners put forward their case, and either have got bail or have got paid. But, the other three collisions all happening within a very short time of each other—in one case only a few hours, and in the other case only a few days—I do not think it would be equitable or fair to give any priority for such as that. With regard to the *Squawk* case, if I had to decide whether there were laches or not, I should want to have all the facts before me. So far as the facts in this case are concerned, if anybody had to be postponed, certainly a man who waited such a long time as the master of the *Squawk* would have to be postponed, because he had an option whether he should allow the ship to go free of his claim, or for some considerable time. The other people had no option. . . . On the whole, I have come to the conclusion that *pari passu* is the right method of dealing with these different claims.

The "Veritas"

[1900–3] All E.R. Rep. 501

A maritime lien for salvage services previously rendered is postponed to a maritime lien for collision damage.

A vessel was in distress outside the River Mersey. Salvage services were rendered to her, and she was towed into port where she collided with a landing stage belonging to the Mersey Docks and Harbour Board. The vessel was sold, and the proceeds of sale were insufficient to meet the claims of the salvors and of the Board.

Held, by the Probate, Divorce and Admiralty Division, that the claim of the Board had priority, for the salvors took the risk of subsequent claims attaching.

GORELL BARNES, J. (at page 508)

Salvage is not governed merely by a regard to benefit received, but also, on grounds of public policy, by a due regard to the interests of commerce and humanity. At the same time the right to proceed against the *res* is to obtain payment of the reward given for services rendered, and the salvors have had the option of rendering their services, and in deciding to render them are in a position to consider the risks they may run in recovering their award, and whether or not it is advisable to render the services. From the time of rendering the services they are practically in the same relative position as a creditor who has obtained a lien strictly *ex contractu*, and while taking precedence over prior claims *ex contractu* and prior salvage, in my opinion, the considerations I have referred to show that their claims should be postponed to subsequent damage claims; and, in my judgment, it is in the best interests of careful navigation that this should be so.

I can see no satisfactory ground on which the claims of an injured party should be postponed to the claim of one who seeks to obtain a benefit for prior services rendered to what is in the Court commonly spoken of as the "wrong-doing" vessel. Such principle as can be applied and general considerations are, in my judgment, the other way, and even if the damage in this case did not give rise to a maritime lien, but only to a right to proceed *in rem*, it seems to me that the latter right should be enforceable in priority to the salvage claims. For all practical purposes in a case where the damage comes last the position of the injured party, so far as regards claims arising prior to the damage, is much the same, whether he has a lien or only a right of process. I may sum up these remarks thus: There is a right to arrest a ship to obtain reparation for damage done by her which is not affected by prior claims against her arising from hypothecation which creates interests in her along with those of her owners. This right was no doubt enforced by the High Court of Admiralty before the doctrine was entertained in the case of *The Bold Buccleugh*[10] that there was a maritime lien for damage, and, as regards such prior claims, the right would not seem to depend on the existence of a maritime lien for damage. A salvage claim may be regarded as if there had been a hypothecation to secure the reward of the salvors for services rendered, and that reward ought not to be recovered against the *res* to the detriment of a claimant in respect of subsequent damage. The matter is of importance when it is not possible or convenient to proceed against the owners personally, and it would be unreasonable and inequitable to satisfy out of the *res* a claim for a reward for prior salvage services which the salvors elected to render, in preference to a claim in respect of damage done.

The "Inna"

(1938) 60 Ll.L.Rep. 414

A maritime lien in respect of collision damage by a vessel will be postponed to a maritime lien of salvors who subsequently salve her.

An explosion on board a vessel caused her to sink, and damage was done to adjacent premises. Subsequently she was salved, and a question arose as to the priority between the maritime lien of the owners of the premises in respect of the damage and the maritime lien of the salvors.

---

[10] (1852) 7 Moo. P.C.C. 267.

Held, by the Probate, Divorce and Admiralty Division, that the maritime lien of the salvors had priority, for their services had produced the *res* for the other lien to take effect upon.

SIR BOYD MERRIMAN, P. (at page 415)

Which of these two claimants has the priority? It is common ground that it has been assumed for a very long time, by text writers and practitioners in Admiralty, that as between claimants for salvage services and those who have a lien for damage, the lien for damage is preferred to prior salvage claims and is postponed after later salvage claims. There is ample authority for the first of those propositions that the damage is preferred to prior salvage claims; but there is less authority for the other proposition, which is the one which I have to decide. Nevertheless, I should feel that I was somewhat bold, having regard to the consensus of professional opinion on this matter, if I were to hold that those who hold a lien for damage obtained priority over those who subsequently performed salvage services which preserved the property over which the lien is claimed. It must be for some other Court to say that the time has come to decide that maritime lien in respect of damage is to be preferred to a lien for subsequent salvage services which, in fact, produced any *res* at all for the other lien to take effect upon.

The "Russland"

(1924) 130 L.T. 763

An accrued maritime lien in respect of salvage has priority over the possessory lien of a shiprepairer who has effected repairs to the salved vessel.

A vessel was in distress. Salvage services were rendered to her by salvors, and she was ultimately placed in a shiprepairers' yard. The vessel was sold, and the proceeds of sale were insufficient to pay the claims of the salvors and the cost of the repairs. The shiprepairers contended that their possessory lien for repairs had priority over the maritime lien in respect of salvage.

Held, by the Probate, Divorce and Admiralty Division, that the salvors' maritime lien had priority, even though they had benefited from the repairs.

HILL, J. (at page 766)

The whole of their claim is for work done supported by a possessory lien. As to possession, the law is clear that the repairer takes subject to salvage liens already accrued. In my opinion that follows from *The Immacolata Concezione*[11] (wages); *The Gustav*[12] (wages); and *The Tergeste*[13] (wages and disbursements).

---

[11] (1883) 9 P.D. 37.
[12] (1862) Lush. 506.
[13] [1903] P. 26.

It was suggested on the authority of a passage in Halsbury's Laws of England, Vol. xxvi, at pp. 624–5, that because work has benefited the salvors it can be allowed as against them. The authorities referred to are *The Aline*[14] cited in *The Bold Buccleuch.*[15] But, however fair it may be that the salvors should recognise the [shiprepairers'] claim, I can find no principle in law which enables me to prefer [their] claim to an accrued maritime lien for salvage.

The "Two Ellens"

(1872) 26 L.T. 1

The maritime lien of a mortgagor has priority over the statutory right of a person, who has supplied necessaries to a vessel, to arrest her. Such a person has no maritime lien.

A vessel had been mortgaged. Subsequently necessaries were supplied to her. She was arrested and sold, but the proceeds of sale were insufficient to pay both the claims of the mortgagee and that of the necessaries men.

Held, by the Judicial Committee of the Privy Council, that the mortgagee had priority. The claim of the necessaries men gave them a right to arrest the vessel but not a maritime lien.

MELLISH, L.J. (at page 3)

The first Act which altered this state of the law was the 3 & 4 Vict. c. 65. The 6th section of that Act is in these terms: "Be it enacted, that the High Court of Admiralty shall have jurisdiction to decide all claims and demands whatsoever in the nature of salvage for services rendered to or damage received by any ship or sea-going vessel, or in the nature of towage or for necessaries supplied to any foreign ship or sea-going vessel, and to enforce payment thereof, whether such ship or vessel may have been within the body of a county or upon the high seas at the time when the services were rendered or damage received or necessaries furnished in respect of which such claim is made".

It is clear that previous to the passing of the 3 & 4 Vict. the Court of Admiralty had no jurisdiction in the case of necessaries supplied to a ship, and that the supply of such necessaries did not give any maritime lien upon a ship. It is perfectly true that for many years prior to [the] time of Charles II, the Court of Admiralty had claimed, and to a considerable extent exercised such a jurisdiction; but the Courts of Common Law in the time of Charles II and subsequently had prohibited them from exercising that jurisdiction on the ground that they never possessed it. Subsequently, in the case of *The Neptune*,[16] it was decided by the Privy Council that there was no such jurisdiction.

---

[14] (1840) 1 Wm. Rob. 111.

[15] (1852) Moo. P.C.C. 267.

[16] (1824) 1 Hag. Adm. 227.

Therefore, notwithstanding this jurisdiction was practically exercised for years, it must be taken now to be conclusively the law that the Court of Admiralty, by the law of England, never had jurisdiction over necessaries supplied to a ship. . . . It may be observed that the mortgage of ships is a security which is well known and which has existed in this country for many years. It is quite clear that, according to the decisions of the Courts of Common Law and according to the express provisions of the Merchant Shipping Act, which say that a mortgagee is not to be deemed an owner except for the purpose of enforcing his security, a mortgagee was never liable at Common Law for supplies furnished to the mortgagor while the mortgagor continued in possession of the ship. Then the question is, did the Legislature intend to alter that rule, and to say that, in certain cases specified in this section, instead of the mortgagee having precedence over the material man who had furnished supplies to the ship on the credit of the mortgagor remaining in possession, that rule should be altered, and that the material man should take precedence? Now, in order that the rights of different classes, the subjects of the Queen, should be altered, one certainly would expect that such an alteration should be expressed in tolerably clear terms. The 4th section, which begins this subject, says this: "The High Court of Admiralty shall have jurisdiction over any claim for building, equipping, or repairing of any ship if at the time of the institution of the cause the ship or the proceeds thereof are under the arrest of the Court". Now, it is admitted by Dr Deane, and their Lordships think it is quite clear, that that 4th section does not give any maritime lien, because it only gives jurisdiction in respect of "any claim for building, equipping, or repairing of a ship if at the time of the institution of the cause the ship or the proceeds thereof are under arrest of the Court". Now, it certainly would be absurd to say that the question whether the mortgagee is or is not to take precedence over a person who had either built or repaired or equipped a ship should depend upon the accidental circumstance whether some third person had happened to commence a suit in the Court of Admiralty and arrest the ship. That would certainly be a most irrational construction, and therefore it seems clear that that section at any rate does not give any maritime lien, but merely entitles the person who has done the repairs or built the ship to be paid out of the proceeds, in preference at any rate to the owner, to whom the proceeds would otherwise be given up.

PART II

CARRIAGE OF GOODS BY SEA

(1) IMPLIED UNDERTAKINGS IN VOYAGE CHARTER-PARTIES

Steel *v.* State Line Steamship Co.

(1877) 37 L.T. 333

The shipowner's duty to provide a seaworthy ship is an absolute one.

LORD BLACKBURN (at page 336)

I take it . . . to be quite clear . . . that where there is a contract to carry goods in a ship, whether that contract is in the shape of a bill of lading or any other form, there is a duty on the part of the person who furnishes or supplies that ship . . . unless something be stipulated which should prevent it, that the ship shall be fit for its purpose . . . That is generally expressed by saying that it shall be seaworthy; and I think also that in . . . contracts for sea-carriage, . . . not merely . . . [should they] . . . do their best to make the ship fit . . . but the ship should really be fit.

The "Europa"

[1904–7] All E.R. Rep. 394

Although the vessel is unseaworthy, the shipowner can still rely on the exception clauses, if the loss was not caused by unseaworthiness.

A charter-party stated that the shipowner was not to be liable for damage caused by "collision". When the vessel arrived at the port for discharge, she struck a dock wall. A water-closet pipe was broken and the cargo in the 'tween decks was damaged. The vessel was found to be unseaworthy, but the unseaworthiness did not cause the damage.

Held, by the Court of Appeal, that the shipowners could rely on the exception clause.

BUCKNILL, J. (at page 397)

The exact point decided in *Joseph Thorley Ltd.* v. *Orchis Steamship Co. Ltd.*[1] was that as between shipowner and cargo owner the deviation displaced the bill of lading contract altogether, so that it must now be taken that where [there] has been a deviation, it amounts to a non-performance by the shipowner of a condition precedent, the result of which is that it displaces the original contract whether the deviation had any relation to the loss sustained by the cargo owner or not. We have to decide whether "seaworthiness" is to be classed with non-deviation as a condition precedent, the non-performance of which voids the contract of affreightment, so that in the present case of the *Europa*, she being unseaworthy, even though she had carried all the cargo specified in the bill of lading to the proper destination, yet her owners cannot claim exemption from liability for damage caused, not by the unseaworthiness, but by a peril of the seas or other exception in the bill of lading. . . . Is it true to say that the same considerations apply in this case? We have not found any authority for such a proposition. . . . In our judgment, the cargo owners in the present case are only entitled to recover from the shipowners in respect of such damage as directly resulted from the want of seaworthiness and not for the damage caused by the water which got into the 'tween decks through the collision between the ship and the dock wall, which was covered by the excepted perils in the charter-party, and to the protection of which the shipowner was still entitled, notwithstanding the unseaworthiness of the vessel.

M'Andrew *v.* Adams

(1834) 1 Bing., N.C. 29

The ship must proceed on the voyage with reasonable dispatch.

By the terms of a charter-party dated Oct. 20, 1832, a vessel was to proceed from Portsmouth, where she was then lying, to St. Michaels (in the Azores), and there load a cargo of fruit and return to London. On Nov. 7, instead of proceeding direct to St. Michaels, she went on an intermediate voyage to Oporto, and returned later to Portsmouth, from where she finally sailed for St. Michaels on Dec. 6.

Held, by the Court of Common Pleas, that the shipowner was liable to the charterer for breach of the implied undertaking that the voyage should be commenced within a reasonable time.

TINDAL, C.J. (at page 38)

The broad question is, whether, upon the construction of this charter-party, there has been unnecessary delay in commencing the voyage to St. Michaels. Upon general principles, in all contracts by charter-party, where there is no

[1] [1907] 1 K.B. 660, C.A.

express agreement as to time, it is an implied stipulation that there shall be no unreasonable delay in commencing the voyage; and, after it has been commenced no deviation. And the question here is, whether the [shipowner] sailed within a reasonable time according to the terms of his charter-party. . . . If that be the general rule, where there is any delay in a voyage, it is incumbent on the party to account for it. In many cases it may be difficult to say what is a reasonable or an unreasonable time for commencing a voyage. . . . I think therefore, that, as the commencement of the voyage was, without any justifiable cause delayed till Dec. 6, an action lies for the [charterer].

Kish *v.* Taylor Sons & Co.

[1911–13] All E.R. Rep. 481

Deviation is justified even though necessitated by the ship's unseaworthiness at the commencement of the voyage.

The master of a vessel took on board an excessive load of deck cargo to such an extent that she was rendered unseaworthy. As a result of the unseaworthiness she was obliged to deviate from her normal route in order to proceed to a port for repairs.

Held, by the House of Lords, that the deviation was justifiable, and that the shipowners were entitled to rely on the clause in the charter-party entitling them to a lien on the cargo for dead freight.

LORD ATKINSON (at page 486)

What the [shipowners] contend is, in effect, this, that justifiable deviation does not avoid the contract; that, to use the language of LORD WATSON[2] . . . "it is the presence of the peril and not its causes" which justify it, and that it is, therefore, immaterial whether the unseaworthiness of the ship or her negligent navigation contributed directly to the peril or not. Judged by that test it is not disputed that the deviation in the present case was justifiable, and, if so, that the contract of affreightment was not void *ab initio*, so that the question for decision resolves itself into this: Is it the presence of the peril and not its cause which determines the character of the deviation, or must the master of every ship be left in this dilemma, that whenever, by his own culpable act, or a breach of contract by his owner, he finds his ship in a perilous position, he must continue on his voyage at all hazards, or only seek safety under the penalty of forfeiting the contract of affreightment? Nothing could, it would appear to me, tend more to increase the dangers to which life and property are exposed at sea than to hold that the law of England obliged the master of a merchant ship to choose between such alternatives.

---

[2] In *Strang, Steel & Co.* v. *A. Scott & Co.* (1889) 14 App. Cas. 601.

Scaramanga *v.* Stamp

(1880) 42 L.T. 840

Deviation to save human life is always justified, but not one to save property unless this is expressly stipulated.

A ship deviated to assist another in distress, but instead of merely saving the crew, attempted to earn salvage by towing the distressed vessel into port, and in the attempt, went ashore herself and was lost with her cargo.

Held, by the Court of Appeal, that the shipowner was liable for the loss of the cargo, for the deviation was unjustifiable. He could not rely on the exception of "perils of the sea" contained in the charter-party.

COCKBURN, C.J. (at page 844)

Deviation for the purpose of saving life is protected, and involves neither forfeiture of insurance nor liability to the goods' owners in respect of loss which would otherwise be within the exception of "perils of the seas". And, as a necessary consequence of the foregoing, deviation for the purpose of communicating with a ship in distress is allowable, inasmuch as the state of the vessel in distress may involve danger to life. On the other hand, deviation for the sole purpose of saving property is not thus privileged, but entails all the usual consequences of deviation. If, therefore, the lives of the persons on board a disabled ship can be saved without saving the ship, as by taking them off, deviation for the purpose of saving the ship will carry with it all the consequences of an unauthorised deviation. But where the preservation of life can only be effected through the concurrent saving of property, and the *bona fide* purpose of saving life forms part of the motive which leads to the deviation, the privilege will not be lost by reason of the purpose of saving property having formed a second motive for deviating. . . . The impulsive desire to save human life when in peril is one of the most beneficial instincts of humanity, and is nowhere more salutary in its results than in bringing help to those who, exposed to destruction from the fury of winds and waves, would perish if left without assistance. To all who have to trust themselves to the sea, it is of the utmost importance that the promptings of humanity in this respect should not be checked or interfered with by prudential considerations as to injurious consequences, which may result to a ship or cargo from the rendering of the needed aid. It would be against the common good, and shocking to the sentiments of mankind, that the shipowner should be deterred from endeavouring to save life by the fear, lest any disaster to ship or cargo, consequent on so doing, should fall on himself. . . . Deviation for the purpose of saving property stands obviously on a totally different footing. There is here no moral duty to fulfil, which, though its fulfilment may have been attended with danger to life or property, remains unrewarded. There would be much force, no doubt, in the argument that it is to the common interest of merchants and insurers, as well as of shipowners, that ships and cargoes, when in danger of perishing, should be saved, and consequently that, as matter [*sic*] of policy, the same latitude should be allowed in respect of the saving of property as in respect of the saving of life, were it not that the law has provided another, and a very adequate motive for the saving of property, by securing to the salvor a liberal proportion of the property. . . . It would obviously be most unjust if the shipowner could thus take the chance of highly remunerative gain at the risk and possible loss of the merchant or the insurer, neither of whom derive any benefit from the preservation of the property saved.

James Morrison & Co. Ltd. *v.* Shaw, Savill and Albion Co. Ltd.

(1916) 115 L.T. 508

Where a deviation is unjustified, the shipowner cannot rely on the exception clauses in the contract, but he may be entitled to the exceptions available to a common carrier.

A bill of lading[3] contained an exception of "King's enemies". The vessel deviated and was torpedoed by a submarine, and the cargo was lost.

Held, by the Court of Appeal (affirming the decision of BAILHACHE, J.), that the shipowners could not rely on the exception clause in the bill of lading, nor could they rely on the exception of King's enemies accorded to a common carrier, since they could not show that the loss would have taken place even though no deviation had been made.

In the High Court

BAILHACHE, J. ((1916) 114 L.T. 746, at page 749)

From the point of deviation, at any rate, the shipowner becomes at best a common carrier. The [shipowners] say that they are common carriers, with the Common Law exceptions of act of God and King's enemies in their favour. Let me assume that. Of what use are those exceptions to the [shipowners] in this case? As I understand it, the law stands thus. When a ship deviates and loss or damage to cargo occurs, either by act of God, or, as here, by the King's enemies, it is not open to her owners to set up either exception. Those exceptions apply and apply only to a carrier who is performing his contract, and never to a carrier who is breaking it, unless he can show that the loss or damage must have occurred in any event. . . . That he can obviously never do in such a case as the present. The most that can be said is that the [vessel] might have been torpedoed if she had continued on her course . . . , and that avails the [shipowners] nothing.

---

[3] The same principle is applicable in the case of voyage charter-parties. The case has been selected because it is a good illustration of the rule to be applied to both types of contracts of affreightment.

In the Court of Appeal

PHILLIMORE, L.J. ((1916) 115 L.T. 508, at page 512)

As the accident occurred at the time and place when it did, the ship being then on her deviating course, the shipowner is responsible unless he can show that the loss or damage would have occurred if she had been on her proper course. . . . There are circumstances in which conceivably this could be proved, but it could not be and was not proved in this case.

Mitchell, Cotts & Co. *v*. Steel Bros. & Co. Ltd.

[1916–17] All E.R. Rep. 578

Goods are "dangerous" if they are liable to cause the forfeiture or detention of the ship.

The charterers loaded a cargo of rice on board a vessel, and sent her to a port where they knew that it could not be discharged without the permission of the British Government. They did not inform the shipowners of this. Permission was refused and the ship was delayed.

Held, by the King's Bench Division, that the charterers were liable for damages for the delay.

ATKIN, J. (at page 579)

The shipowners say that this is analogous to the case of shipping goods which are known to the charterers to be dangerous, in which case the charterers would be responsible for such damage as happened to the ship or shipowners in the course of the voyage. . . .

I think there can be no question but that the shipment of goods upon an illegal voyage, i.e., upon a voyage that cannot be performed without violating the law of the flag of the country or the law of the place where the goods are to be carried to—a shipment of goods which would involve the ship in consequences either of forfeiture or delay—is precisely analogous to a shipment of dangerous goods which might cause the destruction of the ship. What is the full extent of the shipper's obligation? It appears to me that it amounts to this, that he stipulates that he will not ship goods which involve the risk of unusual danger or delay to the ship, which the owner does not know of or might not reasonably know of without communicating to the owner facts which are within his knowledge indicating that there is such a risk. I do not say that his obligation is not wider than that.

(2) TIME CHARTER-PARTIES

Palace Shipping Co. Ltd. *v.* Gans Steamship Line

[1914–15] All E.R. Rep. 912

Generally, a time charterer is only entitled to send the vessel to safe ports. What is a safe port is a question of fact.[4]

A time charter-party signed in 1913 said that the vessel must only be used between "safe ports". In 1915 she was ordered to Newcastle two days after the German Government had threatened the destruction of all merchant ships in the waters around Great Britain. The shipowners contended that Newcastle was not a "safe port".

Held, by the Court of Appeal, that the "safe port" must be one that was both physically and politically safe. But, on the facts, Newcastle was a "safe port".

SANKEY, J. (at page 913)

It is admitted by both parties that Newcastle itself was safe, but the [shipowners] say that the dangers of the voyage there were such as to make the port unsafe within the meaning of the charter-party. The [charterers], on the other hand, contend that the dangers of the voyage are not material to the question whether the port was a safe one, and, further, that such dangers as either existed or might be apprehended on the voyage were not of a character to make the port unsafe. . . . In my view, the word "safe", when used in connection with the word "port", implies that the port must be both physically and politically safe, and I think that the action either of nature or war may render a port unsafe. I have only to deal with the agency of war in the present case. At the moment no English port would be a safe port for a German vessel. Neither is a place which a vessel can only go to at a certain risk of confiscation a safe port: see the observations of BLACKBURN, J., in *Ogden* v. *Graham.*[5] There does not appear to be any sound distinction between a port to which a vessel is proceeding with a liability to be sunk or confiscated by enemy vessels lying thereat or in the approaches thereto and a port to which a vessel is proceeding with a liability to be sunk or confiscated by enemy vessels at a greater distance. Modern inventions like wireless telegraphy and submarines have quite altered old rules and old conceptions, and I am of opinion that dangers likely to be incurred on a voyage to a port may be taken into account in considering the question whether such port is safe to go to or not. In each case it is a question of fact and a question of degree.

---

[4] See further as to "safe port" *Leeds Shipping Co. Ltd.* v. *Société Française Bunge* [1958] 2 Lloyd's Rep. 127, C.A., p. 76, *post*. For damage caused by entering an unsafe port, see *Reardon Smith Line Ltd.* v. *Australian Wheat Board* [1956] A.C. 266; [1956] 1 All E.R. 456, P.C., p. 78, *post*.

[5] (1861) 1 B. & S. 773.

Kodros Shipping Corporation *v*. Empresa Cubana de Fletes: The "Evia" (No. 2)

[1982] 2 Lloyd's Rep. 307

Where a charter-party requires the vessel to use safe ports only, the port, at the time when the order to go there is given, must be prospectively safe.

A vessel under a time charter-party, which required the charterers to use safe ports only, was ordered by them to proceed to Basrah. She arrived there on Aug. 20, 1979, and discharge of the cargo was completed on Sept. 22. But she was unable to leave as a result of the outbreak of large-scale hostilities between Iran and Iraq. The shipowners claimed damages from the charterers.

Held, by the House of Lords, that there would be judgment for the charterers, for Basrah was prospectively safe at the time of nomination, and the unsafety was due to an unexpected and abnormal event after her arrival. They were not under a secondary obligation to make a fresh nomination because such an order would have been ineffective.

LORD ROSKILL (at page 319)

My Lords, on the view of the law which I take, since Basrah was prospectively safe at the time of nomination, and since the unsafety arose after her arrival and was due to an unexpected and abnormal event, there was at the former time no breach of cl. 2 by the [charterers].

But, my Lords, since your Lordships' House gave leave to appeal in order that this branch of the law should be fully explored, I think your Lordships may wish further to consider whether, notwithstanding the rejection of the views of MUSTILL, J. and ROBERT GOFF, J., and of ACKNER, L.J., there is a residual obligation upon a charterer, whether for time or voyage, given that he has fully complied with his obligation at the time of nomination. My Lords, unless there is something unusual in the relevant express language used in a particular charter-party, the charterer's obligation at the time of nomination which I have been discussing must, I think, apply equally to a voyage charterer as to a time charterer. But in considering whether there is any residual or remaining obligation after nomination it is necessary to have in mind one fundamental distinction between a time charterer and a voyage charterer. In the former case, the time charterer is in complete control of the employment of the ship. It is in his power by appropriate orders timeously given to change the ship's employment so as to prevent her proceeding to or remaining at a port initially safe which has since it was nominated become unsafe. But a voyage charterer may not have the same power. If there is a single loading or discharging port named in the voyage charter-party then, unless the charter-party specifically otherwise provides, a voyage charterer may not be able to order that ship elsewhere. If there is a range of loading or discharging ports named, once the voyage charterer has selected the contractual port or ports of loading or discharge, the voyage charter-party usually operates as if that port or those ports had originally been written into the charter-party, and the charterer then has no further right of nomination or renomination. What, then, is the contractual obligation of such charterers whether for time or voyage if the nominated port becomes unsafe after it was nominated?

My Lords, in the case of a time charterer, I cannot bring myself to think that he has no further obligation to the owner even though for the reasons I have given earlier he is not the insurer of the risks arising from the unsafety of the nominated port. Suppose some event has occurred after nomination which has made or will or may make the nominated port unsafe. Is a time charterer obliged to do anything further? What is a voyage charterer to do in similar circumstances? My Lords, this problem seems never to have been judicially considered in any detail; indeed, as I have already stated, in *Reardon Smith Line Ltd.* v. *Australian Wheat Board*[6] the Privy Council expressly declined to consider it.

In my opinion, while the primary obligation of a time charterer under cl. 2 of this charter-party is that which I have already stated, namely, to order the ship to go only to a port which, at the time when the order is given, is prospectively safe for her, there may be circumstances in which, by reason of a port, which was prospectively safe when the order to go to it was given, subsequently becoming unsafe, cl. 2, on its true construction, imposes a further and secondary obligation on the charterer.

In this connection two possible situations require to be considered. The first situation is where, after the time charterer has performed his primary obligation by ordering the ship to go to a port which, at the time of such order, was prospectively safe for her, and while she is still proceeding towards such port in compliance with such order, new circumstances arise which render the port unsafe. The second situation is where, after the time charterer has performed his primary obligation by ordering the ship to go to a port which was, at the time of such order, prospectively safe for her, and she has proceeded to and entered such port in compliance with such order, new circumstances arise which render the port unsafe.

In the first situation it is my opinion that cl. 2, on its true construction, (unless the cause of the new unsafety be purely temporary in character) imposes on the time charterer a further and secondary obligation to cancel his original order and, assuming that he wishes to continue to trade the ship, to order her to go to another port which, at the time when such fresh order is given, is prospectively safe for her. This is because cl. 2 should be construed as requiring the time charterer to do all that he can effectively do to protect the ship from the new danger in the port which has arisen since his original order for her to go to it was given.

In the second situation the question whether cl. 2, on its true construction, imposes a further and secondary obligation on the time charterer will depend

---

[6] [1956] 1 All E.R. 456, P.C.

on whether, having regard to the nature and consequences of the new danger in the port which has arisen, it is possible for the ship to avoid such danger by leaving the port. If, on the one hand, it is not possible for the ship so to leave, then no further and secondary obligation is imposed on the time charterer. This is because cl. 2 should not be construed as requiring the time charterer to give orders with which it is not possible for the ship to comply, and which would for that reason be ineffective. If, on the other hand, it is possible for the ship to avoid the new danger in the port which has arisen by leaving, then a further and secondary obligation is imposed on the time charterer to order the ship to leave the port forthwith, whether she has completed loading or discharging or not, and, assuming that he wishes to continue to trade the ship, to order her to go to another port which, at the time when such fresh order is given, is prospectively safe for her. This is again because cl. 2 should be construed as requiring the time charterer to do all that he can effectively do to protect the ship from the new danger in the port which has arisen since his original order for her to go to it was given.

My Lords, what I have said with regard to these further and secondary obligations under cl. 2 of this charter-party will apply to any other similarly worded "safe port" clauses.

My Lords, on the basis that time charterers were potentially under the further and secondary obligations which I have held that cl. 2 may impose on them, it cannot avail the [shipowners] against the [charterers] since the events giving rise to the unsafety did not occur until after *Evia* had entered Basrah, and an order to leave the port and proceed to another port could not have been effective.

A/S Tankexpress *v.* Compagnie Financière Belge des Petroles S.A.

[1948] 2 All E.R. 939

Where the hire has been paid by cheque instead of in cash and always accepted by the shipowner, he cannot insist on payment in cash unless he first gives the charterer notice to this effect.

A clause in a time charter-party provided that payment of hire was to be made "in cash monthly in advance in London". In default of such payment the shipowners had the right to withdraw the vessel from the service of the charterers. In accordance with the practice which had always been followed, the charterers had sent a cheque every month to the shipowners instead of paying in cash. A cheque was delayed in transmission, and the shipowners claimed that they were entitled to withdraw the vessel because payment had not been made in cash.

Held, by the House of Lords, that the claim failed, for, if they wanted to insist on payment in cash, they must give reasonable notice of such intention.

LORD DU PARCQ (at page 951)

My Lords, it appears to me . . . that the parties had . . . adopted for the time being a substituted mode of performance of the contract which was acceptable to, and accepted by, each of them. If a contract provides for payment in cash, the party to whom payment is due may accept in substitution payment by cheque. Instead of money, a creditor may be willing to accept meal or malt, and he may be willing to postpone the date of performance of a contractual duty. No one would doubt this, if a single payment were due under a contract. One who has plainly manifested his willingness to accept a substituted method of performance cannot, when payment is made in the accepted manner, take advantage of some provision in the contract which gives him a remedy in default of payment. It is true that in the present case your Lordships are concerned, not with a single payment, but with payments which fell due monthly over a long period, but I think it can hardly be disputed that, where periodical payments have to be made, a substituted method of payment which has been "accepted between the parties" from the beginning must be regarded as fully satisfying the requirements of the contract until timely notice is given, by one or other of the parties, that he withdraws his acceptance of it. . . . I conclude, therefore, that, if the charterers, when the time came to make the payment . . . , in fact acted in accordance with the "accepted method", the owners were not entitled, on the ground that, through no fault of the charterers, receipt of the payment was delayed, to exercise a remedy which was open to them only "in default of" the payment stipulated by the contract.

A/S Awilco *v.* Fulvia S.p.A. di Navigazione: The "Chikuma"

[1981] 1 Lloyd's Rep. 371

Where payment of the hire is to be made "in cash", the charterer is not considered to have paid unless what the shipowner receives is the equivalent of cash or as good as cash.

By the terms of a time charter-party the payment of the hire was to be made in cash monthly in advance, otherwise the shipowners could withdraw the chartered vessel from the service of the charterers. One instalment of the hire fell due on Jan. 22, 1976. On that date the sum due was credited to the shipowners' bank account, but interest could not run on it until Jan. 26. On Jan. 24 the shipowners withdrew the vessel. The charterers claimed damages for wrongful withdrawal.

Held, by the House of Lords, that there would be judgment for the shipowners, for the payment which had been made was not payment in cash or its equivalent because the money could not immediately earn interest.

LORD BRIDGE OF HARWICH (at page 375)

The underlying concept is surely this, that when payment is made to a bank otherwise than literally in cash, i.e., in dollar bills or other legal tender (which no one expects), there is no "payment in cash" within the meaning of cl. 5 unless what the creditor receives is the equivalent of cash, or as good as cash. This is supported both by the common sense of the matter and by the judgments in the Court of Appeal affirming the decision of BRANDON, J., in *The Brimnes*.[7]

EDMUND-DAVIES, L.J. (as he then was) said[8]:

> The owners' contention, however, that the tendering of the commercial equivalent of cash would suffice found favour with BRANDON, J. In particular, he concluded that any transfer of funds to M.G.T. for the credit of the owners' account so as to give them the unconditional right to the immediate use of the funds transferred was good payment. In my judgment, that was clearly right . . .

MEGAW, L.J. said[9]:

> Whatever mode or process is used, "payment" is not achieved until the process has reached the stage at which the creditor has received cash or that which he is prepared to treat as the equivalent of cash or has a credit available on which, in the normal course of business or banking practice, he can draw, if he wishes, in the form of cash.

The book entry made by the owners' bank on Jan. 22 in the owners' account was clearly not the equivalent of cash, nor was there any reason why the owners should have been prepared to treat it as the equivalent of cash. It could not be used to earn interest, e.g., by immediate transfer to a deposit account. It could only be drawn subject to a (probable) liability to pay interest. In substance it was the equivalent of an overdraft facility which the bank was bound to make available. I have put the word "probable" in brackets because I attach no significance to its use in the arbitrator's finding. The finding of a probable liability to pay interest must connote a right in the owners' bank to charge interest, which is the decisive factor. It follows, in my view, that on Jan. 22 there was no "payment in cash" by the charterers of the hire then assumed to be due and accordingly the owners, having refused to accept the credit as payment in accordance with cl. 5, were entitled to withdraw the ship, as they did, on Jan. 24.

Mardorf Peach & Co. Ltd. *v*. Attica Sea Carriers Corporation of Liberia: The "Laconia"

[1977] 1 All E.R. 545

A right to withdraw a vessel "failing the punctual and regular payment of the hire" cannot be defeated by a late tender of the hire unless the shipowners waive the breach.

---

[7] [1974] 2 Lloyd's Rep. 241; [1975] Q.B. 929.
[8] *Ibid.*, at pp. 248 and 948 respectively.
[9] *Ibid.*, at pp. 256 and 963 respectively.

A vessel was chartered to the charterers under a time charter-party stating that hire was to be paid in cash semi-monthly in advance, and that "failing the punctual and regular payment of the hire" the shipowners were to be at liberty to withdraw the vessel from the charterers' service. The charterers tendered payment one day late, and the shipowners withdrew the vessel.

Held, by the House of Lords, that the shipowners were entitled to do so. The breach of the obligation to pay in advance could not be cured by a late tender. There was no evidence that the breach had been waived.

LORD WILBERFORCE (at page 548)

My Lords, I cannot find any difficulty or ambiguity in this clause. It must mean that once a punctual payment of any instalment has not been made, a right of withdrawal accrues to the owners. Conversely, it is incapable of meaning that a charterer who has failed to make a punctual payment, can (unless the owners have waived the default) avoid the consequences of his failure by later tendering an unpunctual payment. He would still have failed to make a punctual payment, and it is on this failure and by reason of it that the owners get the right to withdraw. . . .

The result of my conclusions on these points leaves the matter as follows.

1. Under the withdrawal clause, as under similar clauses, including the Baltime clause properly interpreted, a right of withdrawal arises as soon as default is made in punctual payment of an instalment of hire. Whether or not this rule is subject to qualification in a case of punctual but insufficient payment as some authorities appear to hold, is not an issue which now arises and I express no opinion on it.

2. The owners must within a reasonable time after the default give notice of withdrawal to the charterers. What is a reasonable time—essentially a matter for arbitrators to find—depends on the circumstances. In some, indeed many cases, it will be a short time—viz. the shortest time reasonably necessary to enable the shipowner to hear of the default and issue instructions. If, of course, the charter-party contains an express provision regarding notice to the charterers, that provision must be applied.

3. The owners may be held to have waived the default (*inter alia*) if when a late payment is tendered, they chose to accept it as if it were timeous, or if they do not within a reasonable time give notice that they have rejected it.

LORD SALMON (at page 557)

It may be thought that the withdrawal clauses in the New York Produce Exchange, the Baltime and Shelltime forms of charter are unduly harsh on the charterers who may lose a valuable charter by inadvertently failing to pay the hire until a day or so too late. There are, however, other well-known forms of charter available which are far less stringent. If commercial men such as these charterers choose to enter into a charter which turns out to be harsh or unfair, they are nevertheless bound by it. If, as LORD DENNING, M.R. points out,[10] Equity will not interfere by granting them relief, still less is it possible for the Courts to attempt to attain what may appear to them to be a fairer result by torturing the language of the charter in an effort to extract from it a meaning which it does not bear, but might, if it did, lead to a less harsh result.

Certainty is of primary importance in all commercial transactions. I am afraid that ever since 1971 when *The Georgios C.*[11] was decided a great deal of doubt has been generated about the effect of clauses conferring the right on shipowners to withdraw their vessels when charterers fail to pay hire in accordance with the terms of the charter-parties in the well-known New York Produce Exchange, Baltime and Shelltime forms. No such doubt existed between 1948 (when the *Tankexpress* case[12] was decided) and 1971. My Lords, I hope that the doubts which have troubled the waters since 1971 will now be finally dispelled by this decision of your Lordships' House.

Afovos Shipping Co. S.A. *v*. R. Pagnan and F. Lli: The "Afovos"

[1983] 1 Lloyd's Rep. 335

The latest point of time which constitutes punctual payment of an instalment of hire is midnight of the day in question.

A vessel was chartered under a time charter-party. Clause 31 stated: "When hire is due and not received the owners before exercising the option of withdrawing the vessel . . . will give charterers 48 hours' notice". An instalment of hire became due on June 14, 1979. The shipowners gave notice of withdrawal at 16.40 hours on that day. The charterers contended that the notice was premature and therefore of no effect.

Held, by the House of Lords, that the notice was of no effect because the charterers had until midnight of June 14 before the instalment became due.

LORD HAILSHAM OF ST. MARYLEBONE (at page 338)

At what point of time on June 14, 1979, apart from the mitigation of cl. 31, would the right of withdrawal have arisen under cl. 5 of the charter?

On the assumption that, at 16.40 or 16.45 hours on June 14, 1979, the point of time indicated by the answer to the first question had not been reached, were the [shipowners] entitled to send a notice exercising their option under cl. 31 in advance of that point of time?

Of the two questions which must be decided, the second appears to me to be plain beyond argument. Both the grammatical meaning of cl. 31 and the policy

---

[10] In the Court below: [1976] 2 All E.R. 249, C.A., at p. 255.

[11] I.e., *Empresa Cubana de Fletes* v. *Lagonisi Shipping Co. Ltd. The "Georgios C."* [1971] 1 All E.R. 193, C.A.

[12] I.e., *A/S Tankexpress* v. *Compagnie Financière Belge des Petroles S.A.* [1948] 2 All E.R. 939, H.L. See p. 29, *ante*.

considerations underlying the contract require that the moment of time at which the 48 hours' notice must be given did not arise until after the moment of time at which, apart from the clause, the right of withdrawal would have accrued. I agree with the judgments of the Court of Appeal that both the expression "due and received", and the reference to the right as an "option", really only admit of this sense. The argument which appealed to the learned Judge that notice could be given at any time during the last day available for payment of the instalment (i.e. at any time after midnight on June 13/14 or alternatively at some point of time when it was unlikely that the instalment would be paid timeously) failed to make any impression on me at all. The notice can only be given "when hire is due and not received", which cannot arise before the time postulated by the answer given to the first question (whatever that answer may be), and the notice can only be given when there is (or apart from cl. 31 would be) already in existence, an "option" capable of exercise of "withdrawing the vessel from the charter-party", and that option can only be exercised after the arrival of the same point of time.

Even if the point of cl. 31 were ambiguous, which in my judgment it is not, I would be greatly impressed by the view of the Court of Appeal. Quite obviously the clause was inserted in order to save the charterer, who may (as in this case) be quite innocent even of the knowledge that his payment had not been received, from the extremely onerous effects (in this case a cost of $2½ million) of cl. 5, and equally obviously if the [shipowners'] arguments be accepted a premature notice, would have the effect of allowing the shipowner to reduce the effective period of 48 hours' notice by anything up to 24 hours.

In the result, I conclude that the crux of this case depends upon the answer given to the first of two questions I have posed. This was: at what point of time apart from the mitigation of cl. 31 would the right of withdrawal under cl. 5 of the charter have arisen? To put the question in the terms of cl. 5: At what point of time can the charterers be said to have been "failing the punctual and regular payment of the hire"? Since the punctual payment of only one instalment is in question, for the purpose of the present appeal one need only ask the question in the simpler form: "What is the latest point of time on June 14, 1979, which would have constituted punctual payment of the instalment?" To this question I believe that, in principle, only one answer is possible, namely at midnight on the last day available to them for the due and punctual payment of the hire, i.e. June 14, I take it to be a general principle of law not requiring authority that where a person under an obligation to do a particular act has to do it on or before a particular date, he has the whole of that day to perform his duty. No doubt as the hours pass it becomes less and less probable that he will be able to do it. That is the risk he runs. But he is not actually in default until the time arrives.

Scandinavian Trading Tanker Co. AB *v.* Flota Petrolera Ecuatoriana: The "Scaptrade"

[1983] 2 Lloyd's Rep. 253

The court has no jurisdiction to grant relief to the charterer against the exercise by a shipowner of his contractual right under the withdrawal clause to withdraw the vessel where an instalment of hire is not paid by the due date.

A vessel was chartered under a time charter-party. One month's hire became due on July 8, 1979, but the charterers failed to pay it. So the shipowners withdrew her from the charterers' service. The charterers applied for relief against forfeiture.

Held, by the House of Lords, that no relief would be granted.

LORD DIPLOCK (at page 256)

A time charter, unless it is a charter by demise, with which your Lordships are not here concerned, transfers to the charterer no interest in or right to possession of the vessel; it is a contract for services to be rendered to the charterer by the shipowner through the use of the vessel by the shipowner's own servants, the master and the crew, acting in accordance with such directions as to the cargoes to be loaded and the voyages to be undertaken as by the terms of the charter-party the charterer is entitled to give to them. Being a contract for services it is thus the very prototype of a contract of which before the fusion of law and equity a court would never grant specific performance: *Clarke* v. *Price*[13] *Lumley* v. *Wagner*.[14] In the event of failure to render the promised services, the party to whom they were to be rendered would be left to pursue such remedies in damages for breach of contract as he might have at law. But as an unbroken line of uniform authority in this House, from *Tankexpress*[15] to *The Chikuma*[16] has held, if the withdrawal clause so provides, the shipowner is entitled to withdraw the services of the vessel from the charterer if the latter fails to pay an instalment of hire in precise compliance with the provisions of the charter. So the shipowner commits no breach of contract if he does so; and the charterer has no remedy in damages against him.

To grant an injunction restraining the shipowner from exercising his right of withdrawal of the vessel from the service of the charterer, though negative in form, is pregnant with an affirmative order to the shipowner to perform the contract; juristically it is indistinguishable from a a decree for specific performance of a contract to render services; and in respect of that category of contracts, even in the event of breach, this is a remedy that English courts

---

[13] (1819) 2 Wils. Ch. 157.

[14] (1852) 1 De G. M. & G. 604.

[15] I.e. *A/S Tankexpress* v. *Compagnie Financière Belge des Petroles S.A.* [1948] 2 All E.R. 939, H.L. See p. 29, *ante*.

[16] I.e. *A/S Awilco* v. *Fulvia S.p.A. di Navigazione: The "Chikuma"* [1981] 1 Lloyd's Rep. 371, H.L. See p. 30, *ante*.

have always disclaimed any jurisdiction to grant. This is, in my view, sufficient reason in itself to compel rejection of the suggestion that the equitable principle of relief from forfeiture is juristically capable of extension so as to grant to the court a discretion to prevent a shipowner from exercising his strict contractual rights under a withdrawal clause in a time charter which is not a charter by demise.

Moreover, in the case of a time charter it is not possible to state that the object of the insertion of a withdrawal clause, let alone the transaction itself, is essentially to secure the payment of money. Hire is payable in advance in order to provide a fund from which the shipowner can meet those expenses of rendering the promised services to the charterer that he has undertaken to bear himself under the charter-party; in particular, the wages and victualling of master and crew, the insurance of the vessel and her maintenance in such a state as will enable her to continue to comply with the warranty of performance.

This, the commercial purpose of obtaining payment of hire in advance, also makes inapplicable another analogy sought to be drawn between a withdrawal clause and a penalty clause of the kind against which courts of law, as well as courts of equity, before the Judicature Acts had exercised jurisdiction to grant relief. The classic form of a penalty clause is one which provides that upon breach of a primary obligation under the contract, a secondary obligation shall arise on the party in breach to pay the other party a sum of money which does not represent a genuine pre-estimate of any loss likely to be sustained by him as the result of the breach of primary obligation but is substantially in excess of that sum. The classic form of relief against such a penalty clause has been to refuse to give effect to it, but to award the common law measure of damages for the breach of the primary obligation instead. LLOYD, J. in *The Afovos*[17] attached importance to the majority judgments in *Stockloser* v. *Johnson*[18] which expressed the opinion that money already paid by one party to the other under a continuing contract prior to an event which under the terms of the contract entitled that other party to elect to rescind it and to retain the money already paid, might be treated as money paid under a penalty clause, and recovered to the extent that it exceeded to an unconscionable extent the value of any consideration that had been given for it. Assuming this to be so, however, it is incapable of having any application to time charters and withdrawal notices. Moneys paid by the charterer prior to the withdrawal notice that puts an end to the contract for services represent the agreed rate of hire for services already rendered, and not a penny more.

All the analogies that ingenuity has suggested may be discovered between a withdrawal clause in a time charter and other classes of contractual provisions in which courts have relieved parties from the rigour of contractual terms into

---

[17] I.e. *Afovos Shipping Co. S.A.* v. *R. Pagnon and F.Lli: The "Afovos"* [1980] 2 Lloyd's Rep. 469 at p. 479. The case subsequently went to the House of Lords on another point: [1983] 1 Lloyd's Rep. 335. See p. 33, *ante*.

[18] [1954] 1 Q.B. 476.

which they have entered can in my view be shown upon juristic analysis to be false. Prima facie parties to a commercial contract bargaining on equal terms can make "time to be of the essence" of the performance of any primary obligation under the contract that they please, whether the obligation be to pay a sum of money or to do something else. When time is made of the essence of a primary obligation, failure to perform it punctually is a breach of a condition of the contract which entitles the party not in breach to elect to treat the breach as putting an end to all primary obligations under the contract that have not already been performed. In *Tankexpress* this House held that time was of the essence of the very clause with which your Lordships are now concerned where it appeared in what was the then current predecessor of the Shelltime 3 charter. As is well-known, there are available on the market a number of so-(mis)called "anti-technicality clauses", such as that considered in *The Afovos*, which require the shipowner to give a specified period of notice to the charterer in order to make time of the essence of payment of advance hire; but at the expiry of such notice, provided it is validly given, time does become of the essence of the payment.

My Lords, quite apart from the juristic difficulties in the way of recognising a jurisdiction in the court to grant relief against the operation of a withdrawal clause in a time charter, there are practical reasons of legal policy for declining to create any such new jurisdiction out of sympathy for charterers. The freight market is notoriously volatile. If it rises rapidly during the period of a time charter, the charterer is the beneficiary of the windfall which he can realise if he wants to by sub-chartering at the then market rates. What withdrawal of the vessel does is to transfer the benefit of the windfall from charterer to shipowner.

Federal Commerce and Navigation Ltd. *v.* Molena Alpha Inc.: The "Nanfri"

[1978] 2 Lloyd's Rep. 132

Certain types of cross-claim can be pleaded by the charterer against whom a claim for hire is made, and accordingly deductions from hire can be made.

The charterers of a vessel under a time charter-party made deductions from hire due under it.

Held, by a majority of the Court of Appeal, that deductions could be made where the shipowners had wrongly deprived the charterers of the use of the vessel or had prejudiced them in the use of her. Such a right could not be extended to other breaches or default of the shipowners, e.g., damage to cargo arising from the negligence of the crew.[19]

---

[19] The case subsequently went to the House of Lords where it was decided on different grounds without affecting this point: [1979] 1 Lloyd's Rep. 201.

LORD DENNING, M.R. (at page 139)

At one time it was common to describe the sums payable under a time charter-party as "freight". Such description is to be found used by Judges and text book writers of great distinction. But in modern times a change has come about. The payments due under a time charter are usually now described as "hire" and those under a voyage charter as "freight". This change of language corresponds, I believe, to a recognition that the two things are different. "Freight" is payable for carrying a quantity of cargo from one place to another. "Hire" is payable for the right to use a vessel for a specified period of time, irrespective of whether the charterer chooses to use it for carrying cargo or lays it up, out of use. Every time charter contains clauses which are quite inappropriate to a voyage charter, such as the off-hire clause and the withdrawal clause. So different are the two concepts that I do not think the law as to "freight" can be applied indiscriminately to "hire". In particular, the special rule of English law whereby "freight" must be paid in full (without deductions for short delivery or cargo damage) cannot be applied automatically to time charter "hire". Nor is there any authority which says that it must. It would be a mistake to suppose that the House of Lords had time charter hire and so forth in mind when they decided *Aries Tanker Corporation* v. *Total Transport Ltd.: The "Aries"*[20] or *Nova (Jersey) Knit Ltd.* v. *Kammgarn Spinnerei G.m.b.H.*,[21] or that anything said in those cases can bind this Court. Many of us, I know, in the past have assumed that the rule as to "freight" does apply: and some Judges have said so. But now, after full argument, I am satisfied that the "freight" rule does not apply automatically to "time charter" hire: and we have to consider the position on principle.

So I turn to the problem here. A shipowner has contracted to give a charterer the right to use the vessel for a period of time—six years in fact. In return, the charterer has agreed to pay a stated sum of hire monthly in advance. Then let us suppose that, after the charterer has paid his month's hire in advance, the shipowner wrongly declines to allow the charterer to have the use of the vessel for some days during the ensuing month. He may put the vessel perhaps to some more profitable use. He, by his conduct, deprives the charterer of part of the consideration for which the hire was paid. I should have thought it plain that the charterer should in fairness be able to recoup himself by making a deduction from the next month's hire—so as to compensate him for the loss of use for those days—equivalent to the hire of those lost days. Likewise, if the shipowner has been guilty of some other wrongful conduct which has deprived the charterer of the use of the ship during some days—or prejudiced the charterer in the use of the ship—then the charterer should in fairness be able to recoup himself by making a deduction from the next month's hire. If the charterer quantifies his loss by a reasonable assessment

---

[20] [1977] 1 Lloyd's Rep. 334, H.L.
[21] [1977] 1 Lloyd's Rep. 463.

made in good faith—and deducts the sum quantified—then he is not in default. The shipowner cannot withdraw his vessel on account of non-payment of hire nor hold him guilty at that point of any breach of contract. If it subsequently turns out that he has deducted too much, the shipowner can, of course, recover the balance. But that is all. This point of view is supported by a score of Judges versed in commercial matters over the last 30 or 40 years.

This line of cases is so convincing that I would hold that, when the shipowner is guilty of a breach of contract which deprives the time charterer of part of the consideration for which the hire has been paid in advance, the charterer can deduct an equivalent amount out of the hire falling due for the next month.

I would as at present advised limit the right to deduct to cases when the shipowner has wrongly deprived the charterer of the use of the vessel or has prejudiced him in the use of it. I would not extend it to other breaches or default of this shipowner, such as damage to cargo arising from the negligence of the crew.

Greek Government *v.* Minister of Transport: The "Ilissos"

[1949] 1 All E.R. 171

"Deficiency of men" relates to their numerical deficiency and not to their unwillingness to work.

A clause in a time charter-party provided that hire should not be payable if there were a "deficiency of men". The officers and crew refused to sail except in convoy.

Held, by the Court of Appeal, that hire was still payable since "deficiency of men" merely meant numerical insufficiency.

BUCKNILL, L.J. (at page 173)

Looking at the words as they stand, and endeavouring to give them a meaning which businessmen, as ordinary reasonable beings, would give them, I think that "deficiency of men" means deficiency of men and not deficiency of willingness in men to work. There is no doubt that the men on board the ship amounted to a full complement of officers and crew. That is what the owners agreed to provide, and they provided them. By a mere change of mind these men would have been competent at once to work the ship. It was not even as though they were sick. I am not sure that the [trial] Judge is right when he says that sickness might amount to deficiency, but we have not to decide that point because these men were not sick. They were able and competent to do their work, and, therefore, I think, giving the words "deficiency of men" their ordinary sense, the facts in this case do not come within those words.

Hogarth *v.* Miller, Brother & Co.

(1891) 64 L.T. 205

"The working of the vessel" is considered to be hindered even though there is only a partial interference with her working.

A time charter-party provided that hire should not be payable when "the working of the vessel" was hindered. The vessel's high-pressure engine broke down. But she managed to get into port with the assistance of a tug and partly by using her own low-pressure engine. While there her winches were capable of unloading her cargo, although she could not proceed to sea.

Held, by the House of Lords, that hire was not payable while she was being assisted by the tug, for her working had been hindered. But it was payable while the cargo was being unloaded, for her working had not been hindered.

LORD HALSBURY, L.C. (at page 206)

I confess that I entertain no doubt whatever that the vessel was not efficient in any sense for the prosecution of her voyage from Las Palmas to Harburg. . . . That another vessel took her in tow, that another vessel accomplished the voyage and brought this vessel, not as an efficient steamer, but as a floating barge, whereby the goods were brought to Harburg, seems to be nothing to the purpose. I use that phrase because, although I am not aware that it is suggested that the low-pressure engine was used for the purpose of easing the work of the tug, that appears to me to be entirely irrelevant when one is ascertaining whether this vessel of its own independent power was efficient for the purpose of prosecuting the voyage. . . . The vessel was not seaworthy for the purpose of accomplishing her voyage without the assistance of a tug; . . . and in truth, . . . it is clear that the voyage which was accomplished, and the service which it was contemplated this hired vessel was to perform, was performed by another vessel, and that the auxiliary assistance which she gave to that other vessel was not making the vessel herself an efficient vessel for the working of which the hirer was to pay. . . . I should read the contract as meaning . . . that she should be efficient to do what she was required to do when she was called upon to do it, and accordingly, at each period, if what was required of her was to lie at anchor, if it was to lie alongside the wharf, upon each of these occasions, if she was efficient to do it at the time, she would then become, in the language of the contract, to my mind, "efficient", reading with it the other words "for the working of the vessel" . . . It is not denied that during the period that she was lying at Harburg there was . . . machinery at work enabling the hirer to do quickly all that this particular portion of her employment required to be done. It appears to me, therefore, that at that period there was a right in the shipowner to demand payment of the hire, because at that time his vessel was efficiently working; the working of the vessel was proceeding as efficiently as it could with reference to the particular employment demanded of her at the time.

Actis Co. Ltd. *v.* Sanko Steamship Co. Ltd.: The "Aquacharm"

[1982] 1 Lloyd's Rep. 7

"The working of the vessel" is not considered to be hindered where she is prevented from performing her service by an external cause.

The *Aquacharm* was chartered under a time charter-party, which contained a clause stating that "in the event of the loss of time from deficiency of men or stores, fire, breakdown or damage to hull, machinery or equipment or by any other cause preventing the full working of the vessel the payment of hire shall cease for the time thereby lost". Whilst on a voyage from Baltimore to Tokyo she had to pass through the Panama Canal. The Canal authorities would not allow her to proceed because she exceeded the permitted draught as she had too much coal on board. Some of the coal had to be transhipped on to another vessel, which followed her through the Canal. The cargo was then reloaded at the other end. The operation took nine days. The charterers contended that she was "off-hire" for this period as the working of the vessel was prevented.

Held, by the Court of Appeal, that she was not "off-hire" for the vessel remained at all times in herself fully efficient in all respects.

GRIFFITHS, L.J. (at page 10)

The charterers submit that they are not liable to pay for the period of delay as *Aquacharm* was off-hire during that time. Clause 15 of the charter-party provides:

> That in the event of the loss of time from deficiency of men, stores, fire, breakdown or damage to hull, machinery or equipment, grounding, detention by average accidents to ship or cargo, drydocking for the purposes of examination or painting bottom or by any other cause preventing the full working of the vessel, the payment of hire shall cease for the time thereby lost.

The charterers rely upon the words, "any other cause preventing the full working of the vessel". [Counsel], founding himself upon a passage in the judgment of KERR, J. in *Mareva Navigation Co. Ltd.* v. *Canaria Armadora S.A.: The "Mareva S."*[22] submits that the excess draught caused by the amount of cargo she was carrying prevented the full working of the *Aquacharm* because she was unable in that condition to perform the service required of her, namely to pass through the Canal. I do not read KERR, J.'s judgment as supporting the proposition that a ship which is sound in herself is prevented from "full working" because it has loaded too much cargo to pass through a particular waterway, or to enter a particular harbour.

The learned Judge was not considering a situation such as has arisen in this case, and the whole emphasis of his judgment directs one to consider the efficiency of the ship herself in deciding whether or not it is capable of "full working"; see in particular the passage where he said[23]:

---

[22] [1977] 1 Lloyd's Rep. 368.
[23] *Ibid.*, at p. 382.

> . . . But if, for instance, the cargo is damaged as the result of an accident, but the vessel's ability to work fully is not thereby prevented or impaired, because the vessel in herself remains fully efficient in all respects, then I do not think the charterers bring themselves within the clause.

Aquacharm remained at all times in herself fully efficient in all respects. She could not pass through the Canal because the Canal authorities decided she was carrying too much cargo, but that decision in no way reflected upon the *Aquacharm's* efficiency as a ship.

By contrast in *Sidermar S.p.A.* v. *Apollo Corporation: The "Apollo"*[24] a ship was held up by the port health authorities because two of the crew had been taken to hospital with suspected typhus, and the health authority insisted that the ship be disinfected before they would issue a free pratique. MOCATTA, J., held that the vessel was off-hire during that period of delay. A ship suspected of carrying typhus is prevented from working fully until it is cleared, for no responsible person would use it in such a condition. The incapacity of the ship to work in such a case is directly attributable to the suspected condition of the ship itself, and in my view is clearly distinguishable from the present case.

Although obviously not on all fours, the present case is nearer to the decision in *Court Line Ltd.* v. *Dant & Russell Inc.*,[25] when the ship, although sound in herself, was delayed by a boom across the Yangtse River, and it was held that it remained on hire.

As *Aquacharm* remained at all times an efficient ship, she was capable of "full working" within the meaning of the off-hire clause and the charterers do not succeed under this head.

Milburn & Co. *v.* Jamaica Fruit Importing and Trading Co. of London Ltd.

(1900) 83 L.T. 321

The "indemnity clause" in a time charter-party renders the charterer liable for the consequences of the master signing bills of lading under his direction.

By the terms of a time charter-party the charterers were to indemnify the shipowners "against all consequences of the master . . . signing bills of lading". The master signed bills of lading which omitted a clause excepting liability for negligence. The vessel was damaged and by reason of the absence of the clause, the shipowners could not obtain a general average contribution from the owners of the cargo.

Held, by the Court of Appeal, that since the charterers had ordered the master to sign the bills, they must indemnify the shipowners for the loss they had suffered in not recovering the contribution.

---

[24] [1978] 1 Lloyd's Rep. 200.
[25] (1939) 64 Ll.L. Rep. 212.

ROMER, L.J. (at page 326)

It appears that the charterers did ship the . . . goods on terms which . . . materially differed from the terms of the charter-party, inasmuch as those bills of lading left the shipowners responsible for the negligence of the master, officers, and crew of the ship. The consequence has been that the shipowners have lost the right of contribution for general average which, in my opinion, they would have had as against the . . . goods if the latter had been shipped on the terms of the charter-party. That loss has, it appears to me, flowed directly from the bills of lading having been signed by the master by the directions of the charterers in a form which . . . should not have been adopted. That being so, I think the loss is a consequence of the signing of the bills of lading within the meaning of the charter-party, and is accordingly recoverable by the shipowners from the charterers.

Larrinaga Steamship Co. Ltd. *v.* R.

[1945] 1 All E.R. 329

The "employment clause" in a time charter-party does not entitle the charterer to give orders as regards the navigation of the vessel.

A time charter-party provided that the master was to obey the orders of the charterer "as regards employment". The vessel was ordered to leave port by the charterer's representative. The master did so although the weather was very bad. In consequence of the storm she stranded, and sustained serious damage.

Held, by the House of Lords, that the charterer was not liable. The order which had been given was not one as to "employment".

LORD WRIGHT (at page 333)

In my opinion, the "employment" referred to is "employment of the ship". . . . I think the word "employment" . . . means the services which the ship is ordered to perform, such as the voyages to or from particular ports, with particular cargoes or in ballast. . . . [The] sailing orders which . . . were given were, in my opinion, merely dealing with matters of navigation. . . . It was the duty of the master to exercise his judgment in such matters of navigation.

LORD PORTER (at page 336)

[The charterer maintained] that though an order specifying the voyage to be performed is an order as to employment, yet an order as to the time of sailing is not. That order, it is contended, is one as to navigation, or, at any rate, not as to employment. My Lords, this distinction seems to me to be justified: an order to sail from port A to port B is in common parlance an order as to employment, but an order that a ship shall sail at a particular time is not an order as to employment because its object is not to direct how the ship shall be employed, but how she shall act in the course of that employment. If the word were held to include every order which affected not the employment itself but any incident arising in the course of it, almost every other liability undertaken by the charterer would be otiose, since the owners would be indemnified against almost all losses which the ship would incur in prosecuting her voyages. In particular, war and marine risk insurance would be unnecessary, because the charterers would be liable for the losses which were so covered, since the ship would be proceeding on their orders and entitled to an indemnity for all losses caused by following them . . . My Lords, in the present case, I do not think it necessary to determine the exact limitation to be placed on the meaning of the word. It is, I think, enough to say that an order to sail at once, whether wisely or unwisely given, is not within the clause as properly construed.

(3) CONDITIONS AND WARRANTIES

Bentsen *v.* Taylor, Sons & Co. (2)

(1893) 69 L.T. 487

Whether a term in a charter-party amounts to a condition or warranty is a matter of construction, depending on the intention of the parties and the whole of the circumstances.[26]

A ship was described as "now sailed or about to sail from a Pitch Pine Port to the United Kingdom". The charter-party was dated Mar. 29, but, in fact, the vessel did not leave the port concerned until Apr. 23.

Held, by the Court of Appeal, that the description "now sailed or about to sail" was an essential term of the contract, and the charterers would have been able to repudiate the contract, but, in fact, were not entitled to do so since they had waived the breach of this term.

BOWEN, L.J. (at page 488)

But assuming the Court to be of opinion that the statement made amounts to a promise, or in other words a substantive part of the contract, it still remains to be decided by the Court, as a matter of construction, whether it is such a promise as amounts merely to a warranty, the breach of which would sound only in damages, or whether it is that kind of promise the performance of which is made a condition precedent to all further demands under the contract, by the person who made the promise, against the other party—a promise the failure to perform which gives to the opposite party the right to say that he will

---

[26] Whether the classification of "conditions" and "warranties" is to be adopted in every case was considered by DIPLOCK, L.J., in *Hongkong Fir Shipping Co., Ltd.* v. *Kawasaki Kisen Kaisha Ltd.* [1962] 2 Q.B. 26; [1962] 1 All E.R. 474, C.A., p. 48, *post*.

no longer be bound by the contract. . . . There is no way of deciding that question except by looking at the contract in the light of the surrounding circumstances, and then making up one's mind whether the intention of the parties as gathered from the instrument itself, will best be carried out by treating the promise as a warranty, sounding only in damages, or as a condition precedent by the failure to perform which the other party is relieved of liability. . . . Having regard to the time of the year at which it is intended to prosecute the voyage, delay in its commencement, if it is protracted beyond a certain point, may, in many cases, be so vital a matter as to render the voyage impossible, or the risk may be so much increased as to make it no longer possible to have a voyage of the same kind. . . . Is there anything in [the words] so vague or so ambiguous that they cannot fairly be treated as a statement of a condition precedent? I agree that a condition precedent ought to be clearly expressed. The statement is that the ship has "now sailed or is about to sail". Having regard to what we have heard of the history of the port . . . I have not the slightest doubt that, if that statement does not mean that the ship has actually sailed, it does mean that she is loaded or may at all events for business purposes be treated as actually loaded; that she has got past the embarrassments and dangers attendant on loading, and that her sailing is the next thing to be looked for, and with regard to the suggested ambiguity in the phrase "about to sail", when it is read in conjunction with the other words, it seems to me clear that it does not mean that the ship is to sail within a reasonable or indefinite time, a statement which might lead to endless difficulties and expense, but that if she has not already sailed, she is about to sail forthwith. If that is so, . . . I have no hesitation in saying that I believe the phrase to be a condition precedent.

Behn *v.* Burness

(1863) 3 B. & S. 751

The position of a ship at the date of the charter-party is usually considered to be a "condition".

A charter-party stated that a vessel was "now in the port of Amsterdam". In fact, she was 62 miles away from that place.

Held, by the Exchequer Chamber, that the statement amounted to a condition, and, since it had been broken, the charterer was entitled to refuse to load when she arrived at the port of loading.

WILLIAMS, J. (at page 759)

The question on the present charter-party is confined to the statement of a definite fact—the place of the ship at the date of the contract. Now the place of the ship at the date of the contract, where the ship is in foreign parts and is chartered to come to England, may be the only datum on which the charterer can found his calculations of the time of the ship's arriving at the port of load [*sic*]. A statement is more or less important in proportion as the object of the contract more or less depends upon it. For most charters, considering winds, markets and dependent contracts, the time of a ship's arrival to load is an essential fact, for the interest of the charterer. In the ordinary course of charters in general it would be so: the evidence for the [charterer] shows it to be actually so in this case. Then, if the statement of the place of the ship is a substantive part of the contract, it seems to us that we ought to hold it to be a condition . . . unless we can find in the contract itself or the surrounding circumstances reason for thinking that the parties did not so intend. If it was a condition and not performed, it follows that the obligation of the charterer dependent thereon cease at his option . . .

Mitsui O.S.K. Lines Ltd. *v*. Garnac Grain Co. Inc.: "The Myrtos"

[1984] 2 Lloyd's Rep. 499

A clause stating the estimated time of arrival of a vessel has been held to be a condition.

A charter-party stated "vessel to be nominated 20 days prior to vessel's ETA". On June 11, 1980, the shipowners nominated the vessel *Myrtos* and on June 27 the charterers nominated Houston as the loading port. She did not arrive there until July 15. The charterers claimed damages on the ground that the shipowners were in breach of the clause, because she ought to have arrived by July 1.

Held, by the Queen's Bench Division (Commercial Court), that the clause was a condition.

LEGGATT, J. (at page 450)

It is the charterers' principal contention that on a true construction of the charter-party, the words "vessel to be nominated 20 days prior to the vessel's ETA" cannot mean what the owners say. The effect of the owners' contention is that the vessel was to be nominated on the day on which it was estimated that she would arrive 20 days thereafter. Mr Caldin, on behalf of the owners, contends that there are several reasons why the words do not mean what it is claimed, on the charterers' behalf, they do mean. He first submits that the words "estimated time of arrival" (which are the words of the charter-party) do not mean "expected ready to load" and Mr Flaux, for the charterers, would no doubt agree with that. Many of Mr Caldin's submissions were directed to making, or establishing, or reiterating that point, but for my part I have not been persuaded that they constitute a fundamental reason for adopting a different approach to the construction of the words in question than has been adopted in cases where similar phrases were in issue.

According to Mr Caldin's contention, the preamble does not have the effect of requiring an estimated time of arrival to be stated on the nomination of a vessel. It is true that an itinerary was, as it appears, given by the owners at the time when the vessel was nominated, but there was no explicit obligation to give an estimated time of arrival. The best that could be said (according to Mr Caldin) is that such a provision may be implicit in the nomination or in the provision for the nomination. It seems to me, upon a sensible reading of the opening words of the preamble, that what the owners are required to say is, in effect, "This is the vessel which is estimated to arrive at the loading port 20 days from today". Mr Caldin contends that in so far as there is an absolute warranty, relating to readiness to load, it is to be derived from a combination of provisions to be found in many charter-parties; that is to say, one providing for expected date of readiness to load, and the other providing for the vessel to proceed to the loading port with all convenient speed, or utmost dispatch, or whatever other phrase happens to have been chosen. Again, I am not convinced that there is any material distinction for the purpose of considering that submission, between a provision for estimated time of arrival and a provision for expected readiness to load: it is merely that a somewhat different time in course of the vessel's progress is being looked at.

Looking at the words with which I am concerned, it seems to me plain that the phrase, "vessel to be nominated 20 days prior to the vessel's ETA" constitutes a provision analogous with the expected readiness clause to be found not only in *Evera S.A. Commercial* v. *North Shipping Co. Ltd.*[27] itself, but in the other cases cited in it. In deciding the effect of the clause, it appears to me that I am bound by the decision of the Court of Appeal in *Monroe Brothers, Ltd.* v. *Ryan*,[28] and that I should follow DEVLIN, J., in the *Evera* case, unless they are distinguishable. I have already referred to the suggested distinction between an estimated time of arrival and an estimated date of readiness to load, but in my judgment that does not constitute any distinction in principle. It is true that it is less directly helpful to charterers to know when a vessel is to arrive than when she is to present ready, but they will nonetheless benefit in a way contemplated in the *Evera* case if they have a statement of position in the form of a stipulated arrival time because, for example, if the arrival time were not fulfilled, it would entitle the charterers to impugn the reasonableness of the estimate of time of arrival.

The other possible distinction between the present case and the *Evera* case and those cited in it, is that whereas they were concerned with specific vessels, the parties here were contracting in relation to a vessel to be nominated. Here again, I do not consider that the distinction is one which will avail the owners. Once the nomination had occurred, the contractual vessel was identified. There is no reason why the owners should not, upon nomination, assume an

---

[27] [1956] 2 Lloyd's Rep. 367.
[28] [1935] 2 K.B. 28, C.A.

absolute obligation to sail the vessel, from wheresoever she then might be, to the port of loading; and to do so, moreover, at such date as was necessary for her to arrive at the port of loading on the date estimated. It was suggested in argument that the reasoning is circular, because there cannot be an absolute obligation for a vessel to reach the port of loading until she has been nominated, and until she has been nominated it cannot be known how long it will take her to reach the port of loading from wherever she may happen to be. But the owners know that they must have a vessel available to reach the loading port in 20 days from nomination or, more accurately, as here, the loading port range, or area, since at the date of nomination the specific port of loading had not itself yet been identified. Before nomination the charterers know that they can expect the vessel to arrive on a date which will be specified. I can see no reason, in practice or in principle, why the absolute obligation of the owners should not crystallise on nomination. When that is to occur, it is no doubt commercially sensible to provide (as was provided here) that the charterer should have a period of three weeks or so in which to conclude the loading arrangements and thereafter monitor the vessel's progress by reference to such notices of expected readiness to load, and notices of actual time of arrival, as were required by cl. 20 of the charter-party.

I accordingly accede to Mr Flaux's submissions that as in the three cases upon which he relies, the owners' obligation here was to proceed with all convenient speed and that there was nothing in the drafting of this charter-party which detracted from that obligation of the owners.

Hongkong Fir Shipping Co. Ltd. *v.* Kawasaki Kisen Kaisha Ltd.

[1962] 1 All E.R. 474

It is difficult to classify the shipowner's undertaking to supply a seaworthy ship either as a "condition" or as a "warranty".

A time charter-party provided that the vessel was to be "in every way fitted for ordinary cargo service". She kept breaking down because her engine-room staff was incompetent and inadequate, and accordingly, she was unseaworthy.

Held, by the Court of Appeal, that this did not entitle the charterers to repudiate the charter-party, since the clause as to her fitness did not, in the circumstances, amount to a "condition".

DIPLOCK, L.J. (at page 487)

No doubt there are many simple contractual undertakings, sometimes express, but more often because of their very simplicity . . . to be implied, of which it can be predicated that every breach of such an undertaking must give rise to an event which will deprive the party not in default of substantially the whole benefit which it was intended that he should obtain from the contract. And such a stipulation, unless the parties have agreed that breach of it shall not entitle the non-defaulting party to treat the contract as repudiated, is a "condition". So, too, there may be other simple contractual undertakings of which it can be predicated that *no* breach can give rise to an event which will deprive the party not in default of substantially the whole benefit which it was intended that he should obtain from the contract; and such a stipulation, unless the parties have agreed that breach of it shall entitle the non-defaulting party to treat the contract as repudiated, is a "warranty". There are, however, many contractual undertakings of a more complex character which cannot be categorised as being "conditions" or "warranties" if the late nineteenth century meaning . . . used by BOWEN, L.J., in *Bentsen* v. *Taylor, Sons & Co.* (2)[29] be given to those terms. Of such undertakings, all that can be predicated is that some breaches will, and others will not, give rise to an event which will deprive the party not in default of substantially the whole benefit which it was intended that he should obtain from the contract; and the legal consequences of a breach of such an undertaking, unless provided for expressly in the contract, depend on the nature of the event to which the breach gives rise and do not follow automatically from a prior classification of the undertaking as a "condition" or a "warranty". . . . The shipowner's undertaking to tender a seaworthy ship has, as a result of numerous decisions as to what can amount to "unseaworthiness", become one of the most complex of contractual undertakings. It embraces obligations with respect to every part of the hull and machinery, stores and equipment and the crew itself. It can be broken by the presence of trivial defects easily and rapidly remediable as well as by defects which must inevitably result in a total loss of the vessel. Consequently, the problem in this case is, in my view, neither solved nor soluble by debating whether the owners' express or implied undertaking to tender a seaworthy ship is a "condition" or a "warranty". It is, like so many other contractual terms, an undertaking one breach of which may give rise to an event which relieves the charterer of further performance of his undertakings if he so elects, and another breach of which may not give rise to such an event but entitle him only to monetary compensation in the form of damages.

UPJOHN, L.J. (at page 483)

Why is this apparently basic and underlying condition of seaworthiness not, in fact, treated as a condition? It is for the simple reason that the seaworthiness clause is breached by the slightest failure to be fitted "in every way" for service. Thus, . . . if a nail is missing from one of the timbers of a wooden vessel, or if proper medical supplies or two anchors are not on board at the time of sailing, the owners are in breach of the seaworthiness stipulation. It is contrary to common sense to suppose that, in such circumstances, the parties contemplated that the charterer should at once be entitled to treat the contract

---

[29] [1893] 2 Q.B. 274, at p. 280. See p. 44, *ante*.

as at an end for such trifling breaches. . . . It is open to the parties to a contract to make it clear either expressly or by necessary implication that a particular stipulation is to be regarded as a condition which goes to the root of the contract, so that it is clear that the parties contemplate that *any* breach of it entitles the other party at once to treat the contract as at an end. That matter is to be determined as a question of the proper interpretation of the contract.

(4) FRUSTRATION

Bank Line Ltd. *v.* Arthur Capel & Co.

[1918–19] All E.R. Rep. 504

Where a vessel is requisitioned during the currency of a charter-party, the requisition may be sufficient to cause the charter-party to be frustrated.

A time charter-party was signed on Feb. 16, 1915. It was for a period of 12 months from the time when the vessel was placed at the disposal of the charterers. A clause stated that if she were not delivered by Apr. 30, the charterers had the right to cancel the charter-party. The vessel was not ready by Apr. 30, but they did not exercise their right of cancellation. On May 11 the vessel was requisitioned by the Government. She was released from requisition in September, 1915.

Held, by the House of Lords, that the charter-party was frustrated.

LORD FINLAN, L.C. (at page 508)

Did the requisition of the vessel and the detention under it constitute a change of circumstances such as to entitle the owners to treat the charter as at an end? As events show, the release of the vessel could be procured by providing another instead, but there was no obligation on the owners to do this for the purpose of carrying out the charter. . . . In my opinion, the owners were entitled to [state], as they did, that the contract had come to an end, as the detention had lasted so long that if the vessel were delivered in September, it would be on a contract differing most materially from that provided for by the original charter.

LORD SUMNER (at page 514)

In the particular circumstances of *Tamplin's* case[30] the main thing to be considered was the probable length of the total deprivation of the use of the chartered ship compared with the unexpired duration of the charter-party, and I agree in the importance of this feature, though it may not be the main and certainly is not the only matter to be considered. The probabilities as to the

[30] *F.A. Tamplin Steamship Co. Ltd.* v. *Anglo-Mexican Petroleum Products Co. Ltd.* [1916] 2 A.C. 397.

length of the deprivation and not the certainty arrived at after the event are also material. The question must be considered at the trial as it had to be considered by the parties when they came to know of the cause and the probabilities of the delay and had to decide what to do. . . . Rights ought not to be left in suspense or to hang on the chances of subsequent events. The contract binds or it does not bind, and the law ought to be that the parties can gather their fate then and there. What happens afterwards may assist in showing what the probabilities really were, if they had been reasonably forecasted, but when the causes of frustration have operated so long or under such circumstances as to raise a presumption of inordinate delay, the time has arrived at which the fate of the contract falls to be decided. That fate is dissolution or continuance, and, if the charter ought to be held to be dissolved, it cannot be revived without a new contract. The parties are free. . . . Delay even of considerable length and of wholly uncertain duration is an incident of maritime adventure which is clearly within the contemplation of the parties, such as delay caused by ice or neaping, so much so as to be often the subject of express provision. Delays such as these may very seriously affect the commercial object of the adventure, for the ship's expenses and overhead charges are running on, and, even with the benefit of protecting and indemnity club policies, the margin of profit is quickly run off. None the less, this is not frustration; the delay is ordinary in character, and in most cases the charterer is getting the use of the chartered ship. . . . Ultimately the frustration of an adventure depends on the facts of each case, but it is no easy matter so to direct a jury as that they will neither ask themselves what the actual parties thought of at the date of the contract, nor dispose of the case by saying that it would be unreasonable to find a verdict for the claimant, nor be governed only by their notion of what is fair between man and man nor be left in impenetrable doubt as to what the legal direction means. . . . Applying these considerations I am of opinion that the requisitioning of the [vessel] destroyed the identity of the chartered service and made the charter as a matter of business a totally different thing. It hung upon the performance for a time, which was wholly indefinite and probably long. The return of the ship depended on considerations beyond the ken or control of either party.

Admiral Shipping Co. Ltd. *v.* Weidner, Hopkins & Co.

(1917) 115 L.T. 812

A charter-party may be frustrated by the outbreak of war.

A ship was hired under a charter-party for "two Baltic rounds". She was not allowed to leave a Russian port on account of the outbreak of war between Germany and Russia.

Held, by the Court of Appeal, that the delay being of indefinite duration was such as completely to frustrate the adventure, and the charterers were not liable for the payment of the hire.

BANKES, L.J. (at page 819)

It remains, therefore, only to consider whether the doctrine of the frustration of the adventure has any application to [this case]. BAILHACHE, J., defines the doctrine thus[31]:

> The commercial frustration of an adventure by delay means, as I understand it, the happening of some unforeseen delay without the fault of either party to a contract of such a character as that by it the fulfilment of the contract in the only way in which fulfilment is contemplated and practicable is so inordinately postponed that its fulfilment when the delay is over will not accomplish the only object or objects which both parties to the contract must have known that each of them had in view at the time when they made the contract, and for the accomplishment of which object or objects the contract was made. . . .

. . . [This definition] appears to me to be entirely in accordance with the previous decisions upon the point.

Is there anything in the express provisions of these charter-parties or in the intention of the parties as gathered from those provisions which is inconsistent with the implied condition sought to be introduced by the appellants? I think not.

In the present case I find nothing in the charter-parties which appears to me to indicate an intention that the doctrine relied on should be excluded. On the contrary, the intention, apart from the expressed provisions, appears to be the other way. Take, for instance, the payment of the hire. Hire must continue to be paid until the vessel is redelivered at a United Kingdom coal port. No voyage may be undertaken which may involve risk of seizure or capture. Delay in consequence of not being able to start on the homeward voyage in consequence of such risk is not within the cesser of hire clause. It seems to me possible that the parties may from the language they used have contemplated a mere delay in the prosecution of the adventure being at the risk of the charterer, but I cannot gather from that language the intention that the charterer should, after the adventure had become commercially impossible, continue liable to pay the hire for a vessel which by the terms of the charter he was forbidden to bring to the only place at which he could terminate his obligation to pay that hire.

---

[31] In the Court below: (1916) 114 L.T. 171, at p. 175.

(5) BILLS OF LADING

The "Ardennes" (Owner of Cargo) *v*. The "Ardennes" (Owners)

[1950] 2 All E.R. 517

The bill of lading is very good evidence of the contract, but is not the contract itself.

A bill of lading gave the shipowner liberty to proceed by any route and to carry the goods beyond their port of destination. Instead of proceeding direct to London from Cartagena, the ship went first to Antwerp. When she arrived in London, the shipper had to pay a higher import duty since the goods had arrived after the proper time. Before the bill of lading had been issued the shipowner had promised the shipper that the ship would go direct to London.

Held, by the King's Bench Division, that the bill of lading was not in itself the contract between the shipowner and the shipper, and that the shipper was entitled to show that the prior promise constituted the contract on which he could make the shipowner liable for the payment of the higher duty.

LORD GODDARD, C.J. (at page 519)

It is, I think, well settled that a bill of lading is not, in itself, the contract between the shipowner and the shipper of goods, though it has been said to be excellent evidence of its terms: see *Sewell* v. *Burdick*[32] *per* LORD BRAMWELL[33] and *Crooks* v. *Allan*.[34] The contract has come into existence before the bill of lading is signed. The bill of lading is signed by one party only and handed by him to the shipper, usually after the goods have been put on board. No doubt, if the shipper finds that it contains terms with which he is not content or that it does not contain some term for which he stipulated, he might, if there was time, demand his goods back, but he is not, in my opinion, thereby prevented from giving evidence that there was a contract which was made before the bill of lading was signed, and that it was different from that which is found in the document or contained some additional term. He is not a party to the preparation of the bill of lading, nor does he sign it. It is unnecessary to cite further authority than the two cases which I have already mentioned for the proposition that the bill of lading is not itself the contract, and, therefore, in my opinion, evidence as to the true contract is admissible.

---

[32] (1884) 10 App. Cas. 74.
[33] *Ibid.*, at p. 105.
[34] (1879) 5 Q.B.D. 38.

Smith & Co. *v.* Bedouin Steam Navigation Co. Ltd.

[1896] A.C. 70

The bill of lading is prima facie *evidence in favour of an indorsee that the quantity of goods alleged to have been shipped has, in fact, been shipped.*

A bill of lading signed by the master stated that 1,000 bales of jute had been shipped on board. When the goods were delivered to the indorsees of the bill of lading, there was found to be a short delivery of 12 bales.

Held, by the House of Lords, that the shipowners were liable for the short delivery unless they could prove that the 12 bales had not been shipped, and, on the facts, they had not discharged this burden.

LORD HALSBURY, L.C. (at page 76)

To my mind, the cardinal fact is that the person properly appointed for the purpose of checking the receipt of the goods has given a receipt in which he has acknowledged, on behalf of the person by whom he was employed, that those goods were received. If that fact is once established, it becomes the duty of those who attempt to get rid of the effect of that fact to give some evidence from which your Lordships should infer that the goods never were on board at all.

LORD WATSON (at page 77)

The rule of law applicable to this case appears to me to be settled beyond dispute. The master of a ship has no authority to grant bills of lading for goods which were not put on board his vessel; but, when he signs a bill acknowledging the receipt of a specific quantity of goods, the shipowner is bound to deliver the full amount specified, unless he can show that the whole or some part of it was, in fact, not shipped. If the owner is able to satisfy that onus, by proving a short shipment, he is, to that extent, relieved from the obligation which would otherwise attach to him under the bill of lading. . . .

Silver *v.* Ocean Steamship Co. Ltd.

[1929] All E.R. Rep. 611

If the bill of lading states that the goods have been shipped "in apparent good order and condition", the shipowner will be estopped as against an indorsee by such a statement as far as defects which ought to be apparent on reasonable examination.

Cans of frozen eggs were shipped under a bill of lading incorporating The Hague Rules, and were stated to be shipped "in apparent good order and condition". When the cans arrived at the port of discharge, some were found in a damaged condition, being gashed or punctured, while others only had pinhole perforations.

Held, by the Court of Appeal, that the shipowners were estopped as against the indorsees of the bill of lading from showing that the cans had gashes which would have been apparent when the goods were loaded, but they were entitled to show that they had perforations which would not have been apparent on a reasonable examination.

SCRUTTON, L.J. (at page 614)

It has been decided in *Companía Naviera Vascongada* v. *Churchill and Sim*[35] and affirmed in the Court of Appeal in *Brandt* v. *Liverpool, Brazil and River Plate Steam Navigation Co. Ltd.*,[36] that the statement with regard to "apparent good order and condition" estops—as against the person taking the bill of lading for value . . .—the shipowner from proving that the goods were not in apparent good order and condition when shipped and, therefore, from alleging that there were, at shipment, external defects in them which were apparent to reasonable examination.

What was reasonably apparent to the shipowner's servants loading at [the port of loading] at night, but under clusters of electric light? The ultimate damage was classed by the surveyors as (i) serious damage where the tins were gashed or punctured, damage easily discernible in handling each tin; (ii) minor damage, pinhole perforations, which on tins covered with rims were not easily discernible, but which were found when the tins were closely examined. I have considered the evidence and I find that the first class of damage was apparent to reasonable examination; the second, having regard to business conditions, was not apparent. The result of this is that the shipowner is estopped against certain persons from proving or suggesting that there was gash or serious damage when the goods were shipped. He may raise the question whether there was not minor pinprick damage at that time, but having regard to the small quantity of goods rejected for visible damage, I should not estimate the amount of such minor damage at shipment as very high.

Parsons *v.* New Zealand Shipping Co.

[1901] 1 K.B. 548

The Bills of Lading Act 1855 does not preclude the shipowner from showing that the goods shipped were marked otherwise than as stated, unless the marks are material to the description of the goods.

Frozen carcases of lamb were shipped, and the bills of lading, signed by the shipowners' agents, described the goods as "622 X, 608 carcases. 488 X, 226 carcases". On arrival some carcases were found to be marked 522 X and others 388 X. The

[35] [1906] 1 K.B. 237.
[36] [1924] 1 K.B. 575, C.A.

indorsees of the bill of lading claimed that the shipowners were estopped from denying the statements in the bill of lading, and were liable for failing to deliver the carcases shipped.

Held, by the majority of the Court of Appeal, that the description of the goods in the bills of lading did not affect or denote the nature, quality, or commercial value of the goods, and that the shipowners were not precluded by s. 3 of the Bills of Lading Act 1855 from showing that there was a mistake in the description, and that the goods formed a portion of those in fact shipped.

ROMER, L.J. (at page 570)

The [indorsee] . . . contends that the [shipowners] are by s. 3 of the Bills of Lading Act 1855 precluded from going into evidence in order to establish the identity of the carcases tendered with those described in the bill of lading, by reason of the discrepancy between the marks on those carcases and the marks mentioned in the bill of lading. The contention raises a question of general importance as to the meaning and effect of the section, which speaks of a bill of lading "representing goods to have been shipped". Is every reference in a bill of lading to the marks on the goods of necessity part of the description of the goods within the meaning of the section? I think not. . . . Suppose, by way of example, a bill of lading was dealing with five parcels of goods of the same size, quality, and value, and, after describing these goods accurately, it proceeded to state the parcels were numbered consecutively one to five. Could a purchaser refuse to accept delivery of one or two of the parcels, and hold the signer of the bill of lading estopped under the section, because it turned out that the two out of the five which should have been respectively marked figure 3 and figure 4 were both marked figure 4? It appears to me that he could not. . . . Of course, difficult questions may arise on particular bills of lading, whether certain references to marks do or do not form part of the description of the goods within the meaning of s. 3. Those questions will fall to be determined according to the circumstances of the particular cases in which they arise. But, speaking generally, when the section refers to the bill of lading as "representing goods to have been shipped", it is, in my opinion, only contemplating those statements which may be said to describe the goods in the ordinary mercantile sense—that is to say, statements which would substantially affect a purchaser relying on the bill of lading as to the quantity, quality, or value of the goods he was buying. Marks on the goods which, so far as the purchaser is concerned, have no meaning, and could only be referred to in the bill of lading in order to assist in the more sure or speedy identification or delivery of the goods, do not, in my opinion, form part of the description of the goods within the meaning of s. 3, so as to bind the signer of the bill of lading by way of estoppel.

E. Clemens Horst Co. *v.* Biddell Bros.

[1912] A.C. 18

The holder of a bill of lading can transfer the possession of the goods by transferring the bill of lading.

A contract was made for the sale of hops to be shipped from San Francisco to London c.i.f. net cash. The buyer refused to pay for the goods until they were actually delivered.

Held, by the House of Lords, that possession of the bill of lading was in law equivalent to possession of the goods, and that under a c.i.f. contract the seller was entitled to payment on shipping the goods and tendering to the buyer the documents of title.

EARL LOREBURN, L.C. (at page 22)

This is a contract usually called a c.i.f. contract, under which the seller is to ship a cargo of hops and is to contract for freight and to effect insurance. . . . The buyer is to pay cash. But when is he to pay cash? The contract does not say. The buyer says that he is to pay cash against physical delivery and acceptance of the goods when they have come to England. Now s. 28 of the Sale of Goods Act says in effect that payment is to be made against delivery. Accordingly, we have supplied by the general law an answer to the question when this cash is to be paid. But when is there delivery of goods which are on board ship? That may be quite a different thing from delivery of goods on shore. The answer is that delivery of the bill of lading when the goods are at sea can be treated as delivery of the goods themselves, this law being so old that I think it is quite unnecessary to refer to authority for it. Now in this contract there is no time fixed at which the seller is entitled to tender the bill of lading. He therefore may do so at any reasonable time; and it is wrong to say that he might defer the tender of the bill of lading until the ship has arrived; and it is still more wrong to say that he must defer the tender of the bill of lading until after the goods have been landed, inspected, and accepted.

Sanders Brothers *v.* Maclean & Co.

(1883) 11 Q.B.D. 327

The indorsement of only one bill of lading out of a "set" is sufficient to pass the property in the goods.

A buyer of a cargo of iron rails refused to pay for them because only two out of three bills of lading were tendered to him.

Held, by the Court of Appeal, that, apart from a special stipulation, the tender of one bill of lading was sufficient, and he had no right to refuse payment.

BOWEN, L.J. (at page 341)

A cargo at sea while in the hands of the carrier is necessarily incapable of physical delivery. During this period of transit and voyage, the bill of lading by the law merchant is universally recognised as its symbol, and the indorsement and delivery of the bill of lading operates as a symbolical delivery of the cargo. Property in the goods passes by such indorsement and delivery of the bill of lading, whenever it is the intention of the parties that the property should pass just as under similar circumstances the property would pass by an actual delivery of the goods. And for the purpose of passing such property in the goods and completing the title of the indorsee to full possession thereof, the bill of lading, until complete delivery of the cargo has been made on shore to someone rightfully claiming under it, remains in force as a symbol, and carries with it not only the full ownership of the goods, but also all rights created by the contract of carriage between the shipper and the shipowner. It is a key which in the hands of a rightful owner is intended to unlock the door of the warehouse, floating or fixed, in which the goods may chance to be. The above effect and power belong to any one of the set of original bills of lading which is first dealt with by the shipper. . . . It appears to me, accordingly, that a tender is at all events in compliance with the present contract, by which all the effective bills of lading in existence are tendered. If, indeed, the absent original had been misused so as to defeat the title of the indorsees of the tendered residue of the set, the tender would have been bad. But the vendee was not entitled to reject the tender of the only effective documents on the bare chance that a third effective bill of lading might possibly have been dealt with when, in fact, it had not. The person who rejects effective and adequate documents of title on the ground that another document may possibly be outstanding, does so at his own risk.

Scruttons Ltd. *v.* Midland Silicones Ltd.[37]

[1962] 1 All E.R. 1

Generally, only the parties to a bill of lading have any rights under it.

Shipowners issued to the shippers of a drum containing chemicals a bill of lading by the terms of which they were entitled to limit their liability if the goods were damaged through their negligence. The drum was damaged during its loading by stevedores, who claimed to be able to limit their liability in accordance with the terms of the bill of lading.

Held, by the House of Lords, that they were not entitled to do so because they were

---

[37] This case should be contrasted with *New Zealand Shipping Co. Ltd.* v. *A. M. Satterthwaite & Co. Ltd.: The "Eurymedon"* [1974] 1 Lloyd's Rep. 534, P.C. (p. 60, *post*), where it was held that a stevedore could enforce the provisions of the bill of lading because the carrier was acting as the stevedore's agent.

not parties to the bill of lading, and so were liable to pay in full for the damage which had been caused.

VISCOUNT SIMONDS (at page 6)

Learned Counsel for the [shippers] met [the contentions of the stevedores] by asserting a principle which is, I suppose, as well established as any in our law, a "fundamental" principle, as Viscount HALDANE, L.C., called it in *Dunlop Pneumatic Tyre Co. Ltd.* v. *Selfridge & Co. Ltd.*,[38] an "elementary" principle, as it has been called times without number, that only a person who is a party to a contract can sue on it. "Our law" said Lord HALDANE, "knows nothing of a *jus quaesitum tertio* arising by way of contract". Learned Counsel for the [shippers] claimed that this was the orthodox view and asked your Lordships to reject any proposition that impinged on it. To that invitation I readily respond. For me heterodoxy, or, as some might say, heresy, is not the more attractive because it is dignified by the name of reform. Nor will I easily be led by an undiscerning zeal for some abstract kind of justice to ignore our first duty, which is to administer justice according to law, the law which is established for us by Act of Parliament or the binding authority of precedent. The law is developed by the application of old principles to new circumstances. Therein lies its genius. Its reform by the abrogation of those principles is the task not of the Courts of law but of Parliament. . . . If the principle of *jus quaesitum tertio* is to be introduced into our law, it must be done by Parliament after a due consideration of its merits and demerits. I should not be prepared to give it my support without a greater knowledge than I at present possess of its operation in other systems of law.

LORD REID (at page 10)

I think it is necessary to have in mind certain established principles of the English law of contract. Although I may regret it, I find it impossible to deny the existence of the general rule that a stranger to a contract cannot in a question with either of the contracting parties take advantage of provisions of the contract, even where it is clear from the contract that some provision in it was intended to benefit him. . . . There are, it is true, certain well-established exceptions to that rule[39]—though I am not sure that they are really exceptions and do not arise from other principles. But none of these in any way touches the present case.

---

[38] [1915] A.C. 847, at p. 853.

[39] See, e.g., *Les Affréteurs Réunis Sociétè Anonyme* v. *Leopold Walford (London) Ltd.* (1919) 121 L.T. 393, H.L.

New Zealand Shipping Co. Ltd. *v*. A. M. Satterthwaite & Co. Ltd.: The "Eurymedon"

[1974] 1 Lloyd's Rep. 534

If a carrier acts as an agent for a third party, e.g., a stevedore, the third party can enforce the terms of the bill of lading against the shipper if the bill of lading makes it clear that the stevedore is protected by the provisions, and if any difficulties about consideration moving from the third party are overcome.

A bill of lading in respect of a drilling machine stated that the carrier acted as agent "for all persons who are or might be his servants or agents from time to time", and that the limitation of liability provisions in the bill of lading were available to such servant or agent. The machine was damaged while being discharged by stevedores. The stevedores contended that they were entitled to limit their liability under the clause in the bill of lading.

Held, by the Judicial Committee of the Privy Council, that they were so entitled. The bill of lading brought into existence a unilateral bargain which became a full contract when the stevedores discharged the goods. The discharge of the goods for the benefit of the shipper was the consideration for the agreement by the shipper that the stevedores should have the benefit of the limitation provisions in the bill of lading. To give them the benefit of such provisions was to give effect to the clear intentions of a commercial document.

LORD WILBERFORCE (at page 539)

The carrier assumes an obligation to transport the goods and to discharge at the port of arrival. The goods are to be carried and discharged, so the transaction is inherently contractual. It is contemplated that a part of this contract, viz. discharge, may be performed by independent contractors—viz. the appellant. By cl. 1 of the bill of lading the shipper agrees to exempt from liability the carrier, his servants and independent contractors in respect of the performance of this contract of carriage. Thus, if the carriage, including the discharge, is wholly carried out by the carrier, he is exempt. If part is carried out by him, and part by his servants, he and they are exempt. If part is carried out by him and part by an independent contractor, he and the independent contractor are exempt. The exemption is designed to cover the whole carriage from loading to discharge, by whomsoever it is performed: the performance attracts the exemption or immunity in favour of whoever the performer turns out to be. There is possibly more than one way of analysing this business transaction into the necessary components; that which their Lordships would accept is to say that the bill of lading brought into existence a bargain initially unilateral but capable of becoming mutual, between the shippers and the appellant, made through the carrier as agent. This became a full contract when the appellant performed services by discharging the goods. The performance of these services for the benefit of the shipper was the consideration for the agreement by the shipper that the appellant should have the benefit of the exemptions and limitations contained in the bill of lading. . . .

In the opinion of their Lordships, to give the appellant the benefit of the exemptions and limitations contained in the bill of lading is to give effect to the clear intentions of a commercial document, and can be given within existing principles. They see no reason to strain the law or the facts in order to defeat these intentions. It should not be overlooked that the effect of denying validity to the clause would be to encourage actions against servants, agents and independent contractors in order to get round exemptions (which are almost invariable and often compulsory) accepted by shippers against carriers, the existence, and presumed efficacy, of which is reflected in the rates of freight. They see no attraction in this consequence.

(6) THE HAGUE RULES

Mayhew Foods Ltd. *v.* Overseas Containers Ltd.

[1984] 1 Lloyd's Rep. 317

The Rules do not apply to the carriage or storage of the goods before they are shipped. But where the goods are shipped but are subsequently discharged and stored at an intermediate port prior to transhipment on to another vessel, the Rules apply during the period of storage.

The shipowners agreed to carry a refrigerated container of chicken and turkey portions from Uckfield, Sussex, to Jeddah, Saudi Arabia. The container was taken to Shoreham, and on Dec. 5, 1981, was carried to Le Havre on the vessel *Volume*. It was discharged there and on Dec. 11 was loaded on the vessel *Benalder*, which arrived at Jeddah on Dec. 21. Its contents were found to have decayed. The shipowners admitted that this was due to their failure to set the temperature control on the container properly, but sought to rely on the provisions of the bill of lading limiting their liability to a lesser sum than that under the Carriage of Goods by Sea Act 1971, Sched., art. IV, r. 5.

Held, by the Queen's Bench Division (Commercial Court), that the Act applied as soon as the container was shipped at Shoreham, and the shipowners could not limit their liability to the lesser sum. If the shipowners chose to avail themselves of their right under the bill of lading to discharge, store and tranship the goods, those were operations in relation to and in connection with the carriage of goods by sea within the meaning of s. 1(3) of the Act.

BINGHAM, J. (at page 320)

As DEVLIN, J., pointed out in *Pyrene Co. Ltd.* v. *Scindia Steam Navigation Co. Ltd.*,[40] the rights and liabilities under the Rules attach to a contract or part of a contract. The contract here was for carriage of these goods from Uckfield to the numbered berth at Jeddah. The Rules did not apply to inland transport prior to shipment on board a vessel, because under s. 1(3) of the [Carriage of

[40] [1954] 1 Lloyd's Rep. 321, at p. 329.

Goods by Sea Act 1971], they are to have the force of law only in relation to and in connection with the carriage of goods by sea in ships. But the contract here clearly provided for shipment at a United Kingdom port, intended to be Southampton but in the event Shoreham, and from the time of that shipment, the Act and the Rules plainly applied. It does not matter that the vessel on which the container left this country was not *Benalder*, because OCL had liberty to substitute vessels or tranship, and *Benalder* was only the intended vessel. Nor does it matter that the bill of lading was issued some days after the goods had arrived in Le Havre showing *Benalder* and Southampton as the intended vessel and port of shipment. The parties clearly expected and intended a bill of lading to be issued and, when issued, it duly evidenced the parties' earlier contract. Since this bill was issued in a Contracting State and provided for carriage from a port in a Contracting State, I think it plain that the Rules applied once the goods were loaded on board the vessel at Shoreham.

OCL's second submission took as its starting point the fact already noted that the Act and the Rules only apply—". . . in relation to and in connection with the carriage of goods by sea in ships . . ." It was accordingly argued that even if the statutory provisions governed carriage from Shoreham to Le Havre, they did not apply while the goods were lying ashore at Le Havre any more than they applied before the goods were loaded at Shoreham or after they were discharged at Jeddah. In short, it was said that the interval of storage at Le Havre was not carriage by sea and so not covered by the Rules. As persuasive authority for this submission, Counsel relied on *Captain* v. *Far Eastern Steamship Co.*,[41] where a shipowner seeking to rely on the Hague Rules scheduled to the Canadian Carriage of Goods by Water Act was held disentitled to do so because the damage to the cargo had occurred during a lengthy period of storage ashore between two voyages. I do not, however, think that this decision gives much assistance, because the shipper there was told when the contract was made that there would be transhipment, and there were separate bills of lading for the two legs of the journey. The present case is factually different. The answer to this problem is again to be found in the principle that the rights and liabilities under the Rules attach to a contract. They do not apply to carriage or storage before the port of shipment or after the port of discharge, because that would be inland and not sea carriage. But between those ports the contract was, despite the wide language of cl. 21, for carriage by sea. If, during that carriage, OCL chose to avail themselves of their contractual right to discharge, store and tranship, those were, in my judgment, operations "in relation to and in connection with the carriage of goods by sea in ships", to use the language of the Act, or were "within the contractual carriage", to use the language of cl. 21(2) of the bill of lading conditions. It would, I think, be surprising if OCL could, by carrying the goods to Le Havre and there storing the goods before transhipment, rid themselves of liabilities to

[41] [1979] 1 Lloyd's Rep. 595.

which they would have been subject had they, as contemplated, shipped the goods at Southampton and carried them direct to Jeddah, the more so since Mayhew had no knowledge of any voyage to Le Havre. My conclusion is that the Rules, having applied on shipment at Shoreham, remained continuously in force until discharge at Jeddah.

Riverstone Meat Co. Pty. Ltd. *v.* Lancashire Shipping Co. Ltd.

[1961] 1 All E.R. 495

Under the Rules, the carrier must see that the independent contractor whom he employs exercises due diligence to make the ship seaworthy.

A fitter employed by ship repairers negligently refixed some inspection covers on some storm valves. Water entered the valves during the voyage, and damaged the cargo.

Held, by the House of Lords, that the negligence of the fitter was a lack of due diligence to make the ship seaworthy under art. III, r. 1, of The Hague Rules, for which the shipowners were responsible.

VISCOUNT SIMONDS (at page 504)

The plea that the shipowner is not liable for the negligence of an independent contractor failing as a general proposition . . . , it was then urged that it was a question of fact in each case and that, on the facts of the present case, the [shipowners] were not liable for the negligence of the fitter employed by the ship repairers. . . . I must say at once that I find it impossible to distinguish between one independent contractor and another, or between one kind of repair and another. I have no love for the argumentative question "Where is the line to be drawn?", but it would be an impossible task for the Court to examine into the facts of each case and determine whether the negligence of the independent contractor should be imputed to the shipowner. I do not know what criterion or criteria should be used, nor were any suggested. Take the case of repair. Is there to be one result if the necessary repair is slight, another if it is extensive? Is it relevant that the shipowner might have done the work by his own servants but preferred to have it done by a reputable shipyard? These and many other questions that will occur to your Lordships show that no other solution is possible than to say that the shipowners' obligation of due diligence demands due diligence in the work of repair by whomsoever it may be done.

LORD RADCLIFFE (at page 518)

Such general considerations as occur to me appear to favour the cargo owner's claim. He is not in any sense behind the scenes with regard to what is done to the vessel or how or when it is done. His concern with it begins and ends with the loading and discharge of his goods. The carrier, on the other hand, must have some form of ownership of the vessel and some measure of responsibility for seeing that it is fit and in proper condition for the carriage undertaken. He may qualify that responsibility by stipulation, if the law allows him to; or the law may write out the terms of his responsibility for him; but, within those limits, the responsibility is there. I should regard it as unsatisfactory, where a cargo owner has found his goods damaged through a defect in the seaworthiness of the vessel, that his rights of recovering from the carrier should depend on particular circumstances in the carrier's situation and arrangements with which the cargo owner has nothing to do; as, for instance, that liability should depend on the measure of control that the carrier had exercised over persons engaged on surveying or repairing the ship, or on such questions as whether the carrier had, or could have, done whatever was needed by the hands of his own servants or had been sensible or prudent in getting it done by other hands. Carriers would find themselves liable or not liable, according to circumstances quite extraneous to the sea carriage itself.

Maxine Footwear Co. Ltd. *v.* Canadian Government Merchant Marine Ltd.

[1959] 2 All E.R. 740

Under the Rules, the words "before and at the beginning of the voyage" mean the period from at least the beginning of loading until the vessel starts on her voyage.

When the cargo had been loaded in a vessel, she was destroyed by fire before she sailed on her voyage. The fire had been caused by negligence when some scupper pipes had been thawed out by an employee of an independent contractor on the authority of the master of the ship. The bill of lading incorporated The Hague Rules. The shippers claimed to recover damages for non-delivery of the goods. But the shipowners contended that they had exercised due diligence to make the ship seaworthy "before and at the beginning of the voyage" within the meaning of art. III, r. 1, since the ship was seaworthy at the time of loading, and the moment of the beginning of the voyage was never reached.

Held, by the Judicial Committee of the Privy Council, that the obligation to exercise due diligence was a continuing one which the shipowners had not fulfilled, since the negligence had occurred during the relevant period.

LORD SOMERVELL OF HARROW (at page 744)

The further submissions by the [shipowners] were based, as they had to be, on the construction of art. III, r. 1. It was submitted that, under that Article, the obligation is only to exercise due diligence to make the ship seaworthy at two moments of time, the beginning of the loading and the beginning of the voyage. It is difficult to believe that this construction of the word "before" could have been argued but for the fact that this doctrine of "stages" had been laid down in relation to the absolute warranty of seaworthiness in English law. . . . In their Lordships' opinion "before and at the beginning of the voyage" means the period from at least the beginning of the loading until the vessel starts on her voyage. The word "before" cannot, in their opinion, be read as meaning "at the commencement of the loading". If this had been intended, it would have been said. The question when precisely the period begins does not arise in this case, hence the insertion above of the words "at least". On that view the obligation to exercise due diligence to make the ship seaworthy continued over the whole of the period from the beginning of loading until the ship sank. There was a failure to exercise due diligence during that period. As a result, the ship became unseaworthy and this unseaworthiness caused the damage to, and loss of, the [shippers' goods] . . . It is also unnecessary to consider the earlier cases as to "stages" under the Common Law.[42] The doctrine of stages had its anomalies, and some important matters were never elucidated by authority. When the warranty was absolute, it seems at any rate intelligible to restrict it to certain points of time. It would be surprising if a duty to exercise due diligence ceased as soon as loading began only to reappear later shortly before the beginning of the voyage.

Gosse Millerd Ltd. *v.* Canadian Government Merchant Marine Ltd.

[1928] All E.R. Rep. 97

Under the Rules, the carrier must take proper care of the cargo.

A cargo of tinplates was shipped in a vessel under a bill of lading incorporating The Hague Rules. During the voyage she sustained damage, and had to go into dock for repairs. While these were being executed, the hatches were left open so that the workmen could go in and out of the hold more easily. The hatches were not protected when rain was falling, and the tinplates were damaged in consequence.

Held, by the House of Lords, that the shipowners were liable, for they had failed properly and carefully to carry the goods as required by art. III, r. 2, of The Hague Rules. The burden lay on them to prove that they were protected from liability by art. IV, r. 2(*a*). The term "management of the ship" did not include negligence in the management of the hatches.

Lord Hailsham, L.C. (at page 101)

In *Hourani* v. *Harrison*[43] the Court of Appeal had to consider the meaning to be attached to the words of art. IV, r. 2, in a case in which loss was caused by the pilfering of the stevedore's men whilst the ship was being discharged. The Court held that this did not fall within the expression "management of the ship"; but both Bankes, L.J., and Atkin, L.J., discussed the meaning to be placed on the expression. Bankes, L.J., reviews the authorities both in this

[42] See *The Vortigern* [1895–99] All E.R. Rep. 387.
[43] (1927) 32 Com. Cas. 305.

country and in the United States; he points out that the principle laid down in *The Glenochil*[44] has been accepted in the Supreme Court of the United States as being correct, and he adopts and applies that principle to the case which he is then considering. The learned Judge expresses the distinction as being between damage resulting from some act relating to the ship herself and only incidentally damaging the cargo, and an act dealing, as is sometimes said in some of the authorities, solely with the goods and not directly or indirectly with the ship herself. ATKIN, L.J. (says): "That there is a clear distinction drawn between goods and ship; and when they talk of the word 'ship', they mean the management of the ship, and they do not mean the general carrying on of the business of transporting goods by sea". In my judgment, the principle laid down in *The Glenochil*[45] and accepted by the Supreme Court of the United States in cases arising under the American Harter Act, and affirmed and applied by the Court of Appeal in the *Hourani* case[46] under the present English statute, is the correct one to apply. Necessarily, there may be cases on the border line, depending upon their own particular facts; but if the principle is clearly borne in mind of distinguishing between want of care of cargo and want of care of vessel indirectly affecting the cargo, . . . there ought not to be very great difficulty in arriving at a proper conclusion.

The "Morviken"

[1983] 1 Lloyd's Rep. 1

A clause enabling the carrier to limit his liability below the level permitted by The Hague-Visby Rules where they apply is void.

The owners of an asphalt road-finishing machine shipped it at Leith, Scotland, on the Dutch vessel *Haico Holwerda* for carriage to Amsterdam and thence to Bonaire in the Dutch Antilles under a bill of lading which by cl. 2 stated that Dutch law should apply and all actions should be brought before the Court of Amsterdam. At Amsterdam the machine was transhipped on to the Norwegian vessel *Morviken* for carriage to Bonaire. Whilst being discharged at Bonaire it was dropped on to the quay and was damaged to the extent of £22,000. The owners of the machine claimed damages, but the Dutch carriers applied for the action to be stayed in view of the clause set out above. By Dutch law the original Hague Rules, which entitled a carrier to limit his liability to £250, applied whereas under art. IV, r. 5(*a*) of The Hague-Visby Rules as set out in the Carriage of Goods by Sea Act 1971, the sum would be far higher.

Held, by the House of Lords, that the action would not be stayed for the bill of lading was one to which the Hague-Visby rules were expressly made applicable by art. X, and the clause was void under art. III, r. 8 because it lessened the liability of the carrier.

---

[44] [1896] P. 10.
[45] *Supra.*
[46] *Supra.*

LORD DIPLOCK (at page 5)

The bill of lading issued to the shippers by the carriers upon the shipment of the goods at the Scottish port of Leith was one to which the Hague-Visby Rules were expressly made applicable by art. X; it fell within both par. (a) and par. (b); it was issued in a Contracting State, the United Kingdom, and it covered a contract for carriage from a port in a Contracting State. For good measure, it also fell directly within s. 1(3) of the [Carriage of Goods by Sea Act 1971] itself.

The first paragraph of condition 2 of the bill of lading, prescribing as it does for a per package maximum limit of liability on the part of the carriers for loss for damage arising from negligence or breach of contract instead of the higher per kilogram maximum applicable under the Hague-Visby Rules, is *ex facie* a clause in a contract of carriage which purports to lessen the liability of the carriers for such loss or damage otherwise than is provided in the Hague-Visby Rules. As such it is therefore rendered null and void and of no effect under art. III, r. 8.

Empresa Cubana Importada de Alimentos "Alimport" *v.* Iasmos Shipping Co. S.A.: The "Good Friend"

[1984] 2 Lloyd's Rep. 586

By art. IV, r. 1 of the Rules whenever loss of or damage has resulted from unseaworthiness, the burden of proving the exercise of due diligence to make the ship seaworthy lies on the carrier claiming exemption under art. IV.

A vessel was not allowed by the port authorities to discharge a cargo of soya bean meal at Havana on the ground that it was infested with insects which were the subject of quarantine in Cuba, so she proceeded to Tenerife to discharge. The cargo owners claimed damages because the meal had not been landed at Havana, and contended that the vessel was unseaworthy in that the insects were present in her trunking and that the unseaworthiness caused the loss.

Held, by the Queen's Bench Division (Commercial Court), that there would be judgment for the cargo owners for the burden of proving that the shipowners had exercised due diligence to make the ship seaworthy under art. III, r. 1 lay on the shipowners. As they had failed to discharge that burden, they could not rely on the exception of quarantine restrictions set out in art. IV, r. 2(h).

STAUGHTON, J. (at page 588)

In the present case it seems to me that the burden is initially on Alimport, to prove that the cargo was not delivered at Havana in accordance with the terms of the bill of lading; that was established without difficulty, and indeed it was not in dispute. Next, it was for the owners to show that they were protected by one of the exceptions in art. IV, r. 2, of The Hague Rules. The most obvious candidate is (h), quarantine restrictions. (It was not disputed that "loss and damage" in art. IV, r. 2, included the kind of loss claimed by Alimport here, which did not comprise any physical damage to the soya bean meal.) It is proved that the discharge of the cargo at Havana was prevented by quarantine restrictions. Then Alimport have the burden of proving that the loss was caused by unseaworthiness. If they achieve that, the owners are liable (subject to the question of due diligence), since the exceptions in art. IV, r. 2, are subject to the obligation as to seaworthiness in art. III, r. 1: *Maxine Footwear Company Ltd.* v. *Canadian Government Merchant Marine Ltd.*[47] Finally, if Alimport prove that the loss was caused by unseaworthiness, the owners are excused if they can prove that they exercised due diligence to make the ship seaworthy before and at the beginning of the voyage.

There is one aspect of the care which does not fit easily into that analysis. This is the exception of loss or damage arising from inherent defect, quality, or vice of the goods in art. IV, r. 2(m), which is one of the exceptions relied on by the owners. If there is inherent vice, and if it has the effect that the vessel is unseaworthy, the *Maxine Footwear* case would seem logically to lead to the conclusion that the owners are not protected, unless they can establish due diligence. However, I do not find that an altogether plausible result. The explanation may be that that inherent vice and unseaworthiness are mutually exclusive as potential causes of damage: either it was caused by the state of the cargo or by the state of the ship, but it cannot have been caused by both. In that respect, inherent vice would differ from many of the other exceptions in art. IV, r. 2, such as perils of the sea, fire, quarantine restrictions, etc., which can be and often are concurrent causes with unseaworthiness.

I have already concluded that there were live *Trogoderma variabile* on board the vessel at Havana . . . On the evidence as a whole, it seems to me distinctly more probable that there was infestation on board the vessel before loading began, than that the insects came on board with the soya bean meal. Accordingly, I do not find that the owners have established a defence of inherent vice; and I do find it proved that the cause of the prohibition on discharge was the condition of the ship before loading as opposed to the condition of the cargo loaded.

I find it proved that there were substantial residues in the trunking just mentioned, and on the balance of probabilities that these were infested before loading with *Trogoderma variabile*. (*Latheticus oryzae*, for the reason already stated, is not crucial to the determination of this case.) There was also a considerable weight of evidence as to cargo residues elsewhere in the vessel, but some doubt as to whether they were substantial and not such as ought to be found in a well run ship prepared to load soya bean meal. I am inclined to the view that they were, in places, significant. But I need not reach a firm conclusion on that point, because the residues in the No. 2 'tweendeck

[47] [1959] 2 All E.R. 740, P.C.

trunking were the major cause of the troubles which the vessel encountered. If they had not existed, discharge of the soya bean meal at Havana might well have been completed without incident. But there was nothing temporary or minor in the impediment which prevented discharge of the soya bean meal in this case. The condition of the ship constituted a major and permanent obstacle to the completion of the contract voyage. I hold *Good Friend* to have been unseaworthy within art. III, r. 1.

I also find that unseaworthiness caused Alimport's loss. That makes it unnecessary for me to consider further the exceptions in art. IV, r. 2, which are relied on by the owners—that is (a) act, neglect or default of the master, etc., (h) quarantine restrictions, (i) act or omission of the shipper, etc., (p) latent defects and (q) any other cause, etc. They are all subject to the obligation in art. III, r. 1, to use due diligence to make the ship seaworthy. As to inherent vice, which is the exception in art. IV, r. 2(m), I have expressed doubt as to how that exception can be subject to art. III, r. 1; but inherent vice has not been established on the facts. I find that the trunking was in a damaged condition at the time when the vessel was being prepared for loading.

It follows that there was lack of due diligence on the part of the owners, through their master and crew, in failing to look inside the trunking, to detect the residues there, and to take measures to deal with them.

Stag Line Ltd. *v.* Foscolo, Mango & Co. Ltd.

[1931] All E.R. Rep. 666

Under the Rules, the ship is entitled to make any reasonable deviation. What is reasonable will depend upon the circumstances.

In the course of a voyage from Swansea to Istanbul [Constantinople] a vessel deviated from the contractual route in order to land at St. Ives some engineers who had been testing her fuel-saving apparatus. After leaving St. Ives she struck a rock and was lost.

Held, by the House of Lords, that the deviation was not a reasonable one within the meaning of art. IV, r. 4 of The Hague Rules.

LORD ATKIN (at page 673)

A deviation may, and often will, be caused by fortuitous circumstances never contemplated by the original parties to the contract, and may be reasonable though it is made solely in the interests of the ship, or solely in the interests of the cargo, or, indeed, in the direct interest of neither, as, for instance, where the presence of a passenger or of a member of the ship or crew was urgently required after the voyage had begun on a matter of national importance, or where some person on board was a fugitive from justice, and there were urgent reasons for his immediate appearance. The true test seems to be what departure from the contract voyage might a prudent person controlling the voyage at the time make and maintain, having in mind all the relevant circumstances existing at the time, including the terms of contract and the interests of all parties concerned, but without obligation to consider the interests of any one as conclusive. . . . I desire to refrain from expressing an opinion on whether the question whether a deviation is reasonable is a question of law or of fact.

Danae Shipping Corporation *v.* T.P.A.O. and Guven Turkish Insurance Co. Ltd.: The "Daffodil B"

[1983] 1 Lloyd's Rep. 498

Under the Rules the ship is entitled to make any reasonable deviation. What is reasonable will depend upn the circumstances.

While on a voyage from Milazzo, Sicily, to Tutunciftlik, Turkey, the vessel went to Lavrion, a small port on the east coast of Greece, to get a generator repaired instead of going to Piraeus.

Held, by the Queen's Bench Division (Commercial Court), that the deviation was a reasonable one within the meaning of The Hague-Visby Rules, art. IV, r. 4 for Lavrion was just as safe as Piraeus, if not safer, in that if the vessel had been disabled in a crowded seaway while approaching Piraeus the danger of collision with other vessels would have been at least as great, if not greater, than if she had become disabled on entering Lavrion.

LLOYD, J. (at page 501)

Having regard to Captain Papadopoulos's[48] evidence, backed up by the statistics, it would be quite impossible for me to hold that the anchorage at Lavrion is unsafe for short stay laden vessels as large as *Daffodil B*. In the event of a wind of force 8 or more getting up, there would not be the slightest difficulty in the vessel getting out. In expressing the view that the anchorage was unsafe, Captain Michaels[49] was, in my view, despite his great experience, being, as he himself accepted, ultra-cautious. I reject, therefore, the first, and main ground on which the defendants put their case.

But they have a second way in which they put their case. Even if Lavrion was safe for vessels of the size of *Daffodil B*, it was not safe for *this* vessel, with her diesel generator out of order. By going to a confined anchorage, such as Lavrion, with her diesel generator out of order, she was incurring the very same risk she was seeking to avoid in going through the Dardanelles in that condition. Much better, so it is said, that she should go to Piraeus, rather than to Lavrion. Although the deviation to Lavrion involved only an additional five miles outside the direct route, and a deviation to Piraeus would have involved

[48] One of the two pilots employed at Lavrion.
[49] The expert called on behalf of the defendants.

an additional 40 miles, Piraeus is a large port with ample repair facilities available, should shore repairs prove necessary, whereas the repair facilities at Lavrion were limited. Moreover, tugs are available at Piraeus, in the event of a complete breakdown; where at Lavrion they are not. In all the circumstances, therefore, the reasonable and obvious thing to do was to put into Piraeus. The defendants did not contend that putting into Piraeus was the *only* reasonable thing to do. But they did contend that it was not reasonable to go to Lavrion, even if, which they did not accept, it was physically safe to do so.

In the present case the plaintiffs say that, granted the vessel had to put in somewhere for repairs to her diesel generator, Lavrion was just as safe as Piraeus; indeed safer. For if the vessel's remaining generator had broken down when she was approaching Piraeus, and the vessel had become disabled in a crowded sea-way, the danger from collision with other vessels would have been at least as great if not greater, than if the vessel had become disabled on entering Lavrion. In the case of a sudden breakdown, the availability of tugs would make no difference. The damage would already have been done.

It seems to me that there is much force in this contention of the plaintiffs. At the very least the choice between Lavrion and Piraeus, from the safety point of view, must be regarded as nicely balanced; and in favour of Lavrion, it can be said that it involved a smaller deviation from the direct route, and almost certainly less waiting. There are other reasons why Lavrion was more convenient. In my view the arguments in favour of Lavrion are entitled to carry the day. But assuming that the arguments are even, then one comes back to the man who made the decision. Captain Galanos,[50] whose decision it was, knew the port; he knew its capacities as well as its limitations. Neither of the experts on either side had ever visited Lavrion. Of Captain Galanos's skill and knowledge there is no question; and nobody now doubts that the choice was made bona fide.

I hold that the deviation to Lavrion was a reasonable deviation within the meaning of art. IV, r. 4 of The Hague Rules. It follows, that the plaintiffs are entitled to their declaration; and once the vouchers which have been asked for by the defendants have been furnished, there will be judgment in the plaintiffs' favour for $387,304.67.

[50] A port captain employed by the shipowners' managers.

(7) LOADING, DISCHARGE AND DELIVERY

Hunter *v*. Fry

(1819) 2 B. & Ald. 421

Generally, the charterer must load a full and complete cargo and not merely one equal to the ship's burden as stated in the charter-party.

A charter-party stated that the charterer was to load a "full and complete cargo". The vessel was described as "of the burden of 261 tons or thereabouts". The charterer loaded 336 tons, although she might have carried 400 tons of the type of cargo loaded.

Held, by the Court of King's Bench, that the shipowner was entitled to damages for dead freight, for a full cargo had not been loaded.

ABBOTT, C.J. (at page 424)

I am of opinion that the mention of a ship's burden in the description of a ship in the charter-party, in the manner it is here mentioned, is an immaterial circumstance. . . . Here, the [charterer] has not covenanted to load a cargo equivalent to the burden mentioned in the charter-party: he has covenanted to load and put on board a full and complete cargo, and to pay so much per ton for every ton loaded on board. If the covenant had been to pay a gross sum for the voyage, the [charterer] (upon the arrival of the ship at the foreign port) might have insisted that the captain should take on board as much as the ship would safely contain; and the owner, who had covenanted to take a full and complete cargo, would not be justified in saying that he would take no more than the register-tonnage of the ship. It is, indeed, quite impossible that the burden of the ship (as described in the charter-party) should, in every case, be the measure of the precise number of tons which the ship is capable of carrying. That must depend upon the specific gravity of the particular goods; for a ship of given dimensions would be able to carry a larger number of tons of a given species of goods, that were of a great specific gravity, than she would of another of a less specific gravity, and the [charterer] would therefore pay freight in proportion to the specific gravity of the goods. Upon the whole, I am of opinion, that the owner was bound to take on board such a number of tons of goods as the ship was capable of containing without injury; and, therefore, that the [shipowner] is entitled to have a verdict for £918 which is the difference between the sum actually paid for freight, and that which would have been payable if the shipper had loaded on board a full and complete cargo.

Grant & Co. *v*. Coverdale, Todd & Co.

(1884) 51 L.T. 472

Generally, exception clauses concerning loading protect the charterer only if actual loading is prevented, and will not do so where he cannot get the goods to the port.

A ship was to proceed to Cardiff and load iron. The time for loading was to commence as soon as the vessel was ready to load except in case of "strikes, frosts, or other unavoidable accidents preventing loading". Owing to frost, delay occurred in bringing the cargo to the docks.

Held, by the House of Lords, that the charterer was liable for the delay, since the frost did not "prevent the loading".

EARL SELBORNE (at page 473)

This exception in the contract being limited to "accidents preventing the loading", the only question is, what is the meaning of "loading" and whether this particular frost did, in fact, prevent the loading. . . . It would appear to me to be unreasonable to suppose, unless the words make it perfectly clear, that the shipowner has contracted that his ship may be detained for an unlimited time on account of impediments, whatever their nature may be, to those things with which he has nothing whatever to do, which precede altogether the whole operation of loading, which are no part whatever of it, but which belong to that which is exclusively the charterer's business. He has to contract for the cargo, he has to buy the cargo, he has to convey the cargo to the place of loading and have it ready there to be put on board; and it is only when he has done those things that the duty and the obligation of the shipowner in respect of the loading arises. These words in the exception are as large as any words can be; they mention "strikes, frosts, floods, and all other unavoidable accidents preventing the loading". If, therefore, you are to carry back the loading to anything necessary to be done by the charterer in order to have the cargo ready to be loaded, no human being can tell where you are to stop. The bankruptcy, for instance, of the person with whom he has contracted for the supply of the iron, or disputes about the fulfilment of the contract, the refusal at a critical point of time to supply the iron, the neglect of the persons who ought to put it on board lighters to come down the canal for any distance or to be brought by sea, or to put it on the railway or bring it in any other way in which it is to be brought; all those things are, of course, practical impediments to the charterer having the cargo ready to be shipped at the proper place and time; but is it reasonable that the shipowner should be held to be answerable for all those things, and is that within the natural meaning of the word "loading"? Are those things any part of the operation of loading?

H. A. Brightman & Co. *v.* Bunge y Born Limitada Sociedad

(1924) 132 L.T. 188

Where the charterer is under an obligation[51] *to load an alternative cargo, and his original choice becomes impossible to effect, he is entitled to a reasonable time in which to make other arrangements.*

A charter-party contained a clause stating that a cargo of wheat and/or maize and/or rye was to be loaded. After the loading of the wheat had commenced the Argentine Government prohibited the export of wheat.

Held, by the Court of Appeal, that the charterers should be allowed a reasonable time for making provisions to ship an alternative cargo.

ATKIN, L.J. (at page 193)

The . . . claim arises from the prohibition of export of wheat. It was argued on behalf of the shipowners that as the obligation was to load a full and complete cargo of wheat and (or) maize and (or) rye, a prohibition confined to only one could not be said to prevent or delay the loading of the cargo. I think that in such a contract as this there is no such thing as an appropriation of cargo binding shipowner to shipper or shipper to shipowner, nor any question of final election of an option. The shipper retains control of his powers until the final ton is put on the ship, and as he retains his rights so he retains his liabilities. I think, therefore, that the prohibited export of one of the classes of grain cannot be said to prevent the ultimate loading of the cargo. Nevertheless, it may well delay it. The contract is made in relation to well-known business conditions, and it would be surprising to find that a shipper of a cargo who intended to ship wheat should find that he had no protection at all in the event of a sudden prohibition imposed while he was in the process of loading wheat, on the ground that the law presumed that he also had ready for that ship a full cargo of maize and rye. . . . The reasonable construction appears to me to be that in such a case, while the shipper must load a cargo in accordance with his contract, and if he cannot load wheat, must complete with maize or rye, yet if he shows that it took him a reasonable time to change over, he shows that he was delayed for that reasonable time, and if he cannot so load wheat from one of the excepted causes, then he is delayed in loading the cargo by that cause for that reasonable time.

---

[51] Whether the charterer is under an obligation to load an alternative cargo or merely has the option to load one is a matter of construction. See *Reardon Smith Line Ltd.* v. *Minister of Agriculture, Fisheries, and Food* [1963] A.C. 691; [1963] 1 All E.R. 545, H.L., p. 75, *post*.

Reardon Smith Line Ltd. *v*. Ministry of Agriculture, Fisheries and Food

[1963] 1 All E.R. 545

Where the charterer has an unfettered option to load an alternative cargo, he is not bound to exercise it.

A charter-party provided that the charterer was to load "a full and complete cargo . . . of wheat in bulk . . . and/or barley in bulk and/or flour in sacks". The charterer had the option "of loading up to one-third cargo of barley and one-third cargo of flour" at an increased rate of freight. The charterer began to load wheat, but a strike occurred, and further loading was delayed.

Held, by the House of Lords, that the primary obligation under the charter-party was to load wheat, and the charterer was under no liability to load an alternative cargo of barley and flour which were not affected by the strike.

VISCOUNT RADCLIFFE (at page 552)

In my opinion, however, the principle of the *Brightman* case[52] has no application here, because there is here no primary obligation on the charterers to ship a mixed cargo. The primary obligation is to provide a cargo of wheat only, the exceptions clause covers delay in the shipping of wheat, and there is no obligation on the charterers to lose that protection by exercising their option to provide another kind of cargo that is not affected by a cause of delay, even assuming such a cargo to be readily available. . . . There is in this case no duty on the charterers to "switch" from wheat to barley or flour, because their choice of loading barley or flour is unfettered and is not at any time controlled in their hands by an overriding obligation to put on board by a fixed date a full cargo which must include those commodities, if it cannot consist of wheat alone.

LORD DEVLIN (at page 559)

When a contract itself limits and enumerates the obligations, as when it obliges the shipper to ship wheat or barley or flour, it is quite sensible and natural to talk of his having an option to ship any one of these three commodities. There is, however, a narrower sense in which the word can be used and that is to confer a right of choice specially granted to the holder of the option and to be used solely for his own benefit. It is in this sense, I think, that the word is generally used in the business world. . . . Where there is no option in the business sense, the consequence of damming one channel is simply that the flow of duty is diverted into the others and the freedom of choice thus restricted. If then a shipper cannot ship wheat, he must ship either barley or flour. The width of the alternatives is in the contract for the benefit of both

---

[52] *H. A. Brightman & Co.* v. *Bunge y Born Limitada Sociedad* [1924] 2 K.B. 619; 132 L.T. 188, C.A., p. 74, *ante*.

parties and it can be a liability as well as a benefit for the shipper. But where there is a "business option", the legal position is quite different. There is not then one contractual obligation to be performed in alternative ways, but one obligation to be performed in one way, unless the option holder chooses to substitute another way and does so by the effective exercise of his option. In exercising the option, which he has acquired solely for his own advantage, the holder is not bound to consider the convenience or the interest of the other party. If the obligation is to ship a full and complete cargo of wheat with the option to change to barley or flour, and the shipment of wheat is impeded, he is not obliged to change to barley or flour simply because that is the only way in which he could ship a full and complete cargo. So the question here is whether the contractual obligation on the charterer is correctly expressed as an obligation to ship a full and complete cargo of wheat, barley or flour in proportions which can, subject to the specified limits, be selected by the charterer; or whether it is an obligation to ship a full and complete cargo of wheat with an option to the charterer to substitute for that cargo a mixed one. . . . I have reached the conclusion that the charterer's construction is the better one.

Leeds Shipping Co. Ltd. *v.* Société Française Bunge

[1958] 2 Lloyd's Rep. 127

The port nominated by the charterer must be a safe port. What is a safe port will depend upon the circumstances.[53]

A charter-party stated that the vessel was to proceed to "one or two safe ports in Morocco". The charterer directed her to Essaouira [Mogador]. In this port there was a lack of shelter and a liability to the sudden onset of a high wind, which could not be predicted, and which might quickly cause an anchor to drag. The port was very near some rocks and shallows, and the anchorage was very restricted.

Held, by the Court of Appeal, that the port was unsafe.

SELLERS, L.J. (at page 130)

The first question involves an appreciation of the factors, relevant to this case, which have to be considered in relation to the unsafety of a port. It is well established that the safety or unsafety of a port must be assessed in regard to the actual vessel which has been chartered to use the port. The period for consideration is at least the whole period of the vessel's use of the port and may take account of dangers likely to be incurred on the voyage to the port. . . . The safety of the port should be viewed in respect of a vessel

[53] For another illustration see *Palace Shipping Co., Ltd.* v. *Gans Steamship Line* [1916] 1 K.B. 138; [1914–15] All E.R. Rep. 912, C.A., p. 26, *ante*.

properly manned and equipped, and navigated and handled without negligence and in accordance with good seamanship. This may include, where circumstances so require, and if available, the engagement of a pilot or the use of a tug or tugs or, especially if such assistance is not available, consultation with a harbourmaster or some other responsible person with knowledge and experience of the port. . . . If it were said that a port will not be safe unless, in the relevant period of time, the particular ship can reach it, use it and return from it without, in the absence of some abnormal occurrence, being exposed to danger which cannot be avoided by good navigation and seamanship, it would probably meet all circumstances as a broad statement of the law. Most, if not all, navigable rivers, channels, ports, harbours, and berths have some danger from tides, currents, swells, banks, bars, or revetments. Such dangers are frequently minimised by lights, buoys, signals, warnings and other aids to navigation and can normally be met and overcome by proper navigation and handling of a vessel in accordance with good seamanship.

The "Athamas" (Owners) *v.* Dig Vijay Cement Co. Ltd.

[1963] 1 Lloyd's Rep. 287

Whether the ship has reached a place sufficiently near to the point named in the contract will depend on the circumstances.

By the terms of a charter-party a vessel was to discharge her cargo at Phnom-Penh or "so near thereto as she may safely get". She could not get to Phnom-Penh, and had to discharge at Ho Chi Minh City [Saigon] which was 250 miles away.

Held, by the Court of Appeal, that in the circumstances of the case the discharge at Ho Chi Minh City [Saigon] was sufficient compliance with the terms of the charter-party.

PEARSON, L.J. (at page 302)

[The] examination of the authorities has not yielded any precise definition of the range of proximity or vicinity within which the substitute destination must lie in order to be, in relation to the named destination for the ship, "as near thereto as she may safely get". I do, however, derive from these authorities an impression that the range is fairly narrow, and that in an ordinary case a substitute destination 250 miles by water from the named destination would be outside the range of proximity. This, however, is an extraordinary case in that Saigon [Ho Chi Minh City], though 250 miles by water away from Phnom-Penh, is nevertheless the nearest port to Phnom-Penh, at any rate for the purpose of unloading the cargo concerned. It is helpful to consider the question as at the date of the conclusion of the charter-party. The parties would not be deemed necessarily to know that Saigon [Ho Chi Minh City] is the nearest port to Phnom-Penh, but they should be deemed to have general maritime knowledge and therefore to know that that part of the world is sparsely provided with ports, so that there might well be a long distance between the named port and any possible substitute. That differentiates this case from, at any rate, any case where the named port is on the west coast of Europe or in the Mediterranean Sea or in the Black Sea. The question is largely one of degree and to be decided mainly on a basis of commercial knowledge and experience.

SELLERS, L.J. (at page 295)

Distance is relative. Ports on the South China Sea or outposts in a desert could be "near" each other in the estimate of men, who might regard a similar distance along the English Channel or in an English county as remote, although places available for discharge along the English Channel ports would be restricted if a charter-party were in respect of one of the larger ships, and, too, the distance between Plymouth and Southampton might be regarded as relatively small if the voyage were from or to Australia. The requirement is not a near port and not the nearest port but the nearest safe port or place. Such a provision seems, of necessity, to involve consideration of a coastline or length of river where safe facilities for loading or discharging could be found outside and away from the named port.

Reardon Smith Line Ltd. *v*. Australian Wheat Board

[1956] 1 All E.R. 456

A charterer who nominates an unsafe port will be liable for any damage so caused as long as it is not too remote.

The charterer directed the vessel to a port in Western Australia. The vessel arrived at the port, and while loading was being carried out, the wind freshened and soon increased to gale force, and she was severely damaged.

Held, by the Judicial Committee of the Privy Council, that the port was unsafe, and that the master of the ship had acted reasonably in going there. The damage to the vessel flowed from the breach of the charter-party, and consequently the charterer was liable.

LORD SOMERVELL OF HARROW (at page 461)

On the general and difficult question as to the position of the master if and when he realises or suspects danger or the possibility of danger, their Lordships would adopt the following passage from the judgment of DEVLIN, J. [in *Compania Naviera Maropan S.A.* v. *Bowaters Lloyd Pulp and Paper Mills Ltd.*[54]]

[54] [1955] 2 Q.B. 68, at p. 77; [1954] 3 All E.R. 563, at p. 568.

I think, therefore, that the real question is not so much whether a distinction can be drawn between a voyage and a time charter, as whether any charter-party, whether for voyage or for time, is exempt from the application of the ordinary law of contract. I see no reason in principle why it should be, and I do not think that business convenience requires it. Indeed, I think business, whether maritime or otherwise, might be gravely impeded if the ordinary principle were not allowed to operate freely—and by the ordinary principle I mean that, generally speaking, a man is entitled to act in the faith that the other party to a contract is carrying out his part of it properly. It does not lie in the mouth of the promisor to say that a promisee has no right to assume that a promise has been faithfully carried out and should make his own inquiries to see whether it is or not. If everything done under contract had to be scrutinised and tested by the other party before he can safely act on it, many transactions might be seriously held up—in doubtful cases, perhaps indefinitely. Even if the breach is clear, it is vital to the proper conduct of business that the promisee should be able, if he considers the breach a minor one, to proceed without sacrificing his right to be indemnified. . . . Suppose that the master thinks that the nominated berth is barely large enough and that he might scrape his vessel's sides and damage her paintwork. If, . . . it is the only berth that can be nominated, is he to throw up the voyage? . . . It is possible . . . that a prudent master, without knowing for certain whether he was right or not and so acting in the interests of all concerned, might have felt that the risk of damage to the vessel's bottom was outweighed by the certainty of time lost. . . . [It] does not mean that a master can enter ports that are obviously unsafe and then charge the charterers with damage done. The damages for any breach of warranty are always limited to the natural and probable consequences. The point then becomes one of remoteness of damage; or, if it is thought better to put it in Latin, the expressions *novus actus interveniens* and *volenti non fit injuria* are ready to hand. There is also the rule that an aggrieved party must act reasonably and try to minimise his damage. A master who entered a berth which he knew to be unsafe (and which perhaps the charterer had nominated in ignorance of its condition) rather than ask for another nomination and seek compensation for any time lost by damages for detention, might find himself in trouble. So might a master who sought compensation for the time lost in sailing back across the Atlantic because he had not cared to risk damage to his paintwork.

Sunbeam Shipping Co. Ltd. *v.* President of India: The "Atlantic Sunbeam"

[1973] 1 Lloyd's Rep. 482

The charterer will be liable if it is due to his fault that the vessel does not become an "arrived ship".[55]

A vessel was directed to Calcutta. She could not become an "arrived ship" there unless a prior entry had been obtained by the shipowners, and a document called a "jetty challan" was obtained by the charterers from the port commissioners. The prior entry was obtained by the shipowners, but four days were wasted in obtaining the jetty challan. A question arose as to whether the charterers were liable for preventing the vessel from becoming an "arrived ship".

---

[55] As to when a vessel is an "arrived ship", see p. 93, *post*.

Held, by the Queen's Bench Division (Commercial Court), that there was an implied term to that effect.

KERR, J. (at page 488)

It therefore follows that in my view the term to be implied in this case is to the effect that the charterers were bound to act with reasonable dispatch and in accordance with the ordinary practice of the port of Calcutta in doing those acts which had to be done by them as consignees to enable the ship to become an arrived ship. In that connection the burden of proof, as in all cases of allegations of breach of contract, rests on the plaintiff, in this case the owners. But the arbitrators are, of course, entitled to draw inferences adverse to the charterers if there are unexplained periods of delay or inactivity.

Petersen *v*. Freebody & Co.

[1895] 2 Q.B. 294

As a general rule, the shipowner is only bound to deliver over the ship's side.

A cargo of spars was to be discharged "overside into lighters". The consignee provided lighters at the ship's side, but did not employ sufficient men in the lighters to take delivery within the time fixed for unloading. The shipowner sued for damages in respect of the delay.

Held, by the Court of Appeal, that the shipowner was not bound to put the spars on board the lighters. His duty was simply to put them over the rail of the ship and within reach of the men on board the lighters. Consequently the consignee was liable for the delay in unloading.

LORD ESHER, M.R. (at page 297)

Whatever be the circumstances of the delivery, one party is to give, and the other is to take, delivery at one and the same time, and by one and the same operation. It follows that both must be present to take their parts in that operation. Those parts are, the ship has to deliver and the consignee to take delivery—where? Each has to act within his own department. The shipowner acts from the deck or some part of his own ship, but always on board his ship. The consignee's place is alongside the ship where the thing is to be delivered to him. If the delivery is to be on to another ship, he must be on the ship; if into a barge or lighter, on that barger or lighter; if on to the quay, on the quay. Wherever the delivery is to be, the shipowner, on the other hand, must give delivery. If he merely puts the goods on the rail of his ship, he does not give delivery: that is not enough. If, on the other hand, the consignee merely stands on the other ship, or on the barge or lighter, or on the quay, and does nothing, he does not take delivery. The shipowner has performed the principal part of his obligation when he has put the goods over the rail of his ship; but I think he must do something more—he must put the goods in such a position that the consignee can take delivery of them. He must put them so far over the side as that the consignee can begin to act upon them; but the moment the goods are put within the reach of the consignee he must take part in the operation. . . . The delivery, under the charter-party, was to be a delivery in the ordinary way by a joint operation in which each was to take his part. The lay days were exceeded because the consignees had not sufficent men on the lighters to perform their part in that operation. The ship was not in default; and, therefore, the shipowner is entitled to demurrage.

The "Stettin"

(1889) 14 P.D. 142

The master is not justified in delivering to any person who does not produce the bill of lading.

Barrels of oil were shipped under bills of lading making them deliverable "to Mendelsohn or assigns". The shipper retained one bill of lading, and sent the other to his agents to secure payment of the price. The master of the ship delivered the oil to Mendelsohn without production of the bill of lading.

Held, by the Probate, Divorce and Admiralty Division, that the shipowner was liable to the shipper for so delivering.

BUTT, J. (at page 147)

According to English law and the English mode of conducting business, a shipowner is not entitled to deliver goods to the consignee without the production of the bill of lading. I hold that the shipowner must take the consequences of having delivered these goods to the consignee without the production of either of the two parts of which the bill of lading consisted.

Glyn Mills Currie & Co. *v.* East and West India Dock Co.

(1882) 47 L.T. 309

Generally, the master will be justified in delivering the goods to the named consignee or the person who first presents the bill of lading.

Goods were deliverable to "Cottam & Co. or assigns". During the voyage Cottam & Co. deposited one bill of lading with a bank as security for a loan, and with a second bill obtained delivery from a dock company in whose warehouse the goods had been stored after being landed. The bank sued the dock company for wrongful delivery.

Held, by the House of Lords, that the dock company was entitled to deliver the goods on presentation of the second bill of lading, for it had no notice of any dealings with the other bill of lading of the same set.

EARL CAIRNS (at page 312)

The shipowner has to protect himself from that which is liable to cause difficulty or embarrassment to him and the way in which as it appears to me he does protect himself is by stating that although "the master . . . hath affirmed to three bills of lading" . . . yet notwithstanding that fact "one of those bills of lading being accomplished the others shall stand void", which I understand to mean that if upon one of them the shipowner acts in good faith, he will have "accomplished" his contract, will have fulfilled it, and will not be liable or answerable upon any one of the others. If one is produced to him in good faith, he is to act upon that and not to embarrass himself by considering what has become of the other bills of lading.

LORD BLACKBURN (at page 316)

I think, as I have already said, that where the master has notice that there has been an assignment of another part of the bill of lading, the master must interplead or deliver to the one who he thinks has the better right, at his peril if he is wrong. And I think it probably would be the same if he had knowledge that there had been such an assignment, though no one had given notice of it or as yet claimed under it. At all events, he would not be safe, in such a case, in delivering without further inquiry. But I think that when the master has not notice or knowledge of anything but that there are other parts of the bill of lading, one of which it is possible may have been assigned, he is justified or excused in delivering according to his contract to the person appearing to be the assign of the bill of lading which is produced to him.

Monarch Steamship Co. Ltd. *v.* A/B Karlshamns Oljefabriker

[1949] 1 All E.R. 1

Where goods are delivered short of their destination and cannot be obtained elsewhere, the consignee is entitled to the costs of transhipment.

A British ship was chartered to carry soya beans from Manchuria in April, 1939, and in June the charterers were given bills of lading in respect of them and nominated Karlshamn in Sweden as the port of discharge. Under the terms of the charter-party the owners were under contract to supply a seaworthy ship. The ship was unseaworthy, and the voyage was thereby delayed. Soon after the outbreak of war in September, 1939, the ship was ordered by the Admiralty to proceed to Glasgow, where the beans were discharged. They were then forwarded by the consignees (to whom the charterers had transferred the bills of lading which incorporated the terms of the charter-party) to Karlshamn in neutral ships since no similar beans were obtainable there. The cost of transhipment came to over £21,000.

Held, by the House of Lords, that the consignees were entitled to recover the cost of transhipment from the shipowners by way of damages.

LORD PORTER (at page 9)

It must then be asked whether [the consignee] was obliged to accept the beans in some other quarter of the globe, where it did not want them, without any right to recover damages provided it could sell them there at a price as high as it could obtain at the contractual port. I cannot think that it was obliged to accept any such substituted performance. It appears to me to have had the right to require the goods to be delivered at the place stipulated, and, if the shipowner failed to carry out his bargain to deliver there, the direct and natural consequence is that the merchant should arrange for the carriage forward and charge the shipowner with the reasonable cost of doing so. Nor do I think it improves the [shipowner's] position to say it is the [consignee's] duty to minimise or nullify his damages by selling elsewhere. He is entitled to have his contract fulfilled in the manner stipulated and is under no obligation to accept some undesired method of performance. . . . If this view be right, the [consignee] was entitled to recover the expense of forwarding the goods in fulfilment of his contract.

LORD WRIGHT (at page 12)

I agree . . . that the claim for the damages is justified. It, in truth, gives effect to the broad general rule of the law of damages that a party injured by the other party's breach of contract is entitled to such money compensation as will put him in the position in which he would have been but for the breach. In that respect this case is singularly clear, because the contract entitled the [consignee] to have the beans delivered at Karlshamn and the damages claimed and awarded represent simply the sum necessary to effect that result, namely, the cost of transhipment from Glasgow to Karlshamn. The [consignee] was fortunate in being a neutral and in being able to charter neutral tonnage and obtaining from the British Government permits to carry the beans from this country to Sweden. What the [consignee] wanted was the consignment of beans. Their value either in Glasgow or Sweden, where no beans were on the market, would have been a poor consolation, but, as transhipment could be effected, the extra cost incurred for transhipment was the proper subject of monetary compensation. . . . The damages awarded are not special or remote, but are the damages naturally and directly resulting from the [shipowner's] breach of contract. . . .

Rodocanachi, Sons & Co. *v.* Milburn Brothers

(1886) 18 Q.B.D. 67

Where goods are not delivered, the damages are to be calculated on their market value if they had arrived at the port of discharge.

Shipowners had agreed to carry a cargo of cotton seed from Alexandria to the United Kingdom. The cargo was lost by the negligence of the master and they were held liable. The cargo owners brought an action for non-delivery.

Held, by the Court of Appeal, that the measure of damages should be based on the market value of the goods at the place of destination, less the amount of any freight remaining unpaid.

LORD ESHER, M.R. (at page 76)

I think that the rule as to measure of damages in a case of this kind must be this: the measure is the difference between the position of a [shipper] if the goods had been safely delivered and his position if the goods are lost. What, then, is that difference? If the goods are delivered, he obtains them, but in order to obtain them he must pay the freight in respect of which there is a lien on them. If there were no lien, he would be entitled to the goods without paying anything. Upon getting the goods he could sell them. He therefore would get the value of the goods upon their arrival at the port of discharge, less what he would have to pay in order to get them. But what is to be the rule in getting at the value of the goods? If there is no market for such goods, the result must be arrived at by an estimate, by taking the cost of the goods to the shipper and adding to that the estimated profit he would make at the port of destination. If there is a market, there is no occasion to have recourse to such a mode of estimating the value; the value will be the market value when the goods ought to have arrived. But the value is to be taken independently of any circumstances peculiar to the [shipper]. It is well settled that in an action for non-delivery or non-acceptance of goods under a contract of sale the law does not take into account in estimating the damages anything that is accidental as between the [seller] and the [buyer], as for instance an intermediate contract entered into with a third party for the purchase or sale of the goods. It is admitted in this case that, if the [shippers] had sold the goods for more than the market value before their arrival, they could not recover on the basis of that price, but would be confined to the market price, because the circumstance that they had so sold the goods at a higher price would be an accidental circumstance as between themselves and the shipowners; but it is said that, as they have sold for a price less than the market price, the market price is not to govern but the contract price. I think, that if the law were so, it would be very unjust. I adopt the rule laid down in *Mayne on Damages*, which gives the market price as the test by which to estimate the value of the goods independently of any circumstances peculiar to the plaintiff, and so independently of any contract made by him for the sale of the goods. That rule gives the mode of estimating the value which is to be taken for the purpose of arriving at the damages.

C. Czarnikow Ltd. *v.* Koufos

[1967] 2 Lloyd's Rep. 457

Where there has been delay in carrying the goods, the measure of damages is the difference between the market value at the time when they ought to have been delivered and at the time when they were delivered in fact.

A vessel was chartered for a voyage from Constantza to Basrah for the carriage of sugar. She deviated to Berbera to load livestock for the shipowner. If she had not deviated, she would have arrived at Basrah 10 days earlier. The charterers claimed damages for the difference between the market value of the sugar at the due date of delivery and at the actual date of delivery.

Held, by the House of Lords, that they were entitled to this sum.

LORD MORRIS OF BORTH-Y-GEST (at page 472)

If the problem in the present case is that of relating accepted principle to the facts which have been found, I entertain no doubt that if at the time of their contract the parties had considered what the consequences would be if the arrival of the ship at Basrah was delayed, they would have contemplated that some loss to the respondents was likely or was liable to result. The appellant, at the time that he made his contract, must have known that if in breach of contract his ship did not arrive at Basrah when she ought to arrive, he would be liable to pay damages. he would not know that a loss to the respondents was certain or inevitable but he must, as a reasonable businessman, have contemplated that the respondents would very likely suffer loss, and that it would be or would be likely to be a loss referable to market price fluctuations at Basrah. I cannot think that he should escape liability by saying that he would only be aware of a possibility of loss but not of a probability or certainty of it. He might have used any one of many phrases. He might have said that a loss would be likely: or that a loss would not be unlikely: or that a loss was liable to result: or that the risk that delay would cause loss to the respondents was a serious possibility: or that there would be a real danger of a loss: or that the risk of his being liable to have to pay for the loss was one that he ought commercially to take into account. As a practical businessman he would not have paused to reflect on the possible nuances of meaning of any one of these phrases. Nor would he have sent for a dictionary.

The carriage of sugar from the Black Sea to Iraqi ports (including Basrah) is a recognised trade. The appellant knew that there was a sugar market at Basrah. When he contracted with the respondents to carry their sugar to Basrah, though he did not know what were the actual plans of the respondents, he had all the information to enable him to appreciate that a delay in arrival might in the ordinary course of things result in their suffering some loss. He must have known that the price in a market may fluctuate. He must have known that if a price goes down, someone whose goods are late in arrival may be caused loss.

Since in awarding damages the aim is to award a sum which as nearly as possible will put the injured party into the position in which he would have been in if the breach of contract had not caused him loss, and if in all the circumstances he had acted reasonably in an effort to mitigate his loss, I think that it must follow that, where there is delay in arrival, in many cases the actual loss suffered (above the amount of which there ought not to be recovery) can be measured by comparing the market price of the goods at the date when they should have arrived and the market price when they did arrive. That, *prima facie*, is the measure of the damages.

(8) EXCEPTIONS

Hamilton *v.* Pandorf

(1888) 57 L.T. 726

The exception "perils of the sea" covers any accident resulting in damage which lets sea-water into the vessel.

A cargo of rice was shipped under a bill of lading containing an exception of "dangers and accidents of the seas". During the voyage sea-water entered through a pipe which had been gnawed by rats, and damaged the rice. There was no negligence on the part of the shipowners.

Held, by the House of Lords, that the damage had been caused by a peril of the sea; and so the shipowners were not liable.

LORD HALSBURY, L.C. (at page 727)

It is clear that the parties do not mean by such an instrument as we are construing to except all accidents of any kind or description whatsoever which may happen during the particular voyage which both parties are looking forward to. Some effect must be given to the words "perils of the sea". A rat eating a cheese in the hold of a vessel is not a peril of the sea; the sea, or the vessel being on the sea, has nothing to do with the destruction of the cheese. . . . One of the dangers which both parties to the contract would have in their mind would, I think, be the possibility of the water getting into the vessel from the sea upon which the vessel was to sail in accomplishing her voyage—it would not necessarily be by a storm; the parties have not so limited the language of their conduct—it might be by striking on a rock, or by excessive heat, so as to open some of the upper timbers; these and many more contingencies that might be suggested would let the sea in; but what the parties, I think, contemplated was that, if any accident (not wear and tear, or natural decay) should do damage by letting the sea into the vessel, that should be one of the things contemplated by the contract. A subtle analysis of all the events which lead up to and in that sense cause a thing may doubtless remove the first link in the chain so far that neither the law nor the ordinary business of mankind can permit it to be treated as a cause affecting the legal right of the parties to a suit. In this case the existence of the rats on board, their thirst, the hardness of their teeth, the law of gravitation, which caused the water to descend upon the rice, the ship being afloat, the pipe being lead, and its capacity of being gnawed—each of these may be represented as the cause of the water entering; but I do not assent to the view that this contract can have a different meaning attached to it according as you regard each step in the chain of events as the origin out of which the damage ultimately arises. In the class of contract where the shipowner's negligence or misconduct prevents perils of the sea being relied upon, it is not that perils of the sea are different, or that the words ought to have a different meaning attached to them, but because in those cases an additional term exists in the contract, which makes the negligence of the shipowner, or of those for whom he is responsible, a material element; but it is also necessary to give effect to the words "dangers and accidents of the seas". . . . I think the idea of something fortuitous and unexpected is involved in both words, peril or accident; you could not speak of the danger of a ship's decay; you would know that it must decay; and the destruction of the ship's bottom by vermin is assumed to be one of the natural and certain effects of an unprotected wooden vessel sailing through certain seas. One ought, if it is possible, to give effect to all the words that the parties have used to express what this bargain is, and I think in this case it was a danger, accident, or peril, in the contemplation of both parties, that the sea might get in and spoil the rice.

Nobel's Explosives Co. *v.* Jenkins

[1896] 2 Q.B. 326

The exception "restraint of princes" covers not only actual seizure of a vessel but also the likely seizure of her.

Goods were shipped in England for Japan under a bill of lading excepting "restraint of princes". On the day the ship reached Hong Kong, war was declared between Japan and China. The master, therefore, landed at Hong Kong such part of the cargo as was contraband.

Held, by the Queen's Bench Division, that the delivery of the contraband goods in Japan was prevented by the excepted peril, since delivery at the port of destination would expose the ship to real danger of seizure.

MATHEW, J. (at page 330)

The main ground of defence was the exception in the bill of lading of "restraint of princes, rulers or people". A large body of evidence was laid before me to show that if the vessel sailed with the goods on board, she would in all probability be stopped and searched. It was certain in that case that the goods would have been confiscated, and quite uncertain what course the captors would take with the ship and the rest of the cargo. I am satisfied that if the master had continued the voyage with the goods on board, he would have been acting recklessly. It was argued for the [consignees] that the clause did not apply unless there was a direct and specific action upon the goods by sovereign authority. It was said that the fear of seizure, however well founded, was not a restraint, and that something in the nature of a seizure was necessary. But this argument is disposed of by the cases of *Geipel* v. *Smith*[56] and *Rodocanachi* v. *Elliot*.[57] The goods were as effectually stopped at Hong Kong as if there had been an express order from the Chinese Government that contraband of war should be landed. . . . The warships of the Chinese Government were in such a position as to render the sailing of the steamer with contraband of war on board a matter of great danger, though she might have got away safely. The restraint was not temporary. . . . There was no reason to expect that the obstacle in the way of the vessel could be removed in any reasonable time. I find that the captain, in refusing to carry the goods farther, acted reasonably and prudently, and that the delivery of the goods at Yokohama was prevented by restraint of princes and rulers within the meaning of the exception.

Blackburn *v.* Liverpool, Brazil and River Plate Steam Navigation Co.

[1902] 1 K.B. 290

The shipowner can rely on an excepted peril, even if he has been negligent, as long as "negligence" itself is one of the excepted perils.

Sugar was stored in a tank at the bottom of the ship. The engineer negligently let salt water into the tank.

Held, by the King's Bench Division, that the shipowner was not liable because the bill of lading contained an exception of perils of the sea, "whether arising from the negligence of the engineers or otherwise".

WALTON, J. (at page 293)

The [shippers] in this action . . . say that they are entitled to recover . . . damages because the shipowners were bound by their contract to carry and deliver the cargo safely and failed to do so. The [shipowners], on the other hand, contend that the obligation to carry and deliver the cargo safely is subject to the exceptions contained in the bill of lading, among which there is

---

[56] (1872) L.R. 7 Q.B. 404.
[57] (1874) L.R. 9 C.P. 518.

an exception in respect of "loss or damage resulting from any of the following perils (whether arising from the negligence, default, or error in judgment of the . . . engineers . . . or otherwise howsoever) . . . or other peril of the seas, rivers, or navigation of whatever nature or kind soever". The shipowners say that they are exempt because the case comes within that exception. . . . As I understand the law, where there is not a negligence clause, the shipowner is bound absolutely to deliver the goods safely, subject to the exception of perils of the sea and any other exceptions contained in the bill of lading. If he fails to carry the goods safely, but the loss is occasioned by one of the excepted perils, then *prima facie* he is not liable. In the cases before *Hamilton* v. *Pandorf*[58] the contract of the shipowner was not only to carry the goods safely, subject to the excepted perils, but, further, to use all due care and diligence to deliver safely, and therefore the exceptions relieved him from his absolute obligation, but not from the obligation to use due care and diligence, if there was no negligence clause. If the shipowner failed to use due care and diligence, though he was exempt by the exception from his absolute obligation, yet he was not exempt from liability for breach of his contract to use due care and diligence, if there was no negligence clause; and therefore, if a loss was occasioned by want of due care and diligence, the shipowner was liable even if the loss was occasioned by an excepted peril. In the present case there is what is called a "negligence clause", and this shipowner is exempt from liability for loss occasioned by peril of the seas though caused by negligence, and therefore we have not to consider the liability for want of due care and diligence. The only question is whether the loss was occasioned by a "peril of the seas or navigation". If it was, then the shipowner is protected by the exception, although the loss was caused by the negligence of his servant.

(9) GENERAL AVERAGE

Australian Coastal Shipping Commission *v.* Green

[1971] 1 Lloyd's Rep. 16

By Rule C of the York-Antwerp Rules "Only such losses, damages or expenses which are the direct consequence of the general average act shall be allowed as general average".

A vessel was in distress and a tug was employed to tow her to a port of safety. The towage contract included a clause whereby the owners of the vessel agreed to indemnify the tugowners for any loss of the tug. The tow rope parted and fouled the tug's propellers, and she became a total loss. The tugowners claimed damages from the owners of the vessel, who incurred expenses in defending the action.

Held, by the Court of Appeal, that these expenses were general average expenditure,

[58] (1887) 12 App. Cas. 518. See p. 86, *ante*.

for the towage contract was a "general average act" under Rule A of the York-Antwerp Rules, 1950,[59] and the expenses were the direct consequence of such general average act.

LORD DENNING (at page 20)

The "general average act" was, I think, the contract made by the shipowners with the tug. In each case the vessel was in dire peril and the shipowners called upon the tug for help. If the tug had rendered salvage services on the usual terms of "no cure—no pay", the contract would undoubtedly have been a "general average act". If the services had been successful, the owners would have been liable to pay a very high reward: which would count as "general average expenditure". . . .

Instead of entering into such a contract, the shipowners made a towage contract on the United Kingdom Standard Towage Conditions. That was a very reasonable contract to make for both sides. It is well known that there is a substantial risk in towage operations that the tow rope may break and foul the propeller of the tug: and that, if that happens, the tug may run aground or be damaged and have to be rescued. In a salvage agreement, the tugowners take that risk on themselves in return for the chance of a very high salvage reward. In a hiring agreement, at a fixed rate of hire, they cannot be expected to take the risk on themselves. It is only right and fair that they should ask for and receive an indemnity. The benefit to the shipowners is that, if the service is successful, he pays much less than he would under a salvage award: but, in return, he has to give an indemnity to the tugowner. In these circumstances, I have no doubt that the towage contract is a "general average act". It was intentionally and reasonably made for the common safety. . . . If the master, when he does the "general average act", ought reasonably to have foreseen that a subsequent accident of the kind might occur—or even that there was a distinct possibility of it—then the subsequent accident does not break the chain of causation. The loss or damage is the direct consequence of the original general average act.

(10) DEMURRAGE

Hick *v.* Raymond and Reid

[1893] A.C. 22

Where no definite period of lay days has been agreed on, the charterer is only bound to load or unload within a reasonable time.

---

[59] Now Rule A of the York-Antwerp Rules, 1974, which states: "There is a general average act when, and only when, any extraordinary sacrifice or expenditure is intentionally and reasonably made or incurred for the common safety for the purpose of preserving from peril the property involved in a common maritime adventure".

No time was fixed for the unloading of a cargo in the Port of London. The unloading was interrupted because of a dock strike. The consignees tried to get the cargo unloaded by means of other labour, but failed to do so.

Held, by the House of Lords, that the shipowners were not entitled to damages for detention, for the consignees had made all reasonable efforts.

LORD HERSCHELL, L.C. (at page 28)

I think it must be taken that throughout the whole of the time during which the discharge ceased, and the dock company were unable to supply labour to effect it, it was not possible for the [consignees] either to find any other person to provide the labour or themselves to obtain the necessary labour in any other way. If the terms of the bills of lading had required the discharge to be effected in any particular number of days, it is quite clear that the burden of the delay caused by the difficulty of obtaining labour would have fallen upon them, and it would have been no answer to a charge that they had failed to fulfil their obligation, to say that the circumstances had rendered it impossible for them to do so. The bills of lading in the present case contained no such stipulation and, therefore, in accordance with ordinary and well-known principles the obligation of the [consignees] was that they should take discharge of the cargo within a reasonable time. The question is, has the [shipowner] proved that this reasonable time has been exceeded? This depends upon what circumstances may be taken into consideration in determining whether more than a reasonable time was occupied. . . . It appears to me that . . . the only sound principle is that the "reasonable time" should depend on the circumstances which actually exist. If the cargo has been taken with all reasonable dispatch under those circumstances, I think the obligation of the consignee has been fulfilled. When I say the circumstances which actually exist, I, of course, imply that those circumstances, in so far as they involve delay, have not been caused or contributed to by the consignee.

LORD WATSON (at page 32)

When the language of a contract does not expressly, or by necessary implication, fix any time for the performance of a contractual obligation, the law implies that it shall be performed within a reasonable time. The rule is of general application, and is not confined to contracts for the carriage of goods by sea. In the case of other contracts the condition of reasonable time has been frequently interpreted and has invariably been held to mean that the party upon whom it is incumbent duly fulfils his obligation, notwithstanding protracted delay, so long as such delay is attributable to causes beyond his control, and he has neither acted negligently nor unreasonably.

William Alexander & Sons *v.* Aktieselskabet Dampskibet Hansa

[1920] A.C. 88

Where the charterer is bound to load or discharge in a fixed time, he will be excused from liability for delay if there is an exceptions clause in his favour.

A vessel was to discharge a cargo of timber at the rate of not less than one hundred standards per day. Instead of the discharge taking six and one-third days, it took 13 and one-third days because of a shortage of labour at the port.

Held, by the House of Lords, that the charterers were liable for seven days' demurrage, for they were not covered by an exception clause in the charter-party, nor had the shortage of labour arisen through the fault of the shipowner.

VISCOUNT FINLAY (at page 94)

A great many cases were cited laying down the rule that if the charterer has agreed to load or unload within a fixed period of time . . . , he is answerable for the non-performance of that engagement, whatever the nature of the impediments, unless they are covered by exceptions in the charter-party or arise through the fault of the shipowner or those for whom he is responsible. . . . Although no authority upon the point was cited which would in itself be binding upon your Lordships' House, there has been such a stream of authority to the same effect that I think it would be eminently undesirable to depart in a matter of business of this kind from the rule which has been so long applied, even if your Lordships felt any doubt as to the propriety of these decisions in the first instance. I myself have no doubt as to their correctness, and I understand that this is the opinion of all your Lordships.

LORD SHAW OF DUNFERMLINE (at page 97)

My Lords . . . the law is perfectly well settled. In *Randall* v. *Lynch*[60] Lord ELLENBOROUGH stated the position in law which has never been departed from: "I am of opinion that the person who hires a vessel detains her, if at the end of the stipulated lay days he does not restore her to the owner. He is responsible for all the various vicissitudes which may prevent him from doing so". This proposition was repeated in ampler words by Lord SELBORNE in *Postlethwaite* v. *Freeland*[61];

> There is no doubt that the duty of providing, and making proper use of, sufficient means for the discharge of cargo, when a ship which has been chartered arrives at its destination and is ready to discharge, lies (generally) upon the charterer. If, by the terms of the charter-party, he has agreed to discharge it within a fixed period of time, that is an absolute and unconditional engagement, for the non-performance of which he is answerable, whatever may be the nature of the impediments which prevent him

[60] (1809) 2 Camp. 352.
[61] (1880) 5 App. Cas. 599, at p. 608.

from performing it, and which cause the ship to be detained in his service beyond the time stipulated.

This law has been applied over and over again, and is too well settled to be shaken. The risk of vicissitudes which prevent the loading or discharge of cargo within the stipulated lay days lies unconditionally with the charterer. This is the prescription of the general law. To avoid its application either (1) the contract of parties must be absolutely clear; or (2) it must be established that the failure of the charterer's duty arose from the fault of the shipowners or those for whom they are responsible.

E. L. Oldendorff & Co. G.m.b.H. *v.* Tradax Export S.A.: The "Johanna Oldendorff"

[1973] 2 Lloyd's Rep. 285

Under a port charter-party the vessel becomes an "arrived ship" when, if she cannot proceed immediately to a berth, she has reached a position within the port where she is at the immediate and effective disposition of the charterer. If she is at the place where waiting ships usually lie, she is in such a position unless there are some extraordinary circumstances, proof of which lies on the charterer.

A vessel carrying grain under a port charter-party anchored at the Bar anchorage at Liverpool. The anchorage was 17 miles from the usual discharging berth, but was the usual place where grain vessels lay while awaiting a berth.

Held, by the House of Lords, that she was an "arrived ship" when she reached the anchorage, for she was then at the immediate and effective disposition of the charterer.

Lord Reid (at page 291)

I would therefore state what I would hope to be the true legal position in this way. Before a ship can be said to have arrived at a port she must, if she cannot proceed immediately to a berth, have reached a position within the port where she is at the immediate and effective disposition of the charterer. If she is at a place where waiting ships usually lie, she will be in such a position unless in some extraordinary circumstances proof of which would lie in the charterer. . . .

If the ship is waiting at some other place in the port, then it will be for the owner to prove that she is as fully at the disposition of the charterer as she would have been if in the vicinity of the berth for loading or discharge.

Compania Naviera Aeolus S.A. *v.* Union of India

[1962] 3 All E.R. 670

Once a vessel is on demurrage the exceptions clauses relieving the charterer from liability for delay caused do not apply unless there are clear words to that effect.

A vessel had been chartered under a charter-party, which contained a strike clause stating that the time for discharging should not count against the charterers during the continuance of a strike. The vessel began to discharge the cargo, but after the lay time had expired a strike took place which interrupted further unloading.

Held, by the House of Lords, that the charterers could not rely on the strike clause, because it was not sufficiently clearly worded to have the effect of relieving them from the payment of demurrage. Consequently they had to pay demurrage for the whole period after the lay days had expired.

LORD REID (at page 674)

I must fall back on the rule which I have already quoted from the work of SCRUTTON, L.J.[62] [*viz.* "when once a vessel is on demurrage, no exceptions will operate to prevent demurrage continuing to be payable unless the exceptions clause is clearly worded so as to have that effect"]. I do not think that it is an arbitrary rule for this reason. If a strike occurs before the end of the lay time, neither party can be blamed in any way. But, if it occurs after demurrage has begun to accrue, the owner might well say: true, your breach of contract in detaining my ship after the end of the lay time did not cause a strike, but if you had fulfilled your contract, the strike would have caused no loss because my ship would have been on the high seas before it began: so it is more reasonable that you should bear the loss than that I should. So it seems to me right that if the [charterers] are to escape from paying demurrage during this strike, they must be able to point to an exceptions clause which clearly covers this case. In my judgment they cannot do that.

(11) FREIGHT

Hunter *v.* Prinsep

(1808) 10 East 378

Where freight is payable on delivery, it will not be earned unless the goods are actually delivered.

Where the voyage was from Honduras to London, freight was payable "on a right and true delivery of the homeward bound cargo". After being captured by the enemy, the

---

[62] *Scrutton on Charterparties* (16th Edn., 1955, p. 353). Now 19th Edn., 1984, p. 309.

vessel was recaptured and recommenced the voyage, but owing to bad weather she was driven ashore at St. Kitts. The wreck and cargo were put up for sale without the consent of the cargo owner. After paying claims for salvage, the master claimed to retain the balance of the proceeds of sale for freight.

Held, by the Court of King's Bench, that although the ship was prevented by excepted perils from completing the voyage, no freight was payable unless the goods were delivered.

LORD ELLENBOROUGH (at page 394)

The shipowners undertake that they will carry the goods to the place of destination, unless prevented by the dangers of the seas, or other unavoidable casualties: and the freighter undertakes that if the goods be delivered at the place of their destination, he will pay the stipulated freight: but it was only in that event, viz. of their delivery at the place of destination, that he, the freighter, engages to pay anything. If the ship be disabled from completing her voyage, the shipowner may still entitle himself to the whole freight, by forwarding the goods by some other means to the place of destination; but he has no right to any freight if they be not so forwarded; unless the forwarding them be dispensed with, or unless there be some new bargain upon this subject. If the shipowner will not forward them, the freighter is entitled to them without paying anything.

Asfar & Co. *v.* Blundell

[1896] 1 Q.B. 123

Where freight is payable on delivery, it will not be earned unless the goods, when delivered, are in merchantable condition.

A ship carrying dates was sunk in the Thames. The dates were recovered, but in a state which rendered them unfit for human food. They were sold for distilling purposes.

Held, by the Court of Appeal, that no freight was payable because the goods delivered were, for business purposes, something different from those shipped, and were not in merchantable condition.

LORD ESHER, M.R. (at page 127)

The first point taken . . . is that there has been no total loss of the dates, and therefore no total loss of the freight on them. The ingenuity of the argument might commend itself to a body of chemists but not to businessmen. We are dealing with dates as a subject-matter of commerce; and it is contended that, although these dates were under water for two days, and when brought up were simply a mass of pulpy matter impregnated with sewage and in a state of fermentation, there had been no change in their nature, and they were still dates. There is a perfectly well-known test which has for many years been applied to such cases as the present—that test is whether, as a matter of business, the nature of the thing has been altered. The nature of a thing is not necessarily altered because the thing itself has been damaged; wheat or rice may be damaged, but may still remain the things dealt with as wheat or rice in business. But if the nature of the thing is altered, and it becomes for business purposes something else, so that it is not dealt with by business people as the thing which it originally was, the question for determination is whether the . . . original article of commerce has become a total loss. If it is so changed in its nature by the perils of the sea as to become an unmerchantable thing, which no buyer would buy and no honest seller would sell, then there is a total loss. That test was applied in the present case by the learned Judge[63] in the Court below, who decided as a fact that the dates had been so deteriorated that they had become something which was not merchantable as dates. If that was so, there was a total loss of the dates.

Dakin *v.* Oxley

(1864) 10 L.T. 268

The shipowner is entitled to the full freight even though the goods are delivered in a damaged condition.

Coal shipped under a charter-party had, through the negligence of the master, so deteriorated as not to be worth its freight. The charterer therefore abandoned it to the shipowner.

Held, by the Court of Common Bench, that he was nevertheless liable for the freight, his remedy for damage to the coal being by cross-action.

WILLES, C.J. (at page 271)

If [the cargo] has arrived, though damaged, the freight is payable by the ordinary terms of the charter-party; and the question of . . . culpable damage [must be settled] in a distinct proceeding for such damage against the ship, captain, or owner. There would be apparent justice in allowing damage . . . to be set-off or deducted in an action for freight. . . . But our law does not allow deduction in that form, and as at present administered for the sake, perhaps, of speedy settlement of freight and other liquidated demands, it affords the injured party a remedy by cross-action only.

---

[63] Mathew, J.: [1895] 2 Q.B. 196.

De Silvale *v.* Kendall

(1815) 4 M. & S. 37

Advance freight is not repayable even if the ship and her cargo are a total loss.

A vessel was chartered for a voyage from Liverpool to Sao Luiz de Maranhao (Brazil) [Maranham] and back to Liverpool. The ship arrived at Sao Luiz de Maranhao (Brazil) [Maranham], and the shipper paid an advance freight of £192. The vessel sailed on her homeward voyage, but was lost by capture.

Held, by the Court of King's Bench, that the shipper was not entitled to recover the advance freight.

BAYLEY, J. (at page 45)

Wherever there is an express stipulation that the party who is to be entitled to freight shall be paid any portion of it in advance, there ought also to be an express stipulation that the party paying it shall be entitled to recover it back, if freight be not earned, if such be the intention of the parties to the instrument. For without some provision of that sort how are we to raise a new implied contract to that effect? It seems clear that the parties to this instrument have stipulated for a partial payment in advance by way of freight and not as a loan; for after settling the amount and rate of freight to be paid for the voyage out and home, they stipulate that such freight shall be paid as follows, that is, the outward freight to Maranham [Sao Luiz de Maranhao], and as much cash as should be necessary for the ship's disbursements in Maranham [Sao Luiz de Maranhao], to be advanced by the freighter when required, free from interest and commission at the current exchange of the place, and the residue of such freight on the delivery of the homeward cargo. Therefore, taking the whole of the clause together, it seems to me that the payment is to be considered as a payment of so much of the freight in advance. And if that be so, upon what ground is it to be recovered back? It is suggested as a ground, that the freight has failed by the non-performance of the voyage, and thus the plaintiff has derived no benefit from it; but what benefit has the defendant derived? He also has lost as well as the plaintiff, and the question is, whether he is to bear a further loss. Now in order to maintain money had and received, it is in general incumbent upon the plaintiff to show that the defendant has money of the plaintiff which in equity and good conscience he ought not to detain from him. But here the question raised is not whether the defendant has money which he ought not to detain, but whether out of his own money he shall be bound to make good that which the plaintiff has lost. It seems to me that the defendant shall not be so bound.

PART III

COLLISIONS

(1) COLLISION REGULATIONS

The "Billings Victory"

(1949) 82 Ll.L.Rep. 877

Rule 15 of the Collision Regulations states that "When two power-driven vessels are crossing so as to involve risk of collision, the vessel which has the other on her own starboard side shall keep out of the way". The duty of the give-way vessel is to take timely action to keep clear.

The *Billings Victory* and the *Warren Chase* were on course crossing at a fine angle. The *Warren Chase* was the give-way ship. She failed to take action to avoid a collision until the vessels were about half a mile apart.

Held, by the Probate, Divorce and Admiralty Division, that she was in breach of the Rule, for she had taken avoiding action too late.

WILLMER, J. (at page 881)

As to the *Warren Chase*, I do not think the matter admits of any doubt. On a clear night, when vessels sight each other at anything up to four miles, it cannot be right for the give-way vessel to hold her course in face of a stand-on vessel until they have approached to within about half a mile of each other. I do not think it really needs repetition, because it has been said over and over again in this Court that the duty of the give-way vessel is to take timely action to keep clear.

Moreover it is her duty to act, if I may use the expression, handsomely, so as to leave the stand-on vessel in no possible doubt as to what the give-way vessel is doing. If her method of giving way is to alter course, she ought to make a substantial alteration, and ought to be particularly careful to signify that alteration by the appropriate helm signal. It may be said in this case that she could not safely make such alteration of course because she was embarrassed by the presence of the pilot cutter. In that event, she could choose another method of keeping clear, by making a drastic reduction of her speed. Again, a sufficient alteration in her speed would leave the stand-on vessel in no doubt as to what she was doing. That was the duty of the *Warren Chase*, and it was a duty which, as I see it, she signally failed to perform.

The consequence was that when these vessels got to within something like half a mile of each other, the *Warren Chase* had put the *Billings Victory* into a position of no little difficulty and embarrassment. She had no right to do that, and for that she must be held to blame, and seriously to blame.

The "Otranto"

(1931) 144 L.T. 251

By Rule 17(b) of the Collision Regulations: ". . . when, from any cause, the [stand-on] vessel finds herself so close that collision cannot be avoided by the action of the give-way vessel alone, she shall take such action as will best aid to avoid collision".

The *Otranto* sighted the *Kitano Maru* on her port bow at a distance of about seven miles. The *Otranto*, being the stand-on vessel, kept her course. Three minutes before the collision between the two vessels, the *Kitano Maru* had taken no avoiding action. The master of the *Otranto* determined that the *Kitano Maru* could not avoid the *Otranto* by her own action alone, so he starboarded.

Held, by the Probate, Divorce and Admiralty Division, that the master was entitled to act under the Rule, but his action was not in accordance with the requirements of good seamanship for he ought to have stopped and reversed his engines, and any action he took should have been under port helm.

LORD BUCKMASTER (at page 254)

The ship that is bound to keep her course is not entitled to alter it at a moment when there is ample time for the ship that is bound to give way to discharge her duty, for that ship is entitled to rely upon obedience to the rule by the ship that has to keep her course. But, acknowledging to the full the vital consequence of strict obedience, there still remains the fact that these rules were made for the guidance of mariners and not of mathematicians, and that it is not right, by an elaborate process of calculation after the event, to decide that the ship that was bound to keep her course acted a little before the moment that, in fact, she need have done. When two ships are travelling at 16 and 13 knots an hour, the moment when safety has passed and peril has arrived cannot be determined to a hair's breadth. The rule was designed to secure that the standing-on vessel shall maintain her course until the last safe moment. What the safe moment is must depend primarily upon the judgment of a competent sailor, forming his opinion with knowledge of the necessity of obedience to the rule and in face of all the existing facts. Subsequent examination may show that his judgment would not properly have been formed, in which case the rule has been broken without excuse, but the ultimate decision is not to be settled merely by exact calculations made after the event, but by considering these facts as they presented themselves to a skilled man at the time.

In these circumstances, I am not prepared to hold that the captain of the *Otranto* broke any rule when he decided to act. The lives of 560 passengers were in his care, and with such responsibility calculations cannot be expected to be as minute and accurate as when distances, speed, and times are afterwards plotted out in a law Court on a sheet of paper. All the six experienced men who have advised the Courts on this point are in agreement with this conclusion.

But although the captain was entitled to act, I am unable to find that his action was in accordance with the requirements of good seamanship. First, and before all things, he ought to have stopped and reversed his engines. Upon this point the nautical assessors by whom we have been advised are in agreement. This, by itself, might have saved an accident. But, in addition to this, whatever action he took ought to have been under a port helm, which would have tended to draw his vessel into line with the *Kitano Maru* and not opposed to it.

The "Jaladhir"

[1961] 2 Lloyd's Rep. 13

By Rule 34(d) of the Collision Regulations: "When vessels in sight of one another are approaching each other and from any cause either vessel fails to understand the intentions or actions of the other, or is in doubt whether sufficient action is being taken by the other to avoid collision, the vessel in doubt shall immediately indicate such doubt by giving at least five short and rapid blasts on the whistle . . .".

The *Loch Melfort* and the *Jaladhir* collided in the North Sea. They were on crossing courses, and the *Loch Melfort* was the stand-on vessel. It was obvious that the *Jaladhir* was not taking timely action to keep clear, but the *Loch Melfort* failed to sound any warning signal.

Held, by the Probate, Divorce and Admiralty Division, that the *Loch Melfort* was partly to blame because she should have sounded a warning signal.

HEWSON, J. (at page 16)

I have discussed this matter with the Elder Brethren, and they are of the opinion that in the circumstances of the present case it would have been seamanlike to have sounded the permitted signal. I entirely accept the advice of the Elder Brethren in this matter and I do so for several reasons. There were no other vessels in the vicinity at the material time, and, therefore, there was no chance of any misunderstanding or confusion in and about sounding and hearing such a signal; and I further have in mind that, in order to be effective, a warning signal must obviously be sounded well in advance of any manoeuvring signal which a stand-on ship may wish to make to indicate emergency action taken by her. I therefore find that the *Loch Melfort* should have sounded a warning signal at a moment when it was obvious that the *Jaladhir* was not taking timely action to keep clear under Rule [34].

Thomas Stone (Shipping) Ltd. *v*. Admiralty: The "Albion"

[1953] 1 Lloyd's Rep. 239

The Queen's Regulations are binding on Crown ships and set out regulations which are identical with the Collision Regulations. They do not apply, however, to uncommissioned Crown vessels, but they still set a standard to which those in charge of them should conform.

The S.S. *Maystone*, owned by the plaintiffs, collided with the *Albion*, an uncompleted aircraft carrier, in a gale at night in the North Sea. The *Albion* was not exhibiting "Not under command" lights although she was being towed. The plaintiffs sued the Admiralty for the damage caused to the *Maystone*.

Held, by the Court of Appeal, that the *Albion* was solely to blame for the collision. Although the Queen's Regulations did not apply to her because she was not commissioned, she should have carried lights showing that she was "not under command", for the Regulations imposed a standard of care to which those in charge of her should conform.

HODSON, L.J. (at page 247)

Much controversy has raged round the side lights of the *Albion*. Before dealing with this it is right to mention that this case has been pleaded as if the Regulations for Preventing Collisions at Sea applied. The position is that since the *Albion* belonged to the Crown, the Collision Regulations did not apply to her (see Merchant Shipping Act 1894, s. 741), and in her then state, not being commissioned, the Queen's Regulations did not apply. The Collision Regulations should, however, we think, be taken to contain not statutory duties applicable in her case but a standard of care to which those in charge of her should conform.

(2) USE OF RADAR

The "Anna Salen"

[1954] 1 Lloyd's Rep. 475

Radar only remains valuable if it is intelligently used.

WILLMER, J. (at page 488)

I should like to add a footnote to the case. It has been a somewhat unusual case. As I mentioned at the outset of this judgment, this is an unhappy case of collision between two well-found ships, both equipped with every modern aid to navigation, including radar. It is a melancholy reflection that the collision probably would not have happened if the ships had not been equipped with radar. These scientific installations, and particularly radar, are potentially most valuable instruments for increasing safety at sea; but they only remain valuable if they are intelligently used, and if the officers responsible for working them work them and interpret them with intelligence. That is only another way, I think, of saying that a good look-out must be maintained. A good look-out involves not only a visual look-out, and not only the use of ears, but it also involves the intelligent interpretation of the data received by way of these various scientific instruments. This collision ought never to have happened, and certainly would not have happened if both vessels had made intelligent use of the scientific instruments with which they were equipped.

(3) NAUTICAL ASSESSORS

The "Australia"

(1926) 25 Ll.L.Rep. 141

The role of nautical assessors is to give advice only. The Court itself and not the assessors must decide the issue in the case.

VISCOUNT DUNEDIN (at page 143)

I do think it necessary to protest against a view which, if I am not doing them injustice, has seemed to prevail in the Court of Appeal in a recent case, to wit, that the Court is bound to pay more attention to the opinion of its own assessors than to that of those who advised the Court below. There is no hierarchy of assessors. They occupy much the same position as do skilled witnesses, with this difference, that they are not brought forward as the partisans of the one side or the other; and, just as for instance, in a patent case, the Court must take its own choice between the views that may have been put forward by one witness or by another, so if the assessors differ, the Court must make its own choice. In every case the responsibility is with the Court. Personally, I think that while assessors may be used to the full for information, it is a pity if it can be helped to put a question to them in such a shape that it is tantamount to asking them whether they would find for the plaintiff or for the defendant. I cannot forget that when assessors were introduced, ships were sailing ships, and the navigation of a sailing ship is an art which the landsman cannot be expected to understand without much explanation. In these modern times it seems to me that it is much oftener a question of common sense in the application of the rules to avoid collision than a question of seamanship in the true sense of the word.

LORD SUMNER (at page 143)

A mere lawyer, my Lords, might well be forgiven if he felt unable to set his own opinion against that of assessors on so professional a matter. The fact that the Court of Appeal had been advised to the contrary by equally competent advisers might well increase his embarrassment; and when it is remembered that the Trinity Masters had advised the learned President in the sense in which the House is now advised, he might be tempted in his perplexity to renounce the task of judgment. This, however, is exactly what he must not do. Technical advisers are not the judges even of such issues as these. The appointed Court must exercise its function of deciding, and find consolation in a consciousness at any rate of blank impartiality. An opposite road of escape might seem to open, namely, that of accepting, as of course, the advice of the assessors consulted, who are provided for that very purpose by the law itself. In reality there is no escape here. This is what leads to the "intolerable situation", as it is called, of "appeals from assessors to assessors". After all, the technical advice given below is advice available for the consideration of the appellate tribunal, as well as that given by its own assessors. The latter are not substituted for those previously consulted; they are additional to them, and, if one adviser or two advisers are to be preferred, it is because in the judgment of the Court the advice given is such as, in itself, is the more acceptable.

If, as may happen, a Judge cannot decide in his own mind whether or not the advice he receives is sound, his position is simply that the point is not proven, and the loss falls on the party who bears the burden of proof on that issue. It is just as if necessary proof had failed. After all, experience at sea is not everything. Assessors are not chosen for their personal conversance with collisions, and an experienced Judge or counsel may boast that he has, in a sense, been in hundreds of collisions while the assessors have hardly seen tens.

(4) APPORTIONMENT OF BLAME

The "Peter Benoit"

(1915) 114 L.T. 147

By proviso (a) to s. 1(1) of the Maritime Conventions Act 1911 "if having regard to all the circumstances of the case it is not possible to establish different degrees of fault [between two vessels involved in a collision], the liability shall be apportioned equally". The conclusion that it is possible to establish different degrees of fault must be a conclusion proved by evidence.

A collision occurred between two vessels off the mouth of the River Tees. There was no evidence on which the blame could be with any certainty apportioned.

Held, by the House of Lords, that the liability should be apportioned equally.

LORD SUMNER (at page 152)

The conclusion that it is possible to establish different degrees of fault must be a conclusion proved by evidence, judicially arrived at, and sufficiently made out. Conjecture will not do: a general leaning in favour of one ship rather than of the other will not do: sympathy for one of the wrongdoers, too indefinite to be supported by a reasoned judgment, will not do. The question is not answered by deciding who was the first wrongdoer, nor even of necessity who was the last. The Act says, "having regard to all the circumstances of the case". Attention must be paid not only to the actual time of the collision and the manoeuvres of the ship, when about to collide, but to their prior movements and opportunities, their acts, and omissions. Matters which are only introductory, even though they preceded the collision by but a short time, are not really circumstances of the case but only its antecedents, and they should not directly affect the result. As PICKFORD, L.J., observes: " 'The liability to make good the damage or loss shall be in proportion to the degree in which each vessel was in fault.' That must be in fault as regards the collision. If she was in fault in other ways, which had no effect on the collision, that is not a matter to be taken into consideration".

(5) REMOTENESS OF DAMAGE

The "Edison"

[1933] All E.R. Rep. 144

Damages which are too remote cannot be recovered.

A profit earning dredger was sunk in a collision in Patras harbour. The owners claimed (1) the market price of a comparable dredger; (2) the cost of adapting a new dredger and transporting and insuring her from her moorings to Patras; (3) compensation for disturbance and loss in carrying out their contract of dredging the harbour; and (4) a loss due to their inability for financial reasons to buy a substitute dredger and the resulting delay in proceeding with the work.

Held, by the House of Lords, that the owners' claim under heads (1), (2) and (3) succeeded, but that under head (4) failed because such damage was too remote.

LORD WRIGHT (at page 158)

The substantial issue is what in such a case as the present is the true measure of damage[s]. It is not questioned that when a vessel is lost by collision due to the sole negligence of the wrongdoing vessel, the owners of the former vessel are entitled to what is called *restitutio in integrum*, which means that they should recover such a sum as will replace them, so far as can be done by compensation in money, in the same position as if the loss had not been inflicted on them, subject to the rules of law as to remoteness of damage. The respondents contend that all that is recoverable as damages is the true value to the owners of the lost vessel, as at the time and place of loss. Before considering what is involved in this contention, I think it desirable to examine the claim made by the appellants, which found favour with the Registrar and LANGTON, J., and which in effect is that all their circumstances, in particular their want of means, must be taken into account, and hence the damages must be based on their actual loss, provided only that, as the Registrar and the Judge have found, they acted reasonably in the unfortunate predicament in which they were placed, even though but for their financial embarrassment they could have replaced the *Liesbosch* at a moderate price and with comparatively short delay.

In my judgment, the appellants are not entitled to recover damages on this basis. The respondents' tortious act involved the physical loss of the dredger; that loss must somehow be reduced to terms of money. But the appellants' actual loss, in so far as it was due to their impecuniosity, arose from that impecuniosity as a separate and concurrent cause, extraneous to and distinct in character from the tort; the impecuniosity was not traceable to the respondents' acts, and, in my opinion, was outside the legal purview of the consequences of these acts.

The assessment of the value of such a vessel at the time of loss, with her engagements, may seem to present an extremely complicated and speculative problem. But different considerations apply to the simple case of a ship sunk by collision when free of all engagements, either being laid up in port or being a seeking ship in ballast, though intended for employment, if it can be obtained, under charter or otherwise. In such a case the fair measure of damages will be simply the market value, on which will be calculated interest, at and from the date of loss, to compensate for delay in paying for the loss.

The contrasted cases of a tramp under charter or a seeking tramp do not, however, exhaust all the possible problems in which must be sought an answer to the question what is involved in the principle *restitutio in integrum*. I have only here mentioned such cases as the step to considering the problem in the present case. Many, varied and complex are the types of vessels and the modes of employment in which their owners may use them. Hence the difficulties constantly felt in defining rules as to the measure of damages. I think it impossible to lay down any universal formula. A ship of war, a supply ship, a lightship, a dredger employed by a public authority, a passenger liner, a trawler, a cable ship, a tug boat (to take a few instances), all may raise quite different questions before their true value can be ascertained. The question here under consideration is again different; the *Liesbosch* was not under charter nor intended to be chartered, but, in fact, was being employed by the owners in the normal course of their business as civil engineers, as an essential part of the plant which they were using in performance of their contract at Patras.

It follows that the value of the *Liesbosch* to the appellants, capitalised as at the date of the loss, must be assessed by taking into account: (i) the market price of a comparable dredger in substitution; (ii) costs of adaptation, transport, insurance, &c., to Patras; (iii) compensation for disturbance and loss in carrying out their contract over the period of delay between the loss of the *Liesbosch* and the time at which the substituted dredger could reasonably have been available for use in Patras, including in that loss such items as overhead charges, expenses of staff and equipment, and so forth, thrown away, but neglecting any special loss due to the appellants' financial position. On the capitalised sum so assessed interest will run from the date of the loss.

The "Fritz Thyssen"

[1967] 2 Lloyd's Rep. 199

Where a vessel is damaged in a collision due to the negligence of another vessel, and later sinks, the owners of the other vessel are liable only where the sinking is the direct result of the collision.

The *Mitera Marigo* collided with the *Fritz Thyssen* off Ushant, and sustained damage below the waterline. Her master refused assistance from the *Fritz Thyssen* and the salvage tug *Englishman*, which offered to pump out the water. She proceeded on her voyage to Rotterdam, but then altered course for Falmouth because the water in her hold was increasing. She was towed into Falmouth harbour by harbour tugs and moored to a buoy. A noise was heard on board her, and the *Englishman* was then asked to pump. Pumps were started, but 45 minutes later when she cast off from the buoy and prepared to beach, she sank. Her owners claimed damages from the owners of the *Fritz Thyssen* in respect of the loss.

Held, by the Court of Appeal, that the action failed, for her sinking was not the direct result of the collision, but was due to the master's refusal of assistance from the *Englishman*.

WILLMER, L.J. (at page 205)

Having regard to the evidence as to the nature and extent of the damage in the way of No. 1 hold, and in the light of the situation disclosed by the photographs, my view (and I believe it to be the common-sense view) is that this was a ship which throughout was in a situation of the utmost peril. Indeed, when one looks at the photographs, it really does seem almost incredible that a competent master would not have availed himself of any assistance that was available. It is to be remembered that in the nature of things he could have had no proper opportunity to carry out such an inspection of the damage as would enable him to form any reliable view as to the degree of danger to the ship. The stakes, in my judgment, were much too high to justify a gamble on the strength of theoretical calculations as to the ability of the vessel to continue afloat with everything forward of No. 1 hold flooded. We have been told that the property at risk was valued at something like £800,000, and this circumstance alone, in my view, should have been enough to require that no reasonable precaution should be omitted so as to ensure (so far as it could be ensured) that, whatever else happened, the vessel would not be allowed to sink in deep water. Here there was at hand a first-class salvage instrument, ready and willing from five o'clock onwards to tender immediate assistance. Had use been made of her pumps it seems probable, if not certain, that the further increase of water in No. 1 hold would have been checked; indeed, it could have been expected that the water level would have been actually reduced. That would have meant that the vital bulkhead guarding No. 2 hold would have been subjected to no further strain and, even if it had leaked, or even collapsed altogether, the over-all quantity of water in the ship would never have become sufficient to cause her to sink.

In those circumstances, in my judgment, this master took a wholly unjustifiable, and therefore a negligent, risk when he refused the *Englishman*'s offer of assistance, and it is to this act of negligence that the loss of ship and cargo must be attributed.

(6) MEASURE OF DAMAGES

The "Harmonides"

(1903) 87 L.T. 448

Where there is no market for a vessel which is sunk in a collision, the measure of damages is her value to her owners as a going concern at the time of the loss.

The *Waesland* was a passenger vessel engaged in the North Atlantic trade and was sunk in collision. Evidence was given to the effect that it was impossible to say what was the exact market value of an Atlantic liner because they never came into the market unless they were unprofitable or worn out.

Held, by the Probate, Divorce and Admiralty Division, that the measure of damages was her value to her owners as a going concern at the time of the loss, and this sum amounted to £31,000.

GORELL BARNES J. (at page 449)

There is no doubt that in this class of case the best evidence is that of those who know the ship, and the next best evidence that of those who have experience of the market, but who do not know the vessel except from the shipping records. There are other criteria, such as the amount of capital invested, the amount of depreciation, the amount of profits, and so forth. All these matters have to be considered, to my mind, where it is impossible to say that there is a real market test of the value of such a vessel as this. If one goes to the root of the matter, it is clearly obvious that what the owners lose if a vessel like this is run into and sunk is really what it would cost to replace them in the position they were in before the accident. But where a ship like this has gone to the bottom, you cannot, speaking from a business point of view, replace them in the position they were in before, because you cannot replace the vessel which is at the bottom of the sea: you cannot buy another like her in the market; you cannot get another made immediately, and if you bought another ship, she would be new and consequently more valuable, because she would start as a new ship from that day. You would have to start on the basis of her being a new ship and then discount her value down. So that the real test, where there is no market, is, as Mr Aspinall has said, and Mr Pickford agrees, what is the value to the owners, as a going concern, at the time the vessel was sunk? There is no dispute between Counsel as to that. You cannot get at it with any great certainty. Certainly, to my mind, you cannot get at it from the market value. Possibly, for such a ship at such a time there would be no market, and she would have to be sold for old iron. You cannot deal with it like an ordinary commodity being sold every day. You must look at it and see what is the loss to the owners. It has been pointed out that you may look at the original cost, plus the money expended on her, and so forth. That is of assistance, but it is not complete assistance, because it is a rough and ready method. You may look and see also how the ship is paying. But that is not a complete test because you cannot be sure that the way she has been paying will continue. But one thing is absolutely certain, you cannot say the test is her market value. . . . I think the vessel was worth £31,000 and I therefore propose to vary the report by increasing the sum of £18,000 to £31,000.

The "Philadelphia"

(1917) 116 L.T. 794

Where a vessel under charter is a total loss in a collision, the measure of damages is her value at the time of the loss, plus a sum for freight or profits at the end of the voyage fixed by the existing charter-party, subject to proper deductions for contingencies and wear and tear.

The *Ben Lee* was a sailing ship which was lost in collision with the *Philadelphia* in Caernarvon Bay. The *Ben Lee* was under charter with a general cargo for Sydney and Melbourne. The vessel was worth £22,500 at the time of the loss, but her owners maintained that they were entitled to claim £29,370, for this was her value if she had reached Sydney safely.

Held, by the Court of Appeal, that this sum could not be claimed. The measure of damages was the vessel's value at the time of the loss, plus a sum for freight at the end of the voyage, but since the freight had been paid in advance, nothing was recoverable in respect of freight. Deduction must also be made for contingencies and for wear and tear.

SWINFEN EADY, L.J. (at page 799)

It is then said that in working out that value in order to give effect to that rule and to include the value of the charter you must take the value of the ship at its port of arrival; and, in a sense, that is true, and that phrase has been used in various cases; but in my opinion, what is meant by that is that you are to take the value of the ship at the end of the voyage in this sense and meaning; that if you are to give the shipowner the profit that would have been earned by the current charter, you must take into account, on the other hand, the elements that would have to be considered before the profit was arrived at. The first thing which you would have to take into account would be the diminished value of the ship by reason of the wear and tear which arises when the value of the ship at the end of the voyage is ascertained; it does not mean the speculative value of what the ship would probably then fetch in the market if she were then sold and having regard perhaps to the demand for ships and their greatly increased price; it does not mean that at all, but it means that you have to take into account the diminished value of the ship by reason of the wear and tear of the voyage. In the judgment of MOULTON, L.J. in *The Racine*[1] which was quoted, he puts the matter in that way: "The date taken is the conclusion of the voyage. Setting aside other risks, the plaintiff, but for the collision, would at the end of the voyage have been in possession of the ship (diminished in value by the wear and tear of that voyage) and would have been in possession of the freight". In other words, in order to find the value of the charter you must see what the shipowner would have had to lose or provide in order to gain his freight. There would be the wages of the crew in the outward voyage; there would be in a steamship the bunker coal stores, and in every ship, whether a steamship or sailing ship, there would be an allowance for the wear and tear caused by the voyage. In my opinion, in the case of *The Kate*[2] and in the case of *The Racine*[3] it is the amount of the deduction that has to be made for the wear and tear of the voyage that is in the mind of the Court when the expression was used to take the value at the end of the voyage; in

---

[1] [1906] P. 273.
[2] [1899] P. 165.
[3] *Supra.*

every case it means to take the diminished value by reason of having to make the proper allowance for wear and tear of the voyage.

The "Mediana"

[1900–3] All E.R. Rep. 126

Damages for loss of use of a damaged vessel can be claimed where a stand-by vessel takes her place, and are based on the cost of the hire of a similar vessel from a third party in substitution for the damaged vessel.

A lightship was damaged in a collision, and while she was being repaired another lightship belonging to the owners, the Mersey Docks and Harbour Board, which was maintained by them for the purpose of such an emergency, took her place for 74 days.

Held, by the House of Lords, that the owners were entitled to claim £310 6*s*. 0*d*. as damages, i.e., damages of £4 4*s*. 0*d*. per day for the period of 74 days.

LORD SHAND (at page 130)

It was established that the *Orion* was kept expressly for the purpose of meeting such a contingency as happened. It appears that no fewer than 11 cases have occurred during the last 25 years in which a substitute has been called for to replace lightships damaged by collision on the Mersey. If the Mersey Commissioners had hired a ship for the purpose of doing the duty for which this sixth vessel was kept, there could be no answer to the claim for the cost of hire. It seems to me, therefore, if there be no answer in that case, neither can there be any to this.

The "Hebridean Coast"

[1961] 1 All E.R. 82

Where a vessel is damaged and no replacement for her is arranged, her owner's claim for damages for loss of her use is limited to interest on her capital value for the period of her detention for repairs to be effected.

A collier owned by the Central Electricity Generating Board was damaged in a collision, and repairs to her took 11½ days. The Board owned a fleet of ships and chartered others for the transport of coal. But no vessel specifically replaced the collier by carrying the coal which she would have carried. The Board claimed special damages for loss use for the period of 11½ days on the basis of the freight payable for chartering alternative tonnage.

Held, by the House of Lords, that the claim for special damages failed, but general damages based on the capital value of the collier, plus a rate of interest of 7% on the capital, would be awarded.

LORD REID (at page 85)

The appellants then argued that, in any event, they are entitled to general damages, that the method of assessing such damages is a jury question, and that taking the whole matter into consideration as a jury would, a fair method is to take into account what, as a matter of regular practice, the Authority was paying for chartered tonnage. I must confess that I do not understand that. I do not proceed on any supposed distinction in principle between a profit-earning ship and a non-profit-earning ship. The task of assessing damages is easier with a profit-earning ship and depends on the probability that she would have earned so much money if her owner could have used her. With a non-profit-earning ship, there is no direct financial loss, and one must ask what harm was done to the owner by his being deprived of the loss of his ship. Then comes what may be a very difficult task, to put a value in money on the harm which the owner has suffered. But you must first prove the harm. If no harm is proved beyond the mere fact that the owner is deprived of the services of his ship during the period of repairs, the opinion of LORD HERSCHELL in *No. 7 Steam Sand Pump Dredger (Owners)* v. *Greta Holme (Owners): The Greta Holme*[4] appears to have given rise to the practice of awarding damages based on interest on the value of the ship. In this case, if the coal in question was carried in the Authority's own vessels, there is nothing to show that that involved them in any substantial additional expense. The case would be like *Admiralty Comrs.* v. *Susquehanna (Owners), The Susquehanna.*[5] It is only if the coal was carried in chartered ships that there would be any reason for taking into account the cost of so carrying it. But that is just what the appellants have failed to prove. I do not see how general damages can be awarded on the basis of compensating an owner for some kind of harm which he cannot prove that he ever sustained. The award of general damages approved by the Court of Appeal was based on interest on the value of the vessel. The appellants argue that that is a very unsatisfactory basis. So it may be, though it has been in use for a long time; but if the only alternative proposed by the appellants cannot be supported, then I see no other possible course but to use this method with all its disadvantages.

The "Chekiang"

[1926] All E.R. Rep. 114

Where a warship is damaged in a collision, the Crown is entitled to damages for the loss of her use based on a rate of interest on her value at the time of the loss for the period during which she is detained for repairs to be effected.

---

[4] [1897] A.C. 596, H.L.
[5] [1926] A.C. 655, H.L.

The light cruiser *Cairo* was damaged in a collision in Chinese waters. Repairs to her took 20 days. In assessing damages the Registrar assessed the damages at £2,000. This figure was arrived at by allowing 5% per annum for 20 days on the estimated capital value of the vessel at the time of the collision.

Held, by the House of Lords, that this method of assessing the damages was the correct one.

LORD SUMNER (at page 121)

There is no presumption that ships of war are worth to the State what was spent on building them, or that their daily user is worth the cost of running them, for outlay on the Navy is not a matter of commercial investment of money but of State policy. What, for example, is the daily value of the use of a mine-layer or a submarine in time of peace, or what can be made of interest on the capital laid out on the guns and armour of a battleship? In ships of war fashion changes, or, perhaps, I should say the science of war advances, ships are built in a hurry or when prices are high, or are continued in service when they are obsolescent or have proved to be failures, and this for reasons of policy and not of economics. Much depends on the kind of ship; more on the existence of profound peace or the imminence of the outbreak of war. In the last event the value of the time, when collision makes a man-of-war unavailable, may truly be at once vast and inestimable; in some of the others the value of the user may really be no more than that of floating accommodation for officers and crew, who have among other things to be kept under discipline and busy. To all these matters in the appropriate case the Registrar would have to direct his mind. No formula can fit them all and no formula could fail to vary in regard to its factors from time to time. The practical question is whether it can be said that, in applying the principle of *The Greta Holme*[6] to the case of the *Cairo*, the learned Registrar misdirected himself in law. On the record, the learned Registrar had very little evidence about the *Cairo* before him, but there are two things always to be borne in mind about proceedings in the Registry. The great experience of the Registrar and the knowledge of the merchants who assist him make evidence on many topics quite superfluous, and the participation in the proceedings of experienced Counsel constantly justifies the conclusion that, by tacit, if not by express consent, statements are accepted of which no formal proof appears on the note. I think that on the present point there was a large measure of consent, nor was this much contested. It seems to me reasonable to conclude that, whether by the knowledge which he had acquired in the course of his duties or by the advice of the gentlemen who assisted him, or by the acquiescence of Counsel, specially familiar with such matters, or by all of these, the learned Registrar was warranted in assuming that the *Cairo*, a ship about two years old, performing duties and designed to perform duties *inter alia* which appear to

---

[6] [1897] A.C. 596, H.L.

have consisted in patrolling the Yang-tse-Kiang near Hankow and in giving moral rather than material support to British interests, was doing work for which the outlay upon her was economically well designed, and that in allowing a rate of interest, not I think excessive, upon what is really a wasting security, he was committing no error in law.

I am of opinion that, in the present case, there is no ground for interfering with the conclusion of the learned Registrar.

The "Hassel"

[1962] 2 Lloyd's Rep. 139

Where a vessel is damaged in a collision and her owner gets the damage repaired as well as effecting other repairs not caused by the collision, he can only claim damages for her detention during the period when the collision damage was repaired.

A vessel was damaged in a collision, and the damage which she suffered was temporarily repaired at Antwerp. She was later sent to Japan for the execution of permanent repairs. She need not have gone there, but her owners thought that the repairs could be conveniently effected in Japan because various defects in her machinery had become apparent. These were covered by a guarantee clause in the shipbuilding contract made between them and the Japanese shipbuilders, and they could be put right at the same time as the repairs were done. The repairs to the collision damage took 20 days while those relating to the defects took 9½ days. The owners claimed damages for detention during the whole period of 29½ days from the owners of the other vessel.

Held, by the Probate, Divorce and Admiralty Division, that they were entitled in respect of the period of 20 days only.

HEWSON, J. (at page 144)

In such a case as this, where before the collision, the owner, as I find, had intended to lay off the ship for his own purposes from profit earning at or about the time the ship was laid up for repairs to collision damage, damage which did not affect her seaworthiness, and his own repairs were concurrently performed, evidence must be produced by him to satisfy the Court on balance of probabilities that but for the collision the vessel would have continued trading. The onus is on the plaintiff. It is on him who claims to give this satisfaction and, in my view, the plaintiffs in this case have failed to do so. The evidence adduced and the inferences drawn from it lead me to the conclusion that if there had been no collision, the warranty inspection repairs would have been carried out, not necessarily in Japan, but about the time they were, in fact, carried out, with the result that the vessel would have been out of service for the time necessary to execute the warranty inspection repairs.

The evidence shows that inspection and associated repairs would have taken about eight to ten days. There was some evidence from Mr Cook[7] that it could have been nearer 10 days—I think in one part of his evidence he said about 10 days—so I think I shall be doing no injustice in this case if I allow for the period of what I call owner's work 9½ days. The total time allowed by the learned Admiralty Registrar for gas-freeing and collision repairs in Japan was 29½ days. It follows, therefore, that I find that the plaintiffs are entitled to 20 days' detention in Japan attributable to the collision.

---

[7] A surveyor representing the owners' building interests in Japan.

PART IV

SALVAGE, TOWAGE AND PILOTAGE

A. SALVAGE

The "San Demetrio"

(1941) 69 Ll.L.Rep. 5

It is only in exceptional circumstances that the crew of a vessel can claim a salvage award in respect of services to her.

The *San Demetrio* was on fire after being attacked by an enemy raider in 1940 in the South Atlantic. The vessel was abandoned on the master's order. Some of the crew boarded her two days later and extinguished the fire. They brought her safely to a Scottish port.

Held, by the Probate, Divorce and Admiralty Division, that they were entitled to a salvage award.[1]

LANGTON, J. (at page 12)

This class of salvage is, necessarily, of a rare character. It is not often that seamen are called upon to salve their own vessel. The law on the matter was laid down with great strictness as long ago as the time of Dr Lushington, and the law is not in doubt. Four requisites laid down by Dr Lushington[2] have to be fulfilled before seamen can be allowed to claim salvage in respect of their own vessel. The chief of these requisites is that the ship was properly abandoned under the orders of her master. In the present case there has never been the slightest shadow of doubt that all four requisites have been adequately

[1] It was the unanimous request of all on board that the Red Ensign, which the vessel was flying all through the action and until she arrived in port, should be presented to an American member of the crew. LANGTON, J., observed (69 Ll.L.Rep., at p. 12): "I dwell with pleasure on this incident for I am sure that he is of a quality to treasure this bit of bunting, the only flag which remained on the *San Demetrio*. He will remember, as we in England remember, that it was flying at the masthead of the *San Demetrio* when she first met her troubles, that it remained flying through the worst of her misfortunes, and that it still flew when at long last, on November 16, shell-torn and fire-scarred, but undefeated, she came steaming up the sheltered waters of the Clyde".

[2] In *The Florence* (1852) 16 Jur. 572 Dr Lushington said that abandonment (1) must take place at sea, and not upon a coast; (2) must be *sine spe revertendi*; (3) must be *bona fide* for the purpose of saving life; and (4) must be by order of the master, in consequence of danger by reason of damage to the ship and the state of the elements.

fulfilled. The abandonment of this ship was not only a wise and proper act, it was the only possible course that could have been adopted by her master. Moreover, it is clear that at the time when the vessel was abandoned, no one had the slightest hope of returning to her; in fact, no one had the smallest expectation of ever seeing her again.

The "Sandefjord"

[1953] 2 Lloyd's Rep. 557

A pilot is entitled to claim a salvage award in respect of services which he has rendered but the Court in making an award will not encourage pilots to take undue risks by disregarding offers of assistance.

A vessel was stranded on the Goodwin Sands and was in charge of a pilot. He recommended that the master should not accept offers of assistance from tugs which were standing by, but that a kedge anchor should be laid out by a lifeboat. The vessel was refloated by hauling on the anchor. The pilot's services were admitted to be salvage services. The salved values of the vessel and her cargo were £495,000 and £160,000 respectively. The pilot claimed a salvage award.

Held, by the Probate, Divorce and Admiralty Division, that an award of £500 would be made. The Court would not encourage a pilot to take undue risks in advising against the use of tugs, but in the present case the pilot had taken no more than a fair risk.

WILLMER, J. (at page 560)

I have very little doubt that, but for the intervention of the plaintiff, tugs would have been engaged, and the owners of the salved property would have found themselves liable for a large salvage award. I think that the plaintiff's services did prevent, in the events which happened, any such thing occurring. He took a risk in tendering the advice which he did; as it happened, it proved to be a good risk, because the ship came off the sand, and she came off the sand apparently undamaged. Had the risk not come off, the pilot would have exposed himself, I suppose, to the certainty of an inquiry at least, and to the possibility of severe censure by the disciplinary authority. The result might, or might not, have been the withdrawal of his licence. That is a risk which the pilot had to have in mind, and it is a risk which I have had in mind in assessing the reward which he should receive.

Having talked the matter over with the Elder Brother, and bearing in mind what is generally known about the Goodwin Sands and the risks inherent in the stranding of a ship thereon, I entertain no doubt that the pilot took a grave risk. But I do not think that it would be right, or in accordance with public policy, to make an extravagant award in favour of the plaintiff in this case on the basis that he took such a grave risk, because I do not want it to go out from this Court that pilots are to be encouraged lightly to disregard offers of assistance made by tugs whose services are available. The awarding of salvage is governed largely by considerations of public policy and by the desirability of encouraging seafaring folk to take risks for the purpose of saving property. But it is, I think, no part of the business of this Court to encourage pilots, or any other class of seafaring folk, to take undue risks such as may arise if it is thought that they are to be highly rewarded for refusing to accept the assistance of tugs which are offering help.

The "Helmsman"

(1950) 84 Ll.L.Rep. 207

A salvage award cannot be claimed where the salved vessel was in no danger.

The *Helmsman* was moored alongside the *Holberg* for the purpose of supplying oil to her by means of a pipeline. A moderate gale sprung up, and the forward quay moorings of the *Holberg* broke adrift. There was a risk of collision with other vessels. Tugs towed the *Holberg* with the *Helmsman* still fast alongside to another berth. The owners, masters and crews of the tugs claimed a salvage award for the services rendered to the *Helmsman*.

Held, by the Probate, Divorce and Admiralty Division, that the claim failed. The *Helmsman* was never in any danger. She could easily have safely cast off from the *Holberg* if the need to do so had arisen.

PILCHER, J. (at page 216)

I have already described the position of the *Holberg* when the *Homer* was so manoeuvring. The Elder Brethren advise me (and I accept their advice) that at that moment, and for the ensuing quarter of an hour, even if there had been no tugs there, the *Helmsman* could have got away from the side of the *Holberg* quite easily in a couple of minutes; and, that being so, it seems to me to follow that, whatever the plaintiffs' services may have been to the *Holberg*, they were not salvage services rendered to the *Helmsman*, for the reason that the *Helmsman*, being a free agent, was never in any danger at all, and could have cast off from the *Holberg* had she anticipated that she was likely to sustain damage by contact either with vessels at the No. 9 tier or with anything else.

That being so, these claims for salvage fail *in toto*.

The "Rene"

[1955] 1 Lloyd's Rep. 101

A vessel may be entitled to a salvage award in spite of her not contributing to the success of the operation, if it can be proved that the master of the ship in distress has requested performance of a service of a salvage nature.

The *Rene* broke down off the coast of Portugal. The *Alenquer* was in the vicinity and had been asked to keep a look out for her. Later an SOS was flashed from the *Rene* and when the *Alenquer* closed with her, the master requested to be taken in tow. Attempts were made throughout the night to pass a towing hawser, but were unsuccessful. An attempt was made to pass a line to the *Rene*, but during the operation the collision took place, and the *Rene* was badly damaged. Her master requested the *Alenquer* to stand by, and the *Alenquer* did so until the *Rene* had drifted out of all immediate danger. The *Alenquer* claimed a salvage award.

Held, by the Probate, Divorce and Admiralty Division, that the *Alenquer* would have been entitled to a salvage award on the basis that her services had been requested, even though they were unsuccessful, but, on the facts, the claim to salvage had been forfeited, since the *Alenquer* had been seriously to blame in respect of a very substantial collision.

WILLMER, J. (at page 109)

It may perhaps be useful to refer first to what I think is the *locus classicus* on the subject of "engaged services", in order to see how the facts of this case come within the principles enunciated. I refer to the remarks of PHILLIMORE, J., in the well-known case of *The Dart.*[3] There the matter is summed up in three sentences[4]:

> If a salvor is employed to do anything and does it, and the property is ultimately saved, he may claim a salvage award, though the thing which he does, in the events which happen, produces no good effect. If a salvor is employed to complete a salvage and does not, but, without any misconduct on his part, fails after he has performed a beneficial service, he is entitled to a salvage award. If a salvor is employed to do a thing and does not do it, and no doubt uses strenuous exertions and makes sacrifices, but does no good at all, then it seems to me he is not entitled to salvage.

It does seem to be the fact that for sometime, at any rate, although not for very long, the *Alenquer* did continue to stand by the *Rene*, and I think it is clear on both sides' stories that the *Alenquer* did not leave until the *Rene* was quite really out of danger. . . . If that is so, then the *Alenquer* would be entitled to some salvage award on the basis that she deviated from her course and in fact stood by the *Rene* at a request for a period of some hours . . . In the circumstances, I accept the contention that the *Alenquer* brings herself within the first proposition laid down by PHILLIMORE, J., and I come to the conclusion that, other things being equal, she would qualify to obtain a salvage award on the basis of performing services, which she was engaged to perform. It seems to me that the fact of the *Alenquer* being to blame, and seriously to blame, in respect of this very substantial collision, makes it quite impossible for me to make any award of salvage in her favour.

---

[3] (1899) 8 Asp. M.L.C. 481.
[4] *Ibid.*, at p. 483.

The "American Farmer"

(1947) 80 Ll.L.Rep. 672

Salvors must not dispossess prior salvors of the vessel which is in distress, unless there is no reasonable probability that the prior salvors can accomplish successful salvage unaided.

The *American Farmer* was abandoned after a collision in the Atlantic. The *Elizabete* came to her rescue and her crew attempted to tow her. She was sighted by the *American Ranger* which sent a boarding party to her. The *Elizabete* refused to cast off the tow ropes, so the boarding party cut them, and brought the *American Farmer* safely to Falmouth. The *American Ranger* claimed a salvage award.

Held, by the Probate, Divorce and Admiralty Division, that she was entitled to salvage award because she was justified in dispossessing the *Elizabete* by the cutting of the tow rope for there was no reasonable probability that the *Elizabete* would have been able to accomplish successful salvage unaided.

PILCHER, J. (at page 687)

The award which is payable, if any, in this case to the owners of the *Elizabete*, and to her master and crew, must depend largely upon the view which I take on the following point: was there any reasonable probability of the *Elizabete* being able to accomplish this salvage unaided? That is a matter about which I may form a view, but it is essentially a matter which is within the province of the Elder Brethren and consequently it is a matter which I have discussed with them. What they tell me, in substance, is this, that if Captain Millers had kept on towing the *American Farmer* with his four mooring ropes, first one and then the other would have parted as strain was imposed upon them even by comparatively small sheering on the part of the tow, and sooner or later he would have had to use the 5-in. wire. They advise me that there would have been no difficulty in getting the eye of the wire over some appropriate bollard on the *American Farmer* and no difficulty in heaving the wire over to the *Elizabete*; she, of course, had steam and she could have used her winches and hove the wire over to herself and made it fast. They think that if that had been done, there was quite a reasonable chance of the *Elizabete* doing something in the neighbourhood of 50 miles a day, so long as her coal lasted—but, of course, she had not sufficient coal on board to get to any safe port, Cardiff or any nearer port, such as Queenstown, proceeding only at that speed. We know what would, in fact, have happened if the *American Ranger* had not put part of her crew on board the *American Farmer* and the *Elizabete* had been permitted to continue the towage: she would very shortly have been joined by the two salvage tugs, and how long she would have continued her slow progress accompanied by those two highly efficient salvage instruments I do not know, but it may be that she would have gone on until her coal gave out and then have had to hand over the *American Farmer* to the salvage tugs. That is the kind of way in which the Elder Brethren visualise this case, and, speaking for myself, I entirely agree with them. Therefore, there was not in fact any reasonable probability of the *Elizabete* being able to accomplish the service unaided. She could have got the *American Farmer* on a good deal farther, no doubt at a very slow speed, but she would ultimately have had to hand her over to the salvage tugs before she could have brought her to a place of safety.

The next point which I have to consider in reference to both the *Elizabete* and the *American Ranger* and their claims is this: Inasmuch as it is a principle which is always acted upon in this Court that a subsequent salvor is not entitled to disposses a prior salvor provided that the prior has a reasonable prospect of accomplishing the salvage service himself and is not endangering the safety of the salved property, was Captain Johnson, the master of the *American Ranger*, justified in dispossessing Captain Millers, the master of the *Elizabete*, of his prize? I am satisfied myself, and the Elder Brethren agree, that Captain Johnson acted with perfect propriety. He tried persuasion, but persuasion was useless; he was tactful enough to avoid the use of anything more than persuasion, but in the result, without there being any bodily violence offered by either party, Captain Johnson ordered the cutting of the tow ropes of the *Elizabete* and thus effectively dispossessing the *Elizabete* of the *American Farmer*. I think, and the Elder Brethren agree, that Captain Johnson was well justified in acting as he did.

The "Elkhound"

(1931) 39 Ll.L.Rep. 15

The danger to the salved property is one of the matters to be taken into consideration in the making of a salvage award.

The *Elkhound* was an oil tanker which caught fire in the River Thames. Tugs towed her out to sea and held her there until the fire burnt itself out. There was a probability of the cargo exploding, and this would have resulted in the total loss of the vessel. The salved value of property was about £13,000.

Held, by the Probate, Divorce and Admiralty Division, that the danger to the salved property was an element to be taken into account, and a salvage award of £4,500 would be made.

LORD MERRIVALE, P. (at page 18)

I was asked to consult the Elder Brethren on the subject, and they, of course, have had to give attention to many matters of this kind, both administrative and in the course of their experience; and the view which they unhesitatingly take is that there would probably have been an explosion and that probably this vessel would have been sunk and would have become a wreck and the vessel and cargo would have been lost; and I confess that looking at the matter with no other information on the subject than that which common knowledge and the evidence given here afford me, my own view is that there was not that assured immunity from risk which the scientific witness for the defendants believed and asserted in a very convincing way. I have come to the conclusion that there was a very grave peril, that the probability was on the side of explosion, and that, that being so, here is property which is snatched from destruction—very probable destruction.

The question is, what award should be made? Well, the value of the property saved is not less than £13,300. I have considered what should be awarded, and my mind has ranged, before and after I consulted the Elder Brethren, between something in the nature of one-third and something in the nature of one-half, and I have come to the conclusion ultimately that the award, in addition to exceptional awards which I shall mention, should be £4,500.

The "Queen Elizabeth"

(1949) 82 Ll.L.Rep. 803

The value of the salved property is one of the matters to be taken into consideration in the making of a salvage award, even though the value is an exceptionally high one.

The *Queen Elizabeth* ran aground in Southampton Water, and was refloated by tugs which claimed a salvage award in respect of the services which had been rendered. The vessel's value at the time of the casualty was £6,208,000.

Held, by the Probate, Divorce and Admiralty Division, that this value must be taken into account in the making of the award, even though it was an exceptionally high one.

WILLMER, J. (at page 821)

In the course of the argument I asked Counsel specifically to deal with the question of the value of the salved property, because, so far as I know, no case has ever previously come before this Court involving a value even approximating to that with which we have to deal in this case. I was referred to the well-known authorities mentioned in Kennedy[5] at pp. 158–159, which have always been held to be binding statements of the law with regard to value in salvage cases. I think it is proper to observe that the authorities there cited are all cases which were decided in relation to values which in no way bore comparison with those with which we have to deal in this case. On the whole, however, it seems to me that the mere fact that, as a matter of *quantum*, the value in this case is so much higher than anything that was envisaged in those cases, is no reason to depart from the principles therein laid down. In those circumstances,

[5] *The Law of Civil Salvage*, 3rd Edn.

where one has, as we do have in this case, a practical certainty of continuing damage and continuing expense, coupled with a possibility, even if it is not more than a bare possibility, of a much more serious loss, one has to give some real effect to the very high value of the salved property. By that I mean that one must give some effect to it, beyond saying to oneself merely that this is a case in which the value of the salved property at least provides a sufficient and abundant fund out of which to reward the salvors.

I am not saying that you can measure salvage awards as sums in arithmetical proportion in relation to the salved property when you have values of the magnitude that you have in this case, but equally it would not, I think, be right to say that, where you have a value of this size, the addition of a few millions or the subtraction of a few millions would make no difference whatsoever. So long as even an outside chance of anything in the nature of total loss remains, then I think that the increase of value must involve some, although possibly not great, increase in the salvage award over and above what might have been awarded had the value been much smaller.

The "City of Chester"

(1884) 51 L.T. 485

The value of the salving vessel and the danger to which she is exposed are matters to be taken into consideration in the making of a salvage award.

The *City of Chester* was in distress in the Atlantic. The *Missouri* took her in tow and towed her to Halifax. During the towage a heavy sea was running, the *Missouri*'s crankshaft was damaged, and she was considerably strained. The value of the *City of Chester* was £90,000, and that of her cargo and freight was £89,535. The value of the *Missouri* was £83,000 and that of her cargo and freight £104,047.

Held, by the Court of Appeal, that the value of the *Missouri* and the danger to which she was exposed must be taken into account, in the making of the salvage award.

LINDLEY, L.J. (at page 493)

Another circumstance to be considered is the importance of so remunerating salvors as to make it worth their while to succour ships in distress. This consideration renders it necessary to be liberal not only to captains and crews who perform the salvage services, but also to the owners of vessels engaged in those services where such vessels have been injured or exposed to danger. The salving vessel is often herself exposed to imminent peril. The risk of loss or damage to her is often very great, and the damage actually done to her and the loss actually sustained by her owner from delay in her voyage and otherwise may be, and often is, very considerable. Hence, one element in determining the amount to be awarded for salvage services is the value of the salving ship and cargo which have been exposed to risk, and the nature and extent of the risk are other elements for consideration. Where the salving vessel is, as in the present case, a large and valuable steamer, exposed to great risk, the claims of her owner deserve very favourable attention: see *per* Dr Lushington in *The Spirit of the Age*.[6] Unless, where the salving vessel is a valuable steamer, the remuneration awarded to her owner is sufficient to cover this risk, owners of such vessels will naturally discourage their employment in salvage services; a result which would be very disastrous, and which the Court should do what it can to prevent. In order to avoid such a consequence as this it is necessary that the amount of compensation awarded to the owner of the salving ship shall, wherever practicable, be sufficiently large to cover the risk of damage and loss which he ran where fortunately none has been sustained. And where damage and loss have been, in fact, sustained, and its amount can be ascertained, it is necessary that the sum awarded shall, when possible, be large enough to cover such an amount. This amount, however, ought not to be the measure of the remuneration, for the damage actually sustained may be very small, and there may have been serious risk of sustaining much greater damage. Besides which there is always the risk of earning nothing by reason of the loss of the succoured vessel. The amount of loss actually sustained by the owner of the salving ship can therefore seldom, if ever, be the maximum limit of the remuneration to be awarded to him. Neither can such loss be always the minimum limit. It never can be so where the value of the ship and cargo saved is too small to admit of payment in full of the loss in question. And even where the value is sufficient, the salvage service may be so trifling as to render it unreasonable to throw the loss sustained by the salvors on the owners of the property saved. But where the salvage services have been dangerous to the salvors, and have occasioned them serious pecuniary loss, and have been highly valuable to the owners of the property saved, and where the value of the ship and cargo saved is ample not only to defray the loss sustained by the salvors in addition to a proper sum for the services of the master and crew of the salving ship, but also to leave a substantial surplus for the owner of the property saved, in such a case the sum to be awarded to the owner of the salving ship ought to be enough to cover her actual loss and whatever additional risk he ran.

The "Kedah"

(1948) 81 Ll.L.Rep. 217

Where the salvors are guilty of grave misconduct, the Court may refuse to make a salvage award.

[6] (1857) Sw. 286.

The *Kedah* was in distress off the Cornish coast. Salvage services were rendered to her by the tug *Salvonia*, which towed her to Falmouth. Some of the boarding party which she sent to the *Kedah* pilfered some of the vessel's equipment and some of the crew's effects. The members of the boarding party claimed a salvage award.

Held, by the Probate, Divorce and Admiralty Division, that they would have been entitled to an award, but the pilferage constituted misconduct of the gravest kind, which forfeited their right to claim any award at all.

WILLMER, J. (at page 224)

Although I have not been invited to apportion my award between the various interests, I think that it is necessary for me in my own mind to apportion it notionally, and, having arrived at a notional crew's proportion, I have to arrive at some conclusion as to what award would ordinarily have been payable to these particular individuals. Having arrived at the total figure in my own mind, I propose to subtract from the award the whole of that which would have been awarded to the three named men and half of that which would have been awarded to the chief officer—and I shall accompany that with a direction that those men are not to share in the award, except in so far as concerns the half share to the chief officer. The figures, of course, can only be rough. I would just add this, which is one of the unfortunate circumstances in the case. Unhappily these men who are affected were members of the *Salvonia*'s boarding party, and, therefore, the very members of her crew who, in the event of an apportionment, might have been, and I think would have been, entitled to special consideration, as opposed to the other members of the crew. If the amount which I deduct from the total award seems unduly great, it has to be borne in mind that what I am deducting is the proportion appropriate to men whose conduct would otherwise have been particularly meritorious, and such as would probably have entitled them to an unusually large share in the total award.

The "Tojo Maru": Owners of motor tanker "Tojo Maru" *v.* N.V. Bureau Wijsmuller

[1971] 1 All E.R. 1110

Where a ship is damaged by the salvors' negligence, the shipowner is entitled to claim for the full amount of the damage, and his rights are not restricted to a right to set-off the loss against the amount of the salvage award.

A diver operating from the salvors' tug negligently fired a bolt gun causing damage to the salved ship amounting to £331,767. The salvage award was £125,000. The shipowners claimed the full amount of the damage, but the salvors contended that the shipowners could only set-off this sum against the salvage award and therefore were entitled to nothing.

Held, by the House of Lords, that the shipowners were entitled to £206,767 (i.e., £331,767 minus £125,000).

LORD MORRIS OF BORTH-Y-GEST (at page 1125)

The principle that success is necessary for a salvage award will often necessitate a consideration whether the overall result of the operations of a salvor have achieved some success. In this way there will be enquiry whether some good has been the outcome. But I can find no support in principle or in authority for the view that salvors who have negligently caused damage are protected from being out of pocket if the "harm" they have done is counter-balanced by the "good" they have done on some basis such as that the "good" they have done is to be measured as being the value or the improved value of the ship in respect of which their services have been rendered. On the first question posed by WILLMER, L.J., I consider, in agreement with his view which was also the view of the arbitrator, that it was permissible to entertain the owners' counterclaim for damages. Had the salvage operation been conducted without negligence the owners would not have been under the necessity of spending £202,514 on repairs to their ship and would not have suffered loss and damage to the extent of £129,253; they have suffered damages amounting to £331,767. They would, however, have been liable to pay salvage. Had there been no negligence, the salvage award would probably have been more than £125,000. They should be put in the position they would have been in had there been no negligence. Unless there can be limitation of liability, they should receive £331,767 less what would have been the amount of a salvage award that they would have to pay had there been no negligence. The learned arbitrator should be invited to fix that figure.

The "Glengyle"

(1898) 78 L.T. 801

The Court will attach great importance to the fact that the vessel has been salved by professional salvors, and as a matter of policy will give a liberal salvage award.

The *Glengyle* came into collision with another vessel while passing through the Straits of Gibraltar. Two salvage steamers specially built for and employed in salvage services immediately proceeded from Gibraltar, and saved her from certain total loss. The value of the salved vessel was £76,596, and the values of the steamers were £20,000 and £22,000.

Held, by the House of Lords, that a salvage award of £19,000 would be made.

LORD HERSCHELL (at page 802)

The case is a somewhat peculiar one, because the vessel would no doubt have gone to the bottom but for the assistance rendered by the respondents' two tugs or salving steamers—that seems certain; and that the vessel was saved from imminent peril at a risk to the steamers seems almost certain, and at some risk—it may not have been a heavy risk—to the lives of those who were navigating them. Moreover, the destruction of the vessel seems to have been certain unless those steamers had been waiting ready at any moment to respond to a call if there was a vessel in distress. They were steamers of considerable value—the one worth £22,000, and the other word £20,000—with large crews on board (23 in the case of the *Hermes*), with special apparatus ready to be used for salvage purposes, with pumps of unusual power and other appliances—with those always ready, however long a time might elapse between one call and another. I think it impossible to exaggerate the importance to shipping of the presence at a port like Gibraltar of vessels like these, always ready to render the services which they were called upon to render in this case. It is not like the case of a vessel in distress at sea which is fallen in with by other vessels, any one of which would probably be as able as any other to render the required service, the only difference being that the one ship has arrived before the others. It is a case where, but for the presence of these vessels specially prepared for the service, ready for the service at the moment, a vessel would have been lost (as this would have been), but owing to these vessels being ready is saved. Here the vessel and cargo are of great value, £76,000. And I ought to add this, that the crews of the salving steamers were not the ordinary crews of a tug for towage purposes—they were crews especially skilled in salvage work, who were capable of doing the work of divers and various other operations which were necessary if vessels were to be effectually salved. All these were elements to be taken into account, and having been considered, and considered together, the conclusion was arrived at that £19,000 should be awarded for the salvage.

Island Tug and Barge Ltd. *v.* Owners of the S.S. "Makedonia"

[1958] 1 All E.R. 236

Whether taxation is to be taken into account in the assessing of the amount of a salvage award is a question which has not been finally settled.

A company carried on business as professional salvors, and claimed a salvage award in respect of a vessel in distress while on a voyage from Japan to Vancouver. The matter was referred to arbitration, and the arbitrator, holding himself bound by *The Telemachus*[7] awarded £60,000 together with a further sum of £15,000 by way of contribution towards the tax which the salvors would have to pay on the £60,000 awarded.

Held, by the Probate, Divorce and Admiralty Division, (not following *The Telemachus*) that only £60,000 could be awarded, and taxation was not to be taken into account in assessing the amount of the award.

---

[7] [1957] 1 All E.R. 72, P.D.A.

PILCHER, J. (at page 244)

Feeling himself bound by the decision of WILLMER, J., in *The Telemachus*[8] the appeal arbitrator added £15,000 to his award to recompense the claimants for the £18,000 which they would have to pay away in tax. He thus "took the tax aspect into account" in much the same way as the Court and arbitrator "take into account" in arriving at salvage awards the proved expenses of salvors incurred in rendering the salvage services. This is what WILLMER, J., said he was doing in *The Telemachus*,[9] although he did not indicate to what extent the awards he made had been increased by consideration of the tax position of the salvors. I need not say that it is only after the most anxious thought and careful consideration that I have felt compelled to disagree with the views on this topic expressed by WILLMER, J., in *The Telemachus.*[10] I do not feel, as he did, that any principle laid down in *British Transport Commission* v. *Gourley*[11] compels, or even inclines, me to take the view that a salvor, who is already generously rewarded on well-known principles, should have his award further increased so as to indemnify him wholly or in part for the fact that the fiscal law to which he is subject requires him to pay tax on the profit element in his salvage award. If it is right that awards made to salvors, which are already assessed on generous lines, should be exempted in whole or in part from liability to tax, this seems to me to be a matter for consideration by the Legislature. In my humble opinion, it is not the business of the Court to defeat or mitigate the effect of the fiscal laws of this or any other country, more especially where this can only be done at the expense of the owners of the salved property.

For these reasons, I regretfully find myself unable to agree with the judgment of WILLMER, J., in *The Telemachus.*[12]

China Pacific S.A. *v.* Food Corporation of India: The "Winson"

[1982] 1 Lloyd's Rep. 117

Where a cargo has been salved and then stored by the salvors, they may claim the storage expenses as part of the salvage award.

The owners of the vessel *Winson* let her to the charterers under a voyage charter-party for the carriage of a cargo of wheat from the U.S.A. to India. On Jan. 21, 1975, the vessel stranded on a reef in the South China Seas. On Jan. 22 her managing agents signed a "Lloyd's Standard Form of Salvage Agreement—No cure, no pay" with the salvors. The agreement was binding on the shipowners, the charterers and the salvors. The salvors performed salvage services, which resulted in the saving of six parcels of

[8] *Supra.*
[9] *Supra.*
[10] *Supra.*
[11] [1955] 3 All E.R. 796, H.L.
[12] *Supra.*

the wheat. These were taken out of the vessel and off-loaded at Manila. On Apr. 24 the shipowners abandoned the voyage. The salvors claimed against the charterers in respect of the expenses incurred in the off-loading and storage of the salved cargo up to Apr. 24.

Held, by the House of Lords, that there would be judgment for the salvors. The legal relationship of bailor and bailee continued to subsist until possession of the wheat was accepted by the charterers. The salvors owed a duty of care to the charterers to take such measures to preserve the salved wheat from deterioration as a man of ordinary prudence would take for the preservation of his own property. If he fulfilled that duty, he had a right to charge the charterers with the expenses reasonably incurred in doing so.

LORD DIPLOCK (at page 123)

It follows from the existence of the legal relationship of bailor and bailee as a matter of general principle of the law of bailment, which may also be described as hornbook law, that as between the cargo owner and the salvors, the latter as bailees were estopped from denying the title to the goods of the former as their bailor, including as an incident of that title its right to possession. Subject to the lien point, which I am deferring until later, the salvors could not resist a demand for possession of the salved wheat made by the cargo owner upon its arrival at a place of safety by relying upon *jus tertii*, viz. the shipowner's right to possession as against the cargo owner, at any rate until an adverse claim to possession had been made upon them by the shipowner. If demand for possession of the salved wheat had been made upon the salvors by the shipowner (which it never was), the salvors would have complied with it at their peril. Their only safe course would have been to interplead; whereas in returning possession to the cargo owner or in accordance with its directions before any demand for possession was made by the shipowner, they would have run no risk of liability to the latter. So I agree with LLOYD, J.,[13] that (at any rate when, as in the instant case, a salvage contract in Lloyd's open form is entered into on behalf of a sole owner of a bulk cargo) salvors are under a duty at the conclusion of the salvage services to deliver up possession of the salved cargo to the cargo owner or in accordance with his directions.

Upon the assumption, whether correct or not, to which I have already referred as being that upon which this case has been argued throughout, that the salvage services which the salvors had contracted to render to the cargo owner came to an end as respects each parcel of salved wheat when it arrived at a place of safety in Manila Harbour, the legal relationship of bailor and bailee between cargo owner and salvors nevertheless continued to subsist until possession of the wheat was accepted by the cargo owner from the depositaries, who had been the salvors' sub-bailees. Subject always to the question of the salvors' right to the provision of security before removal of the salved wheat from Manila, with which I shall deal separately later, the bailment which up to the

[13] In the High Court.

conclusion of the salvage services had been a bailment for valuable consideration, became a gratuitous bailment; and so long as that relationship of bailor and bailee continued to subsist, the salvors, under the ordinary principles of the law of bailment too well-known and too well-established to call for any citation of authority, owed a duty of care to the cargo owner to take such measures to preserve the salved wheat from deterioration by exposure to the elements as a man of ordinary prudence would take for the preservation of his own property. For any breach of such duty the bailee is liable to his bailor in damages for any diminution in value of the goods consequent upon his failure to take such measures; and if he fulfils that duty, he has, in my view, a correlative right to charge the owner of the goods with the expenses reasonably incurred in doing so.

B. TOWAGE

Elliott Steam Tug Co. Ltd. *v.* New Medway Steam Packet Co. Ltd.

(1937) 59 Ll.L.Rep. 35

In a contract of towage there is an implied term that the vessel to be towed is to be placed in a position where it is reasonably possible for the tug to take her in tow.

The plaintiffs' tug was engaged by the defendants to tow a concrete lighter from a berth at West Mersea to Chatham Buoys. The tug arrived off West Mersea, but found that it was impracticable to reach the lighter because of insufficient water except at high tide. The defendants had taken no steps to bring the lighter into such a position that she could be taken in tow. The plaintiffs claimed damages for breach of an implied term in the contract that the lighter should have been in such a position.

Held, by the King's Bench Division, that the action succeeded.

GODDARD, J. (at page 38)

I think it is right to imply, in such a contract, that the owners of the vessel to be towed would have the vessel in such a position that a tug of the size which they knew would have to be sent to perform the voyage, would be able to take the lighter in tow, and that the lighter was in such a position that a tug could pick it up and take it out.

I think it was the duty, therefore, of the defendants in this case to put the lighter into such a position that a tug of this size could take it out, and that it would have been an unreasonable, and indeed unsafe, manoeuvre for the captain of this tug to have taken his tug up this channel into this place where there was not enough room for him to manoeuvre the vessel with the tug coming down, and he would run a very serious risk, with a falling tide, of being left aground.

I think, therefore, the defendants did not put the lighter in a proper position.

The "Niobe"

(1888) 59 L.T. 257

Under the ordinary contract of towage the tow has control over the tug, and is responsible for any damage done by the tug.

The *Niobe* was being towed by the tug *Flying Serpent* under a towage contract. Both vessels collided with the *Valetta*, but the only damage to the *Valetta* was caused by the *Flying Serpent*. There was a bad look-out on the *Niobe*, and if those on board her had seen the *Valetta* approaching, orders could have been given to the *Flying Serpent* and the collision would have been avoided. The owners of the *Niobe* contended that they were not responsible for the negligence of those on board the *Flying Serpent*, for they were not their servants but were independent contractors.

Held, by the Probate, Divorce and Admiralty Division, that the owners of the *Niobe* were liable for the negligence of the *Flying Serpent*, for the tow had, under the ordinary contract of carriage, control over the tug.

SIR JAMES HANNEN (at page 259)

It appears to me that the authorities clearly establish that the tow has, under the ordinary contract of towage, control over the tug. The tug and tow are engaged in a common undertaking, of which the general management and command belong to the tow, and, in order that she should efficiently carry out this command, it is necessary that she should have a good look-out, and should not allow herself to be drawn, or the tug to go, on a course which will cause damage to another vessel. As Dr Lushington has pointed out, it is essential to the safety of vessels being towed, that there should not be a divided command, and convenience has established that the undivided authority shall belong to the tow. The pilot, if there be one, takes his station on the tow, and the officers of the tow are usually, as in the present case, of a higher class and better able to direct the navigation than those of the tug. The practice which experience has dictated has received the sanction of many legal decisions, and has been recognised in the House of Lords in *Spaight* v. *Tedcastle*[14] where LORD BLACKBURN says that it is the duty of the tug to carry out the directions received from the ship, and in the Privy Council in *The American and The Syria.*[15]

---

[14] (1889) 6 App. Cas. 217.
[15] (1874) L.R. 6 P.C. 127.

The "Impetus": Owners of the m.v. "Blenheim" *v*. Owners of tug "Impetus"

[1959] 2 All E.R. 354

A collision occurs "whilst towing" within the meaning of the United Kingdom Standard Towage Conditions where the tug is ready to receive orders from the tow "to pick up ropes or lines", even though she is not in a position to carry out any order which might have been received.

A collision occurred between the *Blenheim* and the tug *Impetus* for which the *Impetus* was responsible. The *Impetus* had been engaged to tow her under the United Kingdom Standard Towage Conditions,[16] which by condition 3 excluded the tugowner's liability for damage done by the tug "whilst towing". Condition 1 provided that the phrase "whilst towing" "shall be deemed to cover the period commencing when the tug is in a position to receive orders direct from the hirer's vessel to pick up ropes or lines". No order had been given by the *Blenheim* to the *Impetus* to throw a receiving line to the *Blenheim*, but the crew of the *Impetus* were prepared to heave a line, although they were not in a position to do so. Those on board the *Blenheim* were ready to receive the line. The tugowner denied liability on the ground that he was protected by condition 1.

Held, by the Probate, Divorce and Admiralty Division, that the tugowner was protected. The *Blenheim* was ready to give and the *Impetus* ready "to receive orders to pick up ropes or lines", although it was impossible for the *Impetus* immediately to carry out the orders. Consequently the collision had occurred "whilst towing".

KARMINSKI, J. (at page 357)

I have no difficulty in accepting the contention of Counsel for the plaintiffs that the burden in this case is on the defendants to establish that they have brought themselves within the protection of cl. 1 to cl. 3 of the towage conditions. Clausc 1 has, as it seems to me, extended the ordinary meaning of the words "whilst towing" to cover a state of affairs in which towing is contemplated but not being carried out. It is clear on the evidence that at the time of the collision the *Impetus* was in a position to receive the order to heave the line, but was not in a position until after the collision to carry out such an order. The fact that the *Blenheim* on this, as on very many earlier occasions, gave no order is in a sense irrelevant. The question is whether at the time of the collision the *Impetus* was in a position to receive orders from the *Blenheim* to pick up ropes or lines, had such orders been given.

In spite of the interesting argument of Counsel for the plaintiffs to the contrary, I have come to the conclusion that cl. 1 means what it says and that the conditions attach when the tug is in a position to receive orders to pick up ropes or lines. This presupposes that the ship is ready to give such orders, if such orders are required. I cannot, however, accept Counsel's submission that a tug can thereafter put herself outside the conditions by getting into a position

---

[16] The present Conditions are set out in the United Kingdom Standard Conditions for Towage and Other Services (revised 1974). The decision in this case remains unaffected by the revision.

which may for a short period make it impossible for her to carry out such orders. To import such a condition when the tug is already in attendance on the ship, and, therefore, in danger of incurring damage, would, as SCOTT, L.J., pointed out in *W.J. Guy & Son* v. *Glen Line Ltd.*[17] be without justification.

The "Uranienborg"

[1935] All E.R. Rep. 70

A collision does not occur "whilst towing" within the meaning of the United Kingdom Standard Towage Conditions if the tug is not "in a position to receive orders to pick up ropes or lines". For her to be in a position "to receive orders generally" does not bring her within the Conditions.

The plaintiffs were the owners of the tug *Kenia* which had been engaged by the defendants to tow *Uranienborg*, which was owned by them. The contract of towage was made on the United Kingdom Standard Towage Conditions,[18] which by condition 3 stated that the "tugowner shall not, whilst towing, . . . , be liable for damage done by . . . the tug . . . to the hirer's vessel". Condition 1 said that the phrase "whilst towing" "shall be deemed to cover the period commencing when the tug is in a position to receive orders direct from the hirer's vessel to pick up ropes or lines . . .". The *Kenia* collided with the *Uranienborg* and damaged her. The plaintiffs claimed a declaration that they were not liable because the collision occurred "whilst towing". The defendants contended that the plaintiffs were not protected because although the tug was within hailing distance, nobody on board the *Uranienborg* was preparing to give orders with regard to ropes or lines, and the *Kenia*, when she arrived, was trying to avoid a collision, and was not in a position to receive such orders.

Held, by the Probate, Divorce and Admiralty Division, that the declaration would not be granted, for the tug had to be in a position to receive orders to pick up ropes or lines, and not orders generally. Hence the collision had not occurred "whilst towing".

SIR BOYD MERRIMAN, P. (at page 73)

I doubt myself whether the word "position" is only used in the sense of local situation. I think it involves also the conception of the tug being herself in a condition to receive and act upon the orders. But, however that may be, the orders which she is to be in a position to receive are orders to pick up ropes or lines—not orders generally, but those specific orders—and I think that that must have some reference to the intention of those on board the ship to give those orders, and to the readiness of those on board the tug to receive such orders.

On the facts of this case I should be prepared to hold that, even if one were bound to hold that all that matters is the physical position of the tug, I do not

---

[17] [1948] 1 All E.R. 245, C.A.

[18] The present Conditions are set out in the United Kingdom Standard Conditions for Towage and Other Services (revised 1974). The decision in this case remains unaffected by the revision.

think that the moment had arrived. I have already said that there was nobody on board the *Uranienborg* who, at the moment of the *Kenia*'s arrival, was even thinking or preparing to give orders to take or receive, as between the ship and the tug, the ropes or lines. They had not got to that stage; they were not thinking of it. I have seen the officer whose duty it would be to superintend those operations. He had not got anybody standing by; they had not finished discharging; he had already told the other tug that neither the pilot nor the boatmen had come; and the other tug, as I have already said, was lying off some 300 ft. away, at a buoy. [Counsel] says that she plainly, quite plainly, was in a position to receive orders to pick up ropes or lines—she was, in the sense that she was within 300 ft. and within hailing distance, but in no other sense. She knew that the time was not ripe and was acting accordingly, and there is not a tittle of evidence from the *Kenia* that anybody, from the master downwards, on board the *Kenia* was even thinking in terms of ropes and lines at the material time. Certainly, they had come there in order to be available for the towing whenever the towing began. At the moment that this collision occurred they were not thinking of—they had not begun to expect—an order to pick up ropes or lines at all. On the contrary, all that the master was thinking of at that moment was correcting his own errors in going through those barge tiers much too fast and trying to avoid this collision. I find it, whether as a matter of construction of the conditions or on the facts of this case, impossible to hold that at the critical moment this tug was in a position to receive orders with regard to ropes or lines. I think that the least that is involved in arriving at the moment when the period commences is that the tug herself, at any rate, should be able to show that she was in a position to receive and, having received, to comply with these orders in connection with ropes or lines at the material time. I am satisfied that that period had not come in the case of this tug *Kenia*, but I think also that this phrase has got to be read as if there were two parties involved in the matter, and that until the reasonable moment has come at which orders may be expected to be given from the ship, the tug cannot be said to be in a position to receive orders from the ship; but whichever way you look at it—even if you look at it, as I say from the point of view of the tug alone—I am satisfied that on the facts of this case she was not in a position to receive orders and that the towing had not begun.

C. PILOTAGE

W. H. Muller and Co.'s Algemeene Scheepvaart-Maatschappij *v.* Trinity House Corporation

(1924) 132 L.T. 663

Section 31 of the Pilotage Act 1983 only imposes an obligation on a vessel in a compulsory pilotage district to fly the pilot flag. It does not absolutely prohibit

her navigation without a pilot. If no pilot offers his services, there is no duty to pay the pilotage dues.

A vessel flew the pilot flag in the London Pilotage District, but no pilot offered his services. The Corporation of Trinity House sought to charge the shipowners with pilotage dues.

Held, by the King's Bench Division, that the shipowners were under no duty to pay them.

ROWLATT, J. (at page 665)

The main question here is whether when a ship enters the compulsory pilotage area and continues her passage through it to her destination without having taken a pilot, she can be charged with the pilotage dues as a debt, independently of the question whether any offence has been committed. The defendants contend that she can be so charged, and if that contention is wrong, then the whole defence fails, and there is no longer any question as to what rate is chargeable. The question depends on the Pilotage Act 1913 [now the Pilotage Act 1983] and the most material section here in s. 11 [now s. 31].[19] The plaintiffs say that this section covers the whole of the ground, and that the liability being created by the statute and a penalty for breach being provided, there can be no debt. The defendants, on the other hand, say that sub-s. (2) only deals with the case where the pilot has offered, and that whether a pilot offers his services or not, a debt is incurred for pilotage dues in every case, as soon as an inward ship passes the limits with the intention of navigating to London, but that if, in fact, a pilot has offered, then a penalty is incurred in addition under s. 11, sub-s. (2) [now s. 31, sub-s. (2)]. The question is therefore whether s. 11, sub-s. (1) [now s. 31, sub-s. (2)], creates a debt for pilotage dues. As to this I think the true construction is not that no vessel shall navigate unless she has a licensed pilot on board, but that she is under a continuing obligation to fly the pilot flag, and must take a pilot on board if he offers.

To construe the subsection otherwise would be unreasonable, and would place a great responsibility upon the pilotage authority, beside being in conflict with s. 30 [s. 36] which provides for the supersession of a pilot who is not authorised. Even if the position is that she must stop, it does not follow that if she does not stop, she must pay the fees for pilotage, and I cannot see any connection between the two propositions. But the defendants say that even if she

[19] Section 31(1) states: "Every ship . . . while navigating in a pilotage district in which pilotage is compulsory . . . shall be either (a) under the pilotage of a licensed pilot of the district; or (b) under the pilotage of a master . . . or mate possessing a pilotage certificate for the district, . . ." Section 31(2) states: "If any ship . . . in circumstances in which pilotage is compulsory . . . is not under pilotage as required by this section, after a licensed pilot of the district has offered to take charge of the ship, the master . . . shall be liable in respect of each offence to a fine not exceeding double the amount of the pilotage charges that . . . would have been payable in respect of the ship if it had been under pilotage as so required".

is not bound to stop, she must take all reasonable steps to find a pilot, that is to say she must go to the place where she knows the pilots will be assembled, even though that point is at the Sunk and not at the Tongue, which is the nearest route from the nautical point of view. Even if this is true, I am in the same difficulty as before, that if she fails to carry out this obligation, it does not seem to follow that she must pay the pilotage dues.

Babbs *v.* Press

[1971] 2 Lloyd's Rep. 383

An offer for the purposes of the Pilotage Act 1983, s. 36(3) must be an offer made or communicated in relation to the particular movement of the vessel in question.

Press, a licensed waterman, piloted the vessel *Matilde* while changing her moorings in the London Pilotage District which was a compulsory pilotage district. The Trinity House Pilot Station at Gravesend had displayed a pilot flag intended to constitute an offer of pilotage on behalf of all licensed pilots available there. Press was charged with contravening the Pilotage Act 1913, s. 30(3) [now The Pilotage Act 1983, s. 36(3)], which stated that it was an offence for an unlicensed pilot to pilot a vessel in a compulsory pilotage district after a licensed pilot had offered to pilot the ship. Press was discharged on the ground that the evidence did not show that the movement was more than two miles, and in any case the display of the flag was not an offer under s. 30(3) of the Act. The prosecutor appealed.

Held, by the Divisional Court of the Queen's Bench Division, that the appeal would be dismissed, and (*obiter*) that the display of the flag was not an offer.

LORD WIDGERY, L.C.J. (at page 388)

But we have had an interesting and helpful argument on the second point which I referred to, and I think it is right therefore to express certain views upon that, although they must necessarily be obiter. In this Act, as I see it—and I think that Counsel agree—one has running through a general proposition that it is the duty of the pilot to seek out the ship rather than the ship to seek out the pilot. Even where the full rigours of compulsory pilotage apply, it is provided, as I have already said, in s. 11 [now s. 31] that the obligation to take on a licensed pilot does not arise until the offer of a licensed pilot has been made, and one can well see the good sense of that, particularly in 1913 when wireless telegraphy was in its infancy, because one might well ask how could a master of a ship approaching a port provide himself with a pilot unless a pilot came forward and offered his services. So one does get, I think, this important principle that the pilot must seek out the ship and not the ship seek out the pilot. In other words, I do not think that this Act contemplates a situation in which the pilots merely advertise their availability, following upon which it is the duty of the master to find them. Indeed, if that were so, it would be difficult to understand the purpose of s. 30(4) [now s. 36(4)] which I have already read. An extremely sensible exception was made in the subsection, whereby the master of an outward bound ship has got to take steps to get a pilot before he leaves. The reason for that no doubt is that pilots cannot know just when the ship is going to sail and cannot be standing by with an offer of pilotage indefinitely. But in all other instances, the reverse applies, and it seems to me if the appellants are right, and if it is the law that by establishing this base opposite the landing stage, flying a pilot's flag from that base and publishing up and down the river that pilots are there available, if they are right in saying that by virtue of that they issue in effect a global invitation, a global offer, to all masters requiring pilots, that they are available, that would, in fact, be putting the obligation of finding a pilot upon the master instead of in the opposite direction, and, in my judgment, it is not open to Trinity House to support a general offer in those wide terms and circumstances. In my judgment, an offer for the purposes of s. 30(3) [now s. 36(3)] must be an offer made or communicated in relation to the particular movement of the vessel which is in question here.

Whether or not in a given case an offer has been made relative to the particular movement of the vessel will, of course, be a question of fact. I recognise that in many instances an offer may be made simultaneously to a number of vessels at the same time. One visualises a pilot cutter going out from a port, flying the appropriate signals to indicate that it is a pilot cutter, and thereby in effect offering to every passing master the services of a pilot on board a cutter. I am not suggesting that it is not possible for an offer to be made simultaneously to a number of ships in the vicinity, but when one comes to look at the facts of this case, I think that the Justices were wholly justified in reaching the conclusion which they did, that the presence of the pilot station and its flag two miles down the river was not a sufficient offer to the master of the *Matilde* of a licensed pilot at the time when she set off on this short two-mile voyage. To take the contrary view, as I have already said, would be to place the obligation of finding a pilot on the master, and I have no doubt that on the facts which the Justice have found they were correct in taking the view that no sufficient offer relative to the movement had been made at the time when the *Matilde* set off under the control of the respondent.

Clayton *v.* Albertsen

[1972] 2 Lloyd's Rep. 457

Drivers of "roll-on, roll-off" lorries who accompany their vehicles on board a vessel are "passengers" for the purpose of the Pilotage Act 1983, s. 31.

A lorry driver accompanied his vehicle on the Danish "roll-on, roll-off" vessel *Somerset* on a voyage from Denmark to Newcastle. He was accommodated in a cabin in which there were other drivers. He performed no duty in connection with the vessel, but occupied himself with routine maintenance of the vehicle. The vessel entered the Tyne Pilotage District, which was a compulsory pilotage district, without a pilot. The master was charged with an offence under the Pilotage Act 1913, s. 11 [now the Pilotage Act 1983, s. 31], which stated that every vessel carrying passengers in a compulsory pilotage had to be under the pilotage of a licensed pilot. He was discharged by the justices on the ground that the driver was not a passenger. The prosecutor appealed.

Held, by the Divisional Court of the Queen's Bench Division, that the appeal would be allowed and that the case would be remitted to the justices with a direction to convict for, on the evidence, the driver was a "passenger".

MILMO, J. (at page 463)

I can find nothing in the legislation nor in the decided authorities to which we have been referred, which supports the contention that as a matter of law these drivers were other than passengers within the meaning of s. 11 of the Pilotage Act 1913 [now s. 31 of the Pilotage Act 1983]. Indeed, as a matter of law I am of opinion that they clearly were passengers. We have not got the contract of carriage under which the owners of these lorries had their lorries and cargo carried on "roll-on, roll-off" terms which are referred to in the stated case; but, in my view, on the facts as found in the case it is abundantly clear as to what the practice was between the owners of the lorries and the owner of this ship which plied between Newcastle and Denmark, taking on board loaded lorries which were driven on by their drivers on behalf of the owners, then at the port of destination were driven off by drivers on behalf of the owners, and then taken to their inland destination where they discharged their loads. It would seem, however, that there were two practices in operation. In the case with which we are immediately concerned the driver of the lorry drove his lorry on to the vessel, and accompanied the lorry throughout the voyage. Another way in which it emerges that these contracts of freight were implemented was that the lorry would be driven on to the vessel at the port of embarkation, and then would be met by another driver on behalf of the owner who would drive it off at the port of disembarkation. What does appear perfectly plainly is this, that there was provision made by the shipowners for the carriage of drivers whom the lorry owner wished to accompany the lorry throughout the voyage. They were provided with cabin accommodation; they were provided with a separate mess, and they were provided with food. It seems to me that it matters not whether the food supplied was the same food as the food which was provided for the crew. They definitely were not members of the crew, and they took no part whatsoever in the navigation of the vessel itself, and did nothing in connection with the vessel itself. They were being carried on the vessel for one purpose and for one purpose only, namely to take them from the point where they had driven their lorry on to the vessel, and the point at which they were going to drive it off.

In these circumstances I find the conclusion inescapable that these people were passengers, and were nothing other than passengers.

PART V

MARINE INSURANCE

(1) INSURABLE INTEREST

Piper *v.* Royal Exchange Assurance

(1932) 44 Ll.L.Rep. 103

A buyer of a vessel has no insurable interest unless the property in her has passed[1] *to him.*

A yacht in Norway was bought in 1926 "as she lies" by the plaintiff, and was at the risk of the seller until she arrived in London. The plaintiff effected a policy in respect of her, and claimed against the insurers for damage which she sustained by stranding in 1928. The insurers counterclaimed for a sum of money which they had paid to him in respect of damage sustained by her on the voyage from Norway to London in 1926, on the ground that he had no insurable interest in her, since the property in her had not passed to him.

Held, by the King's Bench Division, that the counterclaim succeeded.

ROCHE, J. (at page 116)

It has been contended that the risk of the voyage was upon the plaintiff, Mr Piper. I am satisfied that it was not, upon the evidence afforded by the contemporary documents proceeding from Mr Piper and from the vendor. Mr Piper claimed upon the vendor on the basis that he (the vendor) was liable, and what the vendor wrote about it was as follows, and it is to be found in the correspondence which is headed "Documents obtained from Messrs Webster", under date Sept. 17, or, rather, the letter of Sept. 17 is a letter from Messrs Webster citing to Mr Piper a letter from the owner or his son in these terms: "The yacht has been sold as it was in Norway with delivery England, and my father is consequently only responsible for any damage that occurs on the voyage to England. The vessel was insured for the voyage, and the insurance company therefore take over my father's responsibility in this respect". That is quite right and that is my finding as to the legal position.

---

[1] Under the Sale of Goods Act 1979, ss. 16–18. See generally Chalmers, *Sale of Goods Act 1979* (18th Edn. 1981), pp. 140–152.

Now, in those circumstances the underwriters say: "We insured the plaintiff through the broker on the basis that he had an interest, and we paid him on the basis that he had an interest".

Thomas Cheshire & Co. *v*. Vaughan Bros. & Co.

(1920) 123 L.T. 487

A p.p.i. policy is void even though the assured may, in fact, have had an insurable interest.

Exporters of some nitrate from South America instructed their brokers to effect a p.p.i. policy on their prospective profits. The brokers did so, but the policy was unenforceable against the insurers because they failed to disclose a material fact. When they were sued by the exporters for damages for negligence, they pleaded that they were not liable because the policy, being p.p.i., was in any event void under the Marine Insurance Act 1906, s. 4.

Held, by the Court of Appeal, that this defence succeeded, even though the exporters had an insurable interest in fact.

Scrutton, L.J. (at page 493)

Then, secondly, [Counsel] says, [section] 4 of the Marine Insurance Act 1906 is not really so strict as it appears to be. It says: "(1) Every contract of marine insurance by way of gaming or wagering is void: (*a*) Where the assured has not an insurable interest as defined by this Act, and the contract is entered into with no expectation of acquiring such an interest; or (*b*) where the policy is made 'interest or no interest', or 'without further proof of interest than the policy itself'." That only means, if I understand [Counsel's] argument, that it is *prima facie* a gaming and wagering contract and you may defeat it if you can show you either had a real interest or a probability of obtaining it. That is, in effect, to read sub-s. (*a*) of s. 2 into sub-s. (*b*). I see no ground for cutting down the section in that way. It seems to me Parliament has said: "If you put this clause in your policy without more, we deem it to be a gaming and wagering policy, because it is a gaming and wagering clause". In my view, therefore, the second point fails.

(2) NON-DISCLOSURE

Container Transport International Inc. *v*. Oceanus Mutual Underwriting Association (Bermuda) Ltd.

[1984] 1 Lloyd's Rep. 476

By s. 18(2) of the Marine Insurance Act 1906 "Every circumstance is material which would influence the judgment of a prudent insurer in fixing the premium or determining whether he will take the risk". The word "judgment" is used in the sense of "the formation of an opinion".

KERR, L.J. (at page 492)

The duty of disclosure, as defined or circumscribed by ss. 18 and 19 [of the Marine Insurance Act 1906], is one aspect of the overriding duty of the utmost good faith mentioned in s. 17. The actual insurer is thereby entitled to the disclosure to him of every fact which would influence the judgment of a prudent insurer in fixing the premium or determining whether he will take the risk. The latter words, as [Counsel] rightly said, must comprise any terms, and not only the level of premium, which an insurer might require in the wording of the cover, e.g. warranties, franchises, deductibles, exceptions, etc. The word "judgment"—to quote the *Oxford English Dictionary* to which we were referred—is used in the sense of "the formation of an opinion". To prove the materiality of an undisclosed circumstance, the insurer must satisfy the Court on a balance of probability—by evidence or from the nature of the undisclosed circumstance itself—that the judgment, in this sense, of a prudent insurer would have been influenced if the circumstance in question had been disclosed. The word "influenced" means that the disclosure is one which would have had an impact on the formation of his opinion and on his decision-making process in relation to the matters covered by s. 18(2).

One must bear in mind that the issue is as to the relevance, and not as to the weight, of any evidence which may be adduced in order to show that an undisclosed circumstance was material. Such evidence may be given by the actual insurer who—ex hypothesi—has accepted the risk in ignorance of the undisclosed fact. For him, it may be relatively easy to say simply: "Had I known this, I would have declined the risk, or imposed such-and-such a term, or charged such-and-such a premium". But this is not the nature of the evidence to which s. 18(2) is directed, nor is such evidence required from any witness who may be called on the question of materiality. The section is directed to what would have been the impact of the disclosure on the judgment of the risk formed by a hypothetical prudent insurer in the ordinary course of business; see the remarks of BLACKBURN, J., in *Ionides* v. *Pender*.[2] He is in a hypothetical position, and evidence to support the materiality of the undisclosed circumstances, from this point of view, is therefore often given by an independent expert witness whose evidence has to be assessed by the Court long after the event. He, or the actual insurer, or both, may then be asked: "What would have been your reaction if you had known of this undisclosed fact?" Both would in my view give relevant evidence on materiality if they replied: "I would then have regarded the risk in a different light. I would have

[2] (1874) L.R. 9 Q.B. 531, at p. 539.

taken this circumstance into account. As a first step I might have asked some questions before making up my mind about the risk. What my final decision would have been, I cannot now say for certain. I might have declined the risk altogether, or increased the premium, or altered the terms in some other way". And it would make no difference if the witness went on: "I might even have taken a chance, or given credit for the frankness of the disclosure, by writing the risk as I did. But I should obviously have been told about this fact before being asked to make up my mind".

The weight which the Court would give to such evidence is then a matter for the Court.

Thames and Mersey Marine Insurance Co. *v*. Gunford Ship Co. Ltd.

(1911) 105 L.T. 312

The fact that the assured, in addition to effecting a hull policy, has also taken out a policy on freight and disbursements has been held to be a material one which he must disclose to the insurers.

The assured effected a valued policy in respect of a vessel for a voyage from Hamburg to Santa Rosalia, the sum insured being £18,500, while her real value was only £9,000. But the insurance company was not told that the assured had also taken out policies to a large amount on freight and disbursements. She was wrecked off the Brazilian coast.

Held, by the House of Lords, that the insurance company could avoid liability on the ground of non-disclosure of a material fact.

LORD SHAW (at page 317)

The case as presented, although it touched and could not but touch this fundamental ground, was taken as an issue on the duty of disclosure, and I accordingly proceed to treat it on that footing. So dealing with it, I do not find myself able to agree with the judgment of either House of the Court of Session. It follows upon the nature of the argument there presented that no duty rests upon the owners, or agent, to disclose to the insurers of the hull facts of the character found in this case. I cannot assent or give any countenance to such a view. The learned Lord Ordinary says: "I cannot see that there is any duty whatever on the part of the assured to disclose to the underwriter on hull, who accepts the vessel at a declared value, that he is also effecting insurances upon freight and disbursements". The opinion of all your Lordships is to an opposite effect and I humbly agree with that opinion. So far as the effecting of insurances upon freight is concerned that is sound business because it is grounded upon a stipulation for true indemnity; but so far as disbursements, wherever they are duplications of freight, are concerned, these, when freight has already been insured, form no part of a contract of indemnity, but the insurance upon them is merely a gamble discountenanced by sound principle and not enforceable by law. It forms a distinct temptation of self-interest to business and to conduct which are nefarious. In point of fact, however, these illegitimate dangerous and unenforceable policies are entered upon because of the knowledge that in the majority of cases if the hazard placed against the life of the vessel be won, the stake will be paid. The competition in the underwriting world seems to be such that, with premiums paid down, no questions will be asked, and nothing will be said should loss ensue. It is this which, in fact, constitutes the peril to property and life, and I am not surprised that in this case witnesses like Mr Douglas, speaking apparently with the authority of large associations of underwriters, condemned the practice. "If I had known", says Mr Douglas, "that so much was on the vessel, I would not have touched her with a 6 ft. pole, because I consider that such insurances are a direct incentive to loss". In another passage Mr Douglas remarks with force, "She is insured for loss and not against loss". As I have observed, the practice is continued because underwriters pay upon such policies. They go by the much-abused name of "honour"; and the illegitimate "honour" policies constitute that incentive of self-interest towards the destruction of the vessel which the law holds, quite apart from proof of fraud in the specific transaction, to be enough to make the policy void. It appears to me—differing in this by a very wide diameter from the judgment of the Court below—that when insurances of that illegitimate character are also effected by the owner and insurer of the hull, the duty of disclosure of that material fact is plain. Their non-disclosure can, in my humble judgment, be pleaded as an answer to liability upon any policy effected over the hull.

George Cohen, Sons & Co. *v.* Standard Marine Insurance Co. Ltd.[3]

(1925) 21 Ll.L.Rep. 30

By s. 18(3)(b) of the Marine Insurance Act 1906 "the insurer is presumed to know matters of common notoriety or knowledge, and matters which an insurer in the ordinary course of his business, as such, ought to know", and such matters need not be disclosed by the assured.

An obsolete battleship was insured while being towed from Chatham to Brake (in Germany) where she was to be broken up. She went ashore off the Dutch coast. The insurers sought to avoid liability on the ground that the assured had failed to disclose a material fact, i.e., that the vessel would have no steam power with which to assist her steering gear.

Held, by the King's Bench Division, that there was no need for the assured to

[3] Another aspect of this case, viz., whether she was an actual total loss, is considered at p. 163, *post*.

disclose the fact, for it was a matter of common notoriety that vessels of this type were sent to sea in this condition.

ROCHE, J. (at page 38)

Under the very provisions of sub-s. (3)(*b*) and (*c*), matters have not to be disclosed which are known, or presumed to be known, to the insurer, or circumstances as to which information is waived. Here, having regard to the evidence as to the frequency with which vessels of this character, dismantled warships, are sent to sea without any steam at all, and having regard to the knowledge that the underwriters certainly had that the vessel was not going to have steam for the main purposes of the voyage and for propulsion, I think it was a matter which they must have known, or must be presumed to have known. Whenever one of these vessels goes to sea, and apparently their number has been considerable, casualties have been not unknown, and, apparently also from the evidence before me, underwriters have interested themselves in these matters. I think they must be presumed or taken to have known that a vessel such as this, at any rate, might be going to sea in the condition in which the *Prince George* went to sea. In those circumstances the inference that I draw is that they waived—they asked about a good many of the things—disclosure of any further facts as to what was proposed to be done with regard to the *Prince George* before she went to sea.

St. Margaret's Trust Ltd. *v.* Navigators and General Marine Insurance Co. Ltd.

(1949) 82 Ll.L.Rep. 752

By s. 18(3) of the Marine Insurance Act 1906 "in the absence of inquiry the following circumstances need not be disclosed, namely: . . . (b) any circumstance which is known to the insurer . . .".

The insurance company knew of the age, type, condition and agreed value of a ketch, and the intended manner in which she was going to be laid up.

Held, by the King's Bench Division, that it was unnecessary for the assured to describe the neglected state of her topsides caulking.

MORRIS, J. (at page 762)

In the present case, the defendant company had insured this craft when she was owned by the Hardway Company. They had insured her without survey when she was in a mud berth at Fareham Creek, and they had insured her without survey after she was moved to deep water moorings at Gosport. When asked for a quotation assuming that the craft was to be used as a houseboat, they said: "Our quotation then is 2 per cent., provided that there is a satisfactory survey on the under water part of the hull and the moorings". Afterwards the defendants were told that the quotation was not sought for the craft to be used as a houseboat, but it was sought for her when in mud berth and for a time when she would be out of commission, during which time she would be worked on by Mr Griffin, who was an experienced man in connection with yachts. The defendants knew that the *Vishela* was an old craft: that she was 43 years old.

In all those circumstances, in my judgment, it was not material for Mr Griffin to go into a description of the craft, or in particular to make reference to the state of the caulking of her topsides.

Mann, McNeal and Steeves Ltd. *v.* General Marine Underwriters Ltd.

(1920) 124 L.T. 778

By s. 18(3) of the Marine Insurance Act 1906 "in the absence of inquiry the following circumstances need not be disclosed, namely . . . (c) any circumstance as to which information is waived by the insurer . . .".

A wooden ship was insured for a voyage from America to France and back again. Part of the cargo which she had contracted to carry from America consisted of petrol, but the assured did not disclose this fact.

Held, by the Court of Appeal, that in the circumstances of the case, the insurers had waived disclosure of the contract to carry the petrol by not making inquiry.

BANKES, L.J. (at page 780)

In the first place, I think that the evidence as to the practice in relation to the non-disclosure of the character of cargo when effecting a policy on hull does not only justify, but requires, the Court to hold that an underwriter waives any information in relation to what may be fairly described as a parcel of ordinary cargo of lawful merchandise, which this parcel was. In the second place, I think that the plea of waiver can be supported on the ground indicated by LORD ESHER, M.R. in *Asfar & Co.* v. *Blundell*,[4] where in dealing with the question of concealment he says: "But it is not necessary to disclose minutely every material fact; assuming that there is a material fact which he"—the assured—"is bound to disclose, the rule is satisfied if he discloses sufficient to call the attention of the underwriters in such a manner that they can see that if they require further information they ought to ask for it". In my opinion, the disclosure in the present case that this vessel was a wooden vessel with auxiliary motor engines was a disclosure of the fact that it was proposed to carry cargo from the United States to France in a vessel specially and dangerously liable to fire damage, and that such a disclosure was, within LORD

[4] [1896] 1 Q.B. 123.

ESHER's language, a sufficient disclosure to put the underwriter on inquiry. Having regard to the language of the material section of the Marine Insurance Act 1906, in which the law relating to concealment is now contained, the conclusion is rather that disclosure had been waived than that it had not been made.

(3) MISREPRESENTATION

Demetriades & Co. *v*. Northern Assurance Co.: The "Spathari"

(1925) 21 Ll.L.Rep. 265

By s. 20(1) of the Marine Insurance Act 1906: "Every material representation made by the assured or his agent during the negotiations for the contract, and before the contract is concluded, must be true. If it be untrue, the insurer may avoid the contract".

The assured stated that the insured vessel was owned by a British subject, but, in fact, she was owned by a Greek. She was registered as British and flew the British flag contrary to the Merchant Shipping Act 1894. A loss occurred. The insurance company repudiated liability on the ground that there had been a misrepresentation of a material fact, viz., the true ownership of the vessel.

Held, by the House of Lords, that the company was entitled to do so.

LORD SHAW OF DUNFERMLINE (at page 169)

A material representation which should have been made, and was not made but was concealed, was that this was a Greek ship. In my opinion, as I have said, it was material enough to avoid the contract if the falsehood in regard to that matter was upon the register. But when we come to the actual fact of the nationality of the vessel, how material it is appears from the evidence of Mr. Harper, the shipping editor of "Lloyd's List and Shipping Gazette", who gives the official statistics with regard to a long period of time, namely the period from Sept. 1, 1920, to Nov. 30, 1921. During that period, 14 British vessels of over 500 tons were lost, and during the same period 27 Greek vessels were lost, that is to say, nearly double the number of Greek vessels to British. But, my Lords, that is not really the substantial comparison. The substantial comparison is the relation of Greek losses to Greek tonnage afloat as compared with British losses compared with British tonnage afloat, and the startling fact is that for every 22,000 Greek tons afloat one vessel was lost, whereas in the case of British registered ships one loss only occurred in the case of 1,570,000 tons afloat, a contrast so startling that it requires very little evidence in a law court to convince me that in the insurance and shipping world any representation which would conceal the Greek nationality of the vessel was a material matter for the contracting parties. That misrepresentation or concealment on that subject having occurred, the defence is completely justified.

(4) PERILS INSURED AGAINST

E.D. Sassoon & Co. *v.* Western Assurance Co.

[1911–13] All E.R. Rep. 438

The term "perils of the sea" does not cover damage by sea water entering a vessel through holes in her caused by natural decay.

Opium was stored in a wooden hulk moored in the river Huant-Pu at Shanghai, and was insured against "perils of the sea". The hulk became leaky due to the natural decay of her hull. Water from the river found its way into her and damaged the opium. The assured claimed that the damage was caused by a "peril of the sea".

Held, by the Judicial Committee of the Privy Council, that the loss was not caused by a "peril of the sea", and that the action failed.

LORD MERSEY (at page 439)

There was no weather, nor any other fortuitous circumstance, contributing to the incursion of the water; the water merely gravitated by its own weight through the opening in the decayed wood and so damaged the opium. It would be an abuse of language to describe this as a loss due to perils of the sea. Although sea water damaged the goods, no peril of the sea contributed either proximately or remotely to the loss. There is ample authority for so holding, but it is sufficient to cite the judgment of LORD HERSCHELL in *Wilson, Sons & Co.* v. *"Xantho" (Cargo Owners)*,[5] where he says[6]:

> I think it clear that the term "perils of the sea" does not cover every accident or casualty which may happen to the subject-matter of the insurance on the sea. It must be a peril "of" the sea. Again it is well settled that it is not every loss or damage of which the sea is the immediate cause that is covered by these words. They do not protect, for example, against that natural and inevitable action of the winds and waves which results in what may be described as wear and tear.

In this case the damage, though doubtless proximately due to sea water, was not in any sense due to sea peril. It does not therefore fall within the policy.

Mentz, Decker & Co. *v.* Maritime Insurance Co. Ltd.

(1909) 101 L.T. 808

By Rule 11 of the Rules for Construction of Policy[7] *"the term 'barratry' includes every wrongful act wilfully committed by the master or crew to the prejudice of the owner, or as the case may be, the charterer". The master is*

---

[5] (1887) 12 App. Cas. 503, H.L.
[6] *Ibid.*, at p. 509.
[7] Set out in Schedule 1 to the Marine Insurance Act 1906.

guilty of barratry if he makes a fraudulent deviation for his own purposes, and the insurer will be liable accordingly.

A vessel was insured while at San Juan del Sur and thence to a port in Costa Rica for loading, and thence to a port of discharge in Europe. She sailed for Punta Arenas, and there received orders to load a cargo at Cocos Island at the instance of the concessionaire of certain rights in respect of which he received payment. On the second voyage the vessel became a total loss.

Held, by the King's Bench Division, that the conduct of the master was barratrous, and the insurer was liable on the policy since loss by barratry was one of the perils insured against.

HAMILTON, J. (at page 810)

The question, therefore, which arises first of all is: In deviating did the captain commit a barratrous act? The Marine Insurance Act in the schedule in para. 11 states that, "The term 'barratry' includes every wrongful act wilfully committed by the master or crew to the prejudice of the owner, or, as the case may be, the charterer". The authorities prior to the Act show that where a captain is engaged in doing that which he must, as an ordinary man of common sense, know to be a serious breach of his duty to his owners, and is engaged in doing it for his own benefit, then he is acting barratrously. He may act quite barratrously in many other ways, but I think it is quite clear that if he is disregarding his duty to his owners and breaking his duty to them for the sake of private purposes and ends, his conduct is barratrous.

Having come to the conclusion that both these adventures were barratrous, it follows that although they were deviations, they did not either of them put an end to the policies. The policies are on foot, and the deviations do not afford any answer at all.

Athens Maritime Enterprises Corpn. *v.* Hellenic Mutual War Risks Association (Bermuda) Ltd.: The "Andreas Lemos"

[1983] 1 All E.R. 590

Piracy means theft at sea involving force or threat of force and may be committed inside territorial waters.

A vessel was insured with a mutual insurance association against loss of her equipment as a result of piracy. While she was in the Chittagong Roads inside the territorial waters of Bangladesh, thieves armed with knives began stealing part of her equipment. The theft was discovered by the crew and the thieves fled. The owners of the vessel claimed an indemnity from the association in respect of the loss of the equipment on the ground that it was lost through "piracy".

Held, by the Queen's Bench Division (Commercial Court), that the claim failed. "Piracy" could be committed inside territorial waters and meant theft at sea involving force or threat of force, and, on the evidence, the theft was a clandestine one and the thieves had used force or the threat of force only to make good their escape after the theft had been discovered.

STAUGHTON, J. (at page 598)

In the face of that authority[8] I cannot accept Counsel for the owners' submission that piracy may be committed anywhere within the Common Law jurisdiction of the Court of Admiralty "in places where great ships go", or "at a place where the tide flows and below all bridges". But I see no reason to limit piracy to acts outside territorial waters. In the context of an insurance policy, if a ship is, in the ordinary meaning of the phrase, "at sea" (*per* KENNEDY, L.J.)[9] or if the attack on her can be described as "a maritime offence" (*per* VAUGHAN WILLIAMS, L.J.)[10] then for the business purposes of a policy of insurance she is, in my judgment, in a place where piracy can be committed.

That view is supported to some extent by the Marine Insurance Act 1906, Sch. 1, r. 8: "The term 'pirates' includes passengers who mutiny and rioters who attack the ship from the shore." It is not easy to envisage a ship being attacked by rioters from the shore when she is outside territorial waters, but it could happen, I suppose, when she is "at sea".

The only case to which I was referred that bears directly on the point was *Re Piracy Jure Gentium*[11] and that went no further than holding that an attempt at robbery would amount to piracy, even if the substantive offence were not achieved. But the general tenor of the authorities supports the conclusion that theft without force or a threat of force cannot be piracy. Thus Carver's *Carriage by Sea*[12] has the definition: "Piracy is forcible robbery at sea, whether committed by marauders from outside the ship, or by mariners or passengers within it." The same statement in the fourth edition of *Carver*, was generally approved by KENNEDY, L.J. in *Bolivia Republic* v. *Indemnity Mutual Marine Assurance Co. Ltd.*[13] (Others, including Dr Lushington, would include murder; but that is immaterial for present purposes.) LORD DENNING, M.R. in *Shell International Petroleum Co. Ltd.* v. *Gibbs*[14] said:

> *Pirates and Thieves.* These perils have been very narrowly construed. There were no "pirates" here because there was no forcible robbery. There were no "thieves" here because there were no violent means. This was accepted by Shell and no claim was made in this regard before the judge.

I hold that theft without force or a threat of force is not piracy under a policy of marine insurance.

---

[8] I.e. *Bolivia Republic* v. *Indemnity Mutual Marine Assurance Co. Ltd.* [1909] 1 K.B. 785, C.A.
[9] *Ibid.*, at p. 802.
[10] *Ibid.*, at p. 798.
[11] [1934] A.C. 586, P.C.
[12] 13th Edn. 1982, para. 183.
[13] [1909] 1 K.B. 785, C.A.
[14] [1982] 1 All E.R. 1057 at p. 1062, C.A.

How then stands a case of piracy on the facts? I draw the inference that the armed men who came on board the *Andreas Lemos* intended, and expected, to steal without violence. However, I infer also that they anticipated the possibility of some resistance or interference by a night watchman, and intended to use force or a threat of force if that possibility materialised. I doubt that they expected to be able to defeat the master and crew if it came to a pitched battle.

So much for their intentions. What, in fact, happened was that the theft was complete before they were discovered, or at any rate before any force or threat of force occurred. The contrary is not established by the agreed statement of facts. Counsel for the owners invites me to infer that the fifth mooring line, which was "cut by knife as thieves had not time to pull it out from the forecastle", must have been stolen during or after the first use of force or threat of force. This argument itself has some force, but I do not feel able to draw that inference. The case is, in my judgment, one of clandestine theft which was discovered; force or a threat of force was used by the men to make good their escape.

Section 8(1) of the Theft Act 1968 provides:

> A person is guilty of robbery, if he steals, and immediately before or at the time of doing so, and in order to do so, he uses force on any person or puts or seeks to put any person in fear of being then and there subjected to force.

Archbold's Criminal Pleading, Evidence and Practice states[15]: "Force used only to get away after committing a theft does not seem naturally to be regarded as robbery." This is followed by a discussion as to when theft is first complete, by appropriation. I would, with respect, deprecate any over-elaborate analysis of the sequence of events, either for the purpose of the criminal law or in the context of the present case. That view may perhaps have the support of the Court of Appeal, for Counsel for the owners found in the Supplement to *Archbold* the case of *R.* v. *Hale.*[16] There the Court said[17]: ". . . the act of appropriation does not suddenly cease. It is a continuous act and it is a matter for the jury to decide whether or not the act of appropriation has finished." I gladly follow that test. But I conclude that the act of appropriation had finished in this case when the force or a threat of force was first used, or at any rate the contrary is not proved. The act of appropriation finished when the goods were thrown into the sea, presumably into or near a boat or boats which had brought the armed men. There was no loss by piracy.

That conclusion seems to me to accord with the commercial sense of the matter. The Association, by the word piracy, insures the loss caused to shipowners because their employees are overpowered by force, or terrified into submission. It does not insure the loss caused to shipowners when their night watchman is asleep (as might occur, although it did not in this case) and

---

[15] 40th Edn. 1979, para. 1482.
[16] (1978) 68 Cr.App.Rep. 415.
[17] *Ibid.*, at 418.

thieves steal clandestinely. The very notion of piracy is inconsistent with clandestine theft. Counsel for the owners described this as a prosaic form of piracy: a recent Judge might have preferred the word "anaemic". It is not necessary that the thieves must raise the pirate flag and fire a shot across the victim's bows before they can be called pirates. But piracy is not committed by stealth. This case is very near to the borderline, but it must not on that account be allowed to make bad law.

British and Foreign Marine Insurance Co. *v.* Gaunt[18]

[1921] All E.R. Rep. 447

There are limits to the expression "all risks".

LORD SUMNER (at page 455)

There are, of course, limits to "all risks". They are risks and risks insured against. Accordingly, the expression does not cover inherent vice or mere wear and tear or British capture. It covers a risk, not a certainty; it is something which happens to the subject-matter from without, not the natural behaviour of that subject-matter, being what it is, in the circumstances in which it is carried. Nor is it a loss which the assured brings about by his own act, for then he has not merely exposed the goods to the chance of injury, he has injured them himself.

Compania Naviera Santi S.A. *v.* Indemnity Marine Assurance Co. Ltd.: The "Tropaioforos"

[1960] 2 Lloyd's Rep. 469

The burden of proving a loss by perils of the sea lies on the assured.

A vessel sank in a calm sea. The shipowners alleged that she had struck a submerged object, but the insurers contended that the loss was not due to perils of the sea, and that she had been intentionally cast away. On the question of the burden of proof—

Held, by the Queen's Bench Division (Commercial Court), that the burden of proving a loss by perils of the sea lay on the assured.

PEARSON, J. (at page 473)

As to the burden of proof, the whole question has been reserved in the House of Lords; but, subject to that reservation, it has been established by decisions

---

[18] This case also concerned the extent of the "sue and labour" clause. As to this point, see p. 173, *post*.

of Courts of first instance and the Court of Appeal (with some support from *dicta* in the House of Lords) that the plaintiffs have the burden of proving, in a case such as this, that there was an accidental loss by perils of the seas, although the degree of proof required is only to show a balance of probabilities in favour of an accidental loss by perils of the seas[19] . . .

In assessing the balance of probabilities, due weight must be given to the consideration that scuttling a ship would be fraudulent and criminal behaviour. No doubt one reason for placing the burden of proof on the shipowners in such a case as this is that they are likely to have all, or almost all, the relevant information, and the insurers are likely to have virtually no information initially. The insurers, for their proof of scuttling, or their suggestion that there is strong ground for thinking that there may have been scuttling, have to rely on such information as they can obtain from discovery of documents and from cross-examination of ship's witnesses called by the plaintiffs. That consideration has especial weight in the present case, because the ship's officers failed to preserve any of the log-books, charts, records of soundings, or other ship's papers which might have had evidential value. There was no full report on the casualty by the master. There was not even any complete set of ship's plans, though I accept the expert evidence that it is not unusual, in the case of an old ship, for plans to be missing.

Rhesa Shipping Co. S.A. *v.* Edmunds: The "Popi M"

[1985] 2 Lloyd's Rep. 1

The burden of proving a loss by a peril of the sea lies on the assured.

The vessel *Popi M* was insured under a policy against a loss by a peril of the sea. She sank in a calm sea and fair weather. When the assured claimed under the policy, the insurers repudiated liability on the ground that the loss was due to wear and tear. The assured contended that she had collided with a submarine. The trial Judge considered that the assured's theory was extremely improbable and that that of the insurers was impossible. He then gave judgment for the assured. The insurers appealed.

Held, by the House of Lords, that the appeal would be allowed because the burden of proving a loss by a peril insured against lay on the assured, and that burden had not been discharged.

---

[19] *La Compania Martiartu* v. *Corporation of the Royal Exchange Assurance (The Armus)* [1923] 1 K.B. 650, C.A.; on appeal, [1924] A.C. 850, H.L.; *Anghelatos* v. *Northern Assurance Co. (The Olympia)* (1923) 16 Ll.L.Rep. 252, C.A.; on appeal, (1924) 19 Ll.L.Rep. 255, H.L.; *Banco de Barcelona* v. *Union Marine Insurance Co. (The Cruz)* (1925) 22 Ll.L.Rep. 317 (Greer, J.); *Compania Naviera Vascongada* v. *British and Foreign Marine Insurance Co. Ltd. (The Gloria)* (1936) 54 Ll.L.Rep. 35 (Brandon, J.); *Bank of Athens* v. *Royal Exchange Assurance (The Eftychia)* (1937) 57 Ll.L.Rep. 37; on appeal (1937) 59 Ll.L.Rep. 67, C.A.; *Hornal* v. *Neuberger Products Ltd.* [1957] 1 Q.B. 247, C.A.

LORD BRANDON OF OAKBROOK (at page 5)

The passages which I have quoted from BINGHAM, J.'s judgment amply support the observations about his approach to the case which I made earlier. These observations were to the effect that he regarded himself as compelled to make a choice between the shipowners' submarine theory on the one hand and underwriters' wear and tear theory on the other, and he failed to keep in mind that a third alternative, that the shipowners had failed to discharge the burden of proof which lay on them, was open to him.

As regards the shipowners' submarine theory, BINGHAM, J. stated in terms that he regarded it as extremely improbable, a view with which I think it unlikely that any of your Lordships will quarrel. As regards underwriters' wear and tear theory, it was contended by Counsel for the shipowners that BINGHAM, J. had ruled it out as impossible. The language used by him in different places is, however, ambivalent, and I think that it would be more accurate to say that he regarded the wear and tear theory not as impossible, but as one in respect of which any mechanism by which it could have operated was in doubt.

My Lords, the late Sir Arthur Conan Doyle in his book *The Sign of Four*, describes his hero, Mr Sherlock Holmes, as saying to the latter's friend, Dr Watson: "how often have I said to you that, when you have eliminated the impossible, whatever remains, however improbable, must be the truth?" It is, no doubt, on the basis of this well-known but unjudicial dictum that BINGHAM, J. decided to accept the shipowners' submarine theory, even though he regarded it, for seven cogent reasons, as extremely improbable.

In my view there are three reasons why it is inappropriate to apply the dictum of Mr Sherlock Holmes, to which I have just referred, to the process of fact-finding which a Judge of first instance has to perform at the conclusion of a case of the kind here concerned.

The first reason is one which I have already sought to emphasize as being of great importance, namely, that the Judge is not bound always to make a finding one way or the other with regard to the facts averred by the parties. He has open to him the third alternative of saying that the party on whom the burden of proof lies in relation to any averment made by him has failed to discharge that burden. No Judge likes to decide cases on burden of proof if he can legitimately avoid having to do so. There are cases, however, in which, owing to the unsatisfactory state of the evidence or otherwise, deciding on the burden of proof is the only just course for him to take.

The second reason is that the dictum can only apply when all relevant facts are known, so that all possible explanations, except a single extremely improbable one, can properly be eliminated. That state of affairs does not exist in the present case: to take but one example, the ship sank in such deep water that a diver's examination of the nature of the aperture, which might well have thrown light on its cause, could not be carried out.

The third reason is that the legal concept of proof of a case on a balance of probabilities must be applied with common sense. It requires a Judge of first instance, before he finds that a particular event occurred, to be satisfied on the evidence that it is more likely to have occurred than not. If such a Judge concludes, on a whole series of cogent grounds, that the recurrence of an event is extremely improbable, a finding by him that it is nevertheless more likely to have occurred than not, does not accord with common sense. This is especially so when it is open to the Judge to say simply that the evidence leaves him in doubt whether the event occurred or not, and that the party on whom the burden of proving that the event occurred lies has therefore failed to discharge such burden.

In my opinion BINGHAM, J. adopted an erroneous approach to this case by regarding himself as compelled to choose between two theories, both of which he regarded as extremely improbable, or one of which he regarded as extremely improbable and the other of which he regarded as virtually impossible. He should have borne in mind, and considered carefully in his judgment, the third alternative which was open to him, namely, that the evidence left him in doubt as to the cause of the aperture in the ship's hull, and that, in these circumstances, the shipowners had failed to discharge the burden of proof which was on them.

If ever a case asked to be treated as coming within the dictum with regard to burden of proof of SCRUTTON, L.J., in *La Compania Martiartu* v. *The Corporation of the Royal Exchange Assurance (The Armus)*,[20] this was it. The shipowners failed to establish that the ship was seaworthy, and they only put forward an extremely improbable cause of her loss. In these circumstances the Judge should have found that the true cause of the loss was in doubt, and that the shipowers had failed to discharge the burden of proof which was on them.

British and Foreign Marine Insurance Co. *v.* Gaunt

[1921] All E.R. Rep. 447

Where goods are insured against "all risks" and are damaged, it is sufficient for the assured to show that the loss was caused by a casualty or something accidental. He does not have to prove the exact nature of the casualty or accident.

A cargo of wool was insured from Patagonia to England under an "all risks" policy. On delivery it was found to have been damaged by wet. The buyers of the wool, to whom the policy had been assigned, claimed an indemnity from the insurers. The buyers proved that the wool was sometimes stored in the open, that it was frequently carried on deck on the local steamers to the port of shipment where it was loaded on to ocean steamers, and that the local steamers had experienced bad weather while the

[20] [1923] 1 K.B. 650, C.A., at p. 657.

wool was in transit. The damage sustained was exceptional. The insurers contended that the buyers had failed to establish affirmatively a loss by a peril insured against.

Held, by the House of Lords, that the action succeeded. Since the policy was against "all risks", it was sufficient for the buyers to show that the loss was caused by a casualty or something accidental without proving the exact nature of the casualty or accident which caused the loss. There was evidence in the present case of an abnormal incident.

LORD BIRKENHEAD, L.C. (at page 450)

We are, of course, to give effect to the rule that the plaintiff must establish his case, that he must show that the loss comes within the terms of his policies; but where all risks are covered by the policy and not merely risks of a specified class or classes, the plaintiff discharges his special onus when he has proved that the loss was caused by some event covered by the general expression, and he is not bound to go further and prove the exact nature of the accident or casualty which, in fact, occasioned his loss.

LORD SUMNER (at page 455)

Finally, the description "all risks" does not alter the general law; only risks are covered which it is lawful to cover, and the onus of proof remains where it would have been on a policy against ordinary sea perils. I think, however, that the quasi-universality of the description does affect the onus of proof in one way. The claimant insured against and averring a loss by fire must prove loss by fire, which involves proving that it is not by something else. When he avers loss by some risk coming within "all risks", as used in this policy, he need only give evidence reasonably showing that the loss was due to a casualty, not to a certainty or to inherent vice or to wear and tear. That is easily done. I do not think he has to go further and pick out one of the multitude of risks covered, so as to show exactly how his loss was caused. If he did so, he would not bring it any the more within the policy. These considerations answer the appellants' complaint that the plaintiffs were meagre with their proof. So they were, but it was enough for them to prove some casualty insured against.

(5) EXCEPTED PERILS

Canada Rice Mills Ltd. *v*. Union Marine and General Insurance Co. Ltd.

[1940] 4 All E.R. 169

By s. 55(1) of the Marine Insurance Act 1906: "Subject to the provisions of this Act, and unless the policy otherwise provides, the insurer is liable for any loss proximately caused by a peril insured against . . .".

A cargo of rice was insured for a voyage from Rangoon to the Fraser River, and was stowed in the holds of a vessel ventilated partly by cowl ventilators and hatches. Owing to rough weather the ventilators and hatches had to be closed, and the rice became overheated. The assured claimed for a loss under the policy, which covered perils of the sea, on the ground that action taken to prevent the perils of the sea affecting the goods was itself a loss due to perils of the sea.

Held, by the Judicial Committee of the Privy Council, that the claim succeeded, for the loss had been proximately caused by a peril insured against.

LORD WRIGHT (at page 177)

There remains the second question—namely, whether the damage which was caused, not by the incursion of seawater, but by action taken to prevent the incursion, is recoverable as a loss by perils of the seas. It is curious that, so far as their Lordships know, there is no express decision on this point under a policy of marine insurance, but, in their Lordships' judgment, the question should be answered in the affirmative as they think the jury did. The answer may be based on the view that where the weather conditions so require, the closing of the ventilators is to be regarded, not as a separate or independent cause, interposed between the peril of the sea and the damage, but as being such a mere matter of routine seamanship necessitated by the peril that the damage can be regarded as the direct cause of the peril. In *The Thrunscoe*,[21] where a cargo of oats and maize had been damaged by the closing of the ventilators owing to heavy weather, it was held that the damage was caused by perils of the seas. The severity of the weather (there referred to as exceptional, though the adjective is immaterial) was described by SIR FRANCIS JEUNE, P., as the proximate cause of the damage, because the closing of the ventilators was due to that cause, and GORELL BARNES, J., described it as the direct cause. It is true that the case dealt with the exceptions in the bill of lading, to which the doctrine of *causa proxima* does not apply in the same way as in insurance law, but it is now established by such authorities as *Leyland Shipping Co.* v. *Norwich Union Fire Insurance Society*[22] and many others that *causa proxima* in insurance law does not necessarily mean the cause last in time, but what is "in substance" the cause[23] or the cause "to be determined by commonsense principles"[24] The same rule has been reiterated by the House of Lords several times since then, most strikingly, perhaps, in *P. Samuel & Co.* v. *Dumas*,[25] where it was held by a majority of the Lords that, where a ship insured by the mortgagee was lost by being scuttled by the deliberate act or procurement of the mortgagor, it was not in insurance law to be deemed a loss by perils of the seas. The proximate cause was the intentional and fraudulent act which let in the seawater and sank the vessel. In cases of fire insurance, it has been said that loss caused from an apparently necessary and *bona fide* attempt to put out

---

[21] [1897] P. 301.
[22] [1918] A.C. 350, H.L.
[23] *Ibid.*, at p. 355.
[24] *Ibid.*, at p. 362.
[25] [1924] All E.R. Rep. 66, H.L.

a fire by spoiling goods by water, and in other ways, is within the policy: *per* KELLY, C.B., in *Stanley* v. *Western Insurance Co.*[26] Their Lordships agree with this expression of opinion, and accordingly are prepared to hold that the damage to the rice, which the jury have found to be due to action necessarily and reasonably taken to prevent the peril of the sea affecting the goods, is a loss due to a peril of the sea, and is recoverable as such.

Pateras *v.* Royal Exchange Assurance

(1934) 49 Ll.L.Rep. 400

By s. 55(2)(a) of the Marine Insurance Act 1906: "The insurer is not liable for any loss attributable to the wilful misconduct of the assured".

A vessel was stranded on a rock near the Burling Light off the Portuguese coast. The assured claimed under the policy, but the insurers repudiated liability on the ground that she had been wilfully cast away with the assured's connivance. She was being employed very unprofitably round about the time of the loss. The chief officer, who had been her master, had been succeeded for the voyage, on which she was engaged, by the owner's son.

Held, by the King's Bench Division, that the claim failed because the loss had been caused by the wilful act of the assured.

ROCHE, J. (at page 409)

The interests of the owners point to the desirability of such an end to the ship, and that includes, if it were done that it was not done otherwise than with their consent. The fact was that the vessel was over-insured; she was worth about £5,000 and she was insured against total loss, ship and freight, for about £15,000. That is a matter of which the owners were themselves fully cognisant, but it is not a matter which influences me at all in arriving at my conclusion that the ship was cast away. But when the fact co-exists with a conclusion that the ship was cast away by her navigators, and when it is also clear that the ship was, as most were, navigated very unprofitably about this period, and when I think it is also plain that by an arrangement to which the late Mr Pateras was a party, this master, his son, whom I have found guilty of the conduct which I have described, and who became master for this voyage and arranged, rather unusually, the particular employment which she should go upon, I think the conclusion is inevitable that the late Mr Pateras was a party to what was done.

---

[26] (1868), L.R. 3 Exch. 71, at p. 74.

Wadsworth Lighterage and Coaling Co. Ltd. *v.* Sea Insurance Co. Ltd.

(1929) 34 Ll.L.Rep. 285

By s. 55(2)(c) of the Marine Insurance Act 1906: "Unless the policy otherwise provides, the insurer is not liable for ordinary wear and tear . . .".

A steam barge over 50 years old was insured under a time policy which stated: "This insurance is against the risk of total and/or constructive loss . . . including damage to such vessel . . . by fire, lightning, stranding or sinking". One night the vessel sank in the Coburg Dock, Liverpool. No one was on board at the time. There was no evidence of any accident which caused her to sink. The assured claimed for a total loss.

Held, by the Court of Appeal, that the claim failed since the loss was due to ordinary wear and tear.

SCRUTTON, L.J. (at page 289)

The Act says: "Unless the policy otherwise provides, the insurer is not liable for ordinary wear and tear"; and giving the best consideration I can to the matter, the policy does not seem to provide otherwise; it does not seem to me to provide that the insurer is liable for ordinary wear and tear. It would be very unusual that he should be, and I can find no words which do make him liable for ordinary wear and tear. The result will be, of course, that if the assured on this policy says: "I claim for total loss", the answer is that in the first part of the clause the total loss is only a total loss caused by the perils in the policy, which do not include wear and tear. If, as [Counsel] concluded in his argument, he says: "Very well, if I cannot get total loss, then I want the loss as partial under the latter part of the clause, by sinking", the answer seems to me again to be the same, that it is only sinking by perils insured against, and ordinary wear and tear is not one of the perils insured against in the body of the policy.

F. W. Berk & Co. Ltd. *v.* Style

[1955] 2 Lloyd's Rep. 382

By s. 55(2)(c) of the Marine Insurance Act 1906: "Unless the policy otherwise provides, the insurer is not liable for . . . inherent vice or nature of the subject-matter insured".

A cargo of kieselguhr packed in paper bags was insured for a voyage from Mostaganem, North Africa, to London against all risks of loss and/or damage from whatsoever cause arising. The bags burst while being transferred from the ship's hold to a lighter. The assured claimed to recover from the underwriters the expenses of re-bagging and landing the cargo. The insurers denied liability on the ground that the cargo was packed in defective bags, and that this constituted inherent vice for which they were not liable.

Held, by the Queen's Bench Division, that the insurers were not liable.

SELLERS, J. (at page 387)

I find that the plaintiffs' consignment of kieselguhr was packed in faulty and inadequate bags which leaked because they were insufficient to endure the ordinary contemplated handling and carriage. The faults in the manufacture of the bags could be accounted for by a failure in the machine or in the processes or by the inexperience or negligence of an operative or operatives concerned with making them; but whatever the cause, I find that the evidence establishes that the bags must have been inadequate from the outset.

(6) WARRANTIES

Overseas Commodities Ltd. *v.* Style

[1958] 1 Lloyd's Rep. 546

Under the Marine Insurance Act 1906, s. 33(3): "A warranty[27] *. . . is a condition which must be exactly complied with, whether it is material to the risk or not. If it be not so complied with . . . the insurer is discharged from liability . . .".*

The assured had effected an "all risks" policy in respect of some canned pork. The policy contained a warranty that all the tins were marked by the manufacturers with a code for the verification of the date of manufacture. Many of the tins were not marked in the stipulated manner. The assured discovered that some of the tins were blown, and claimed under the policy.

Held, by the Queen's Bench Division (Commercial Court), that the action failed. The breach of warranty excused the insurers.

MCNAIR, J. (at page 558)

It has long been well-established law that an express warranty requires a strict and literal performance: see now the Marine Insurance Act 1906, s. 33(3). As stated in *Arnould on Marine Insurance*, 14th Edn., s. 632: "Every policy, in fact, in which an express warranty is inserted is a conditional contract, to be binding if the warranty be literally complied with, but not otherwise".

In the language of LORD MANSFIELD in *Hibbert* v. *Pigou* (1783), as reported in *A Treatise on the Law of Insurance*, by Samuel Marshall (1823), Vol. 1, p. 375; and *A Treatise of the Law of Marine Insurance, Bottomry, and*

---

[27] For the purpose of this section a warranty means "a promissory warranty, that is to say, a warranty by which the assured undertakes that some particular thing shall or shall not be done, or that some condition shall be fulfilled, or whereby he affirms or negatives the existence of a particular state of facts": Marine Insurance Act 1906, s. 33(1).

Respondentia (1861), also by Samuel Marshall, p. 280: "... the contract depends on an event taking place. There is no latitude, no equity; the only question is, has that event happened?"

Being satisfied that, as regards both policies, a substantial number of the tins—well exceeding any tolerance that could be disregarded under the *de minimis* rule—were not marked with a code which enabled the true and correct date of manufacture to be established, I have no option but to hold that the breach of the express warranty affords the underwriters a complete defence in this action.

P. Samuel & Co. Ltd. *v.* Dumas

[1924] All E.R. Rep. 66

By s. 34(3) of the Marine Insurance Act 1906: "A breach of warranty may be waived by the insurer."

A vessel was insured under a time policy which contained a warranty that the assured was entitled to insure freight for six months for £13,750. In fact, he insured freight for six months for £27,500. The vessel was lost, and when a claim was made under the policy, the insurers repudiated liability on the ground that there had been a breach of warranty.

Held, by the House of Lords,[28] that there had been a breach of warranty, but that the breach had been waived by the insurers, so they could not rely on it.[29]

VISCOUNT CAVE (at page 74)

But, while I am satisfied that there was a breach of the warranty, I think that the respondent Dumas is prevented from taking advantage of it by the circumstances that he was himself a party to the excessive insurance on freight which constituted the breach. Section 34(3) of the Marine Insurance Act 1906, provides: "A breach of warranty may be waived by the insurer." Now a right may be waived either by express words or by conduct inconsistent with the continuance of the right; and even where there is no actual waiver, the person having the right may so conduct himself that it becomes inequitable for him to enforce it. Here the respondent, who must be assumed to have been aware that the assured was prevented by the terms of the policy of insurance on the vessel from taking out honour policies on the freight for six months for any sum in excess of £13,750, joined in the issue of such policies for double that amount and took his share of the premiums on those policies, and I can conceive no conduct more inconsistent with an intention on his part to enforce

[28] VISCOUNT CAVE and LORD PARMOOR; VISCOUNT FINLAY and LORD SUMNER dissenting. VISCOUNT HALDANE, L.C., expressed no opinion on the matter.

[29] Their Lordships, however, held that the action failed because the vessel had been scuttled, and this was a loss not covered by the policy.

the restriction. It is argued that at the moment when the representative of the respondent initialled the war risk slip, the amount underwritten if apportioned between the ship, freight, and disbursements was not in excess of the amount allowed, but the answer is that the slip then already contained the words: "Hull and machinery, £110,000; freight, f.i.a., £27,500; disbursements, f.i.a., £10,500", and specified the period as six months, so that it was obvious on the face of the document that the underwriters were taking a share in an insurance of that character and amount and expected and intended it to be carried through. Further, when the policy was issued in October, it was known that the full amount specified in the slip had been underwritten; and Mr Dumas through his representatives, who must be taken (in the absence of any evidence to the contrary) to have acted with his authority, was a party to the issue of the policy. In my opinion, the respondent and the other underwriters who took that course are prevented by waiver or acquiescence from treating the marine policy on the vessel as void for breach of the warranty.

Hoffman & Co. *v.* British General Insurance Co.

(1922) 10 Ll.L.Rep. 434

By s. 39(1) of the Marine Insurance Act 1906: "In a voyage policy there is an implied warranty that at the commencement of the voyage the ship shall be seaworthy for the purpose of the particular adventure insured".

A wooden schooner was insured from Oulu (Uleaborg, Finland) to Gweek. She met with contrary winds and put into Elsinore. She left there, but was caught in a heavy summer gale and had to return there, floating on the strength of the buoyancy of her cargo of timber. She was built in 1894 and had undergone her last survey in 1911. In 1914 after a voyage in warm weather she arrived at Oulu (Uleaborg), and loaded a cargo of timber there. War broke out and she could not leave. In 1920 certain repairs, including caulking, were carried out. The assured claimed for a constructive total loss, but the insurers denied liability on the ground that she was unseaworthy at the commencement of the voyage.

Held, by the King's Bench Division, that the action failed. There had been a breach of the implied warranty of seaworthiness required by s. 39(1). The vessel's planks were worm-eaten and the caulking had been badly done.

BAILHACHE, J. (at page 437)

I have come to the conclusion that the vessel had been more affected and strained than anybody at Oulu (Uleaborg) thought, or had the opportunity of finding out, by having remained at Oulu (Uleaborg) for these six years, frozen every winter, thawed every summer, with her cargo in her. I have come to the conclusion also that she was badly worm-eaten. Nobody who gave a seaworthy certificate knew that. I do not mean that the worms had eaten through the planks, but that they were so far worm-eaten that they were weakened. I have come to the conclusion that the caulking which was done was inefficiently and badly done through no fault of the surveyors or the master, but owing to the difficulties there were about getting the services of experienced workmen; and I have come to the conclusion that she needed caulking well and efficiently, not only between the light draught line and the loading line, but right down to the keel. I am very much influenced, but I hope not unduly, by the fact that immediately these repairs were done and the vessel had been re-loaded, she made more water—7 in. against 1 in.—in 24 hours. I am also impressed by the fact that, without heavy weather to account for it, when she had been at sea for six or seven days, she made so much more water that it was necessary to pump her every watch instead of only morning and evening; and I have come to the conclusion that she was altogether too weak to encounter the weather that she did encounter, and that the weather she did encounter was not so abnormal on a voyage of this description at this time of the year as she ought not to have been able to withstand with safety.

Thomas *v*. Tyne and Wear Steamship Freight Insurance Association

(1917) 117 L.T. 55

By the Marine Insurance Act 1906, s. 39(5): "In a time policy there is no implied warranty that the ship shall be seaworthy at any stage of the adventure, but where, with the privity of the assured, the ship is sent to sea in an unseaworthy state, the insurer is not liable for any loss attributable to unseaworthiness."

A vessel was insured under a time policy. The assured was privy to her being sent to sea with an insufficient crew, but did not know of a defect in her hull. The ship was lost on account of such defect.

Held, by the King's Bench Division, that the assured could recover on the policy because the loss had not been caused by the particular unseaworthiness to which he was privy.

ATKIN, J. (at page 56)

The claimant having made a claim under the policy, the [insurers] rely upon s. 39, sub-s. 5, of the Marine Insurance Act 1906 and say that it relieves them from liability. The section provides that: "In a time policy there is no implied warranty that the ship shall be seaworthy at any stage of the adventure, but where, with the privity of the assured, the ship is sent to sea in an unseaworthy state, the insurer is not liable for any loss attributable to unseaworthiness." The [insurers] contended that they were not liable, inasmuch as the ship was sent on her voyage in an unseaworthy condition with the privity of the assured, namely, with an insufficient crew, and that she was lost owing to her unseaworthiness, though the unseaworthiness was in another respect, namely, in respect of the unfitness of her hull. In my view, however, that is not the proper construction of the sub-section, I think it means that the insurer is not to be liable for a loss attributable to unseaworthiness to which the assured was privy. In the case of insurance under a time policy the intention of the Legislature was that the assured should be unable to recover in respect of a loss occasioned by his own fault. That was the rule previous to the Act. In order to prevent the assured recovering under a time policy it was always necessary to show that the loss was the result of some misconduct on the part of assured. The statute has now defined the degree of misconduct necessary to prevent the assured recovering as being the sending of the ship to sea in an unseaworthy state with the privity of the assured. When a ship is sent to sea in a state of unseaworthiness in two particulars, and the assured is privy to the one and not the other, the insurer is not protected unless the loss is caused by the particular unseaworthiness to which the assured was privy. The contrary construction of the section is unreasonable. For example, if a ship were sent on a voyage with a defective equipment and subsequently during the course of the voyage became unseaworthy in some wholly different aspect which caused her loss, according to the [insurers'] contention the assured could not recover.

(7) ASSIGNMENT OF POLICY

William Pickersgill & Sons Ltd. *v*. London and Provincial Marine and General Insurance Co. Ltd.

(1912) 107 L.T. 305

By s. 50(2) of the Marine Insurance Act 1906: "Where a marine policy has been assigned so as to pass the beneficial interest in such policy . . . the defendant is entitled to make any defence arising out of the contract which he would have been entitled to make if the action had been brought in the name of the person by or on behalf of whom the policy was effected."

The assignors of a marine insurance policy failed to disclose a material fact to the insurance company. The insured vessel was lost, and the assignees of the policy, who did not know of the non-disclosure, claimed against the insurance company.

Held, by the King's Bench Division (Commercial Court), that the insurance company was entitled to rely on s. 50(2) and avoid liability under the policy on the ground of non-disclosure, even against an innocent assignee.

HAMILTON, J. (at page 307)

Reliance is placed upon the Marine Insurance Act 1906, s. 50, sub-s. 2. It is pointed out that the words of the Act of 1868 have not been repealed textually, although the Act is repealed by the Act of 1906. There are other differences between s. 1 of the Act of 1868 and s. 50, sub-s. 2, of the Act of 1906, but in particular the words in the Act of 1868 were: "The defendant in any action shall be entitled to make any defence which he would have been entitled to make if the said action had been brought in the name of the person by whom or for whose account the policy sued upon was effected", whereas in the present Act, after the words "to make any defence", the words "arising out of the contract" are inserted. The argument is that this codification expresses the conditions and the whole of the conditions under which and under which alone the defendant defending himself against the assignee of a policy is to be entitled to set up defences. If by the insertion of these words "arising out of the contract" the Legislature intended to deprive underwriters of the right of setting up concealment against an assignee, and leave them with that remedy only against the assignor of the policy, under the form of codification the Legislature, in fact, enacted a drastic and far-reaching alteration in the law of marine insurance.

(8) ACTUAL TOTAL LOSS

George Cohen, Sons & Co. *v*. Standard Marine Insurance Co. Ltd.

(1925) 21 Ll.L.Rep. 30

By s. 57(1) of the Marine Insurance Act 1906: "Where the subject matter insured is destroyed or so damaged as to cease to be a thing of the kind insured, or where the assured is irretrievably deprived thereof, there is an actual total loss".

An obsolete battleship was insured while being towed from Chatham to Brake (in Germany) where she was to be broken up. She went ashore on the Dutch coast. Evidence was given that she could be got off, but the operation would be expensive. The Dutch authorities would not allow her to be moved in case the sea defences in the area were damaged thereby, but their decision was subject to appeal to a higher tribunal.

Held, by the King's Bench Division, that the vessel was not an actual total loss, for the assured had not been irretrievably deprived of her.[30]

ROCHE, J. (at page 33)

My reasons for deciding that the plaintiffs have not been irretrievably deprived thereof are as follows. Having regard to the whole of the evidence, not merely the evidence for the defendants but the evidence given for the plaintiffs by several witnesses, and in particular by Capt. Richards, to whose evidence I attach great importance, I am of opinion that the vessel physically could be got off. It would be a matter of great elaboration and difficulty, but at all events,

---

[30] Another aspect of this case, viz., whether the assured had failed to disclose a material fact, is considered at p. 142, *ante*.

putting the matter at the highest, I am not satisfied that she could not. On the whole I think that she could. It would be an engineering feat requiring considerable preparation and, as I shall subsequently decide, very high expenditure, but it could be done so far as the physical feat was concerned. Though I think Capt. Richards regards it as doubtful, he is not prepared to say that it cannot be done. In these circumstances, there has been no irretrievable deprivation which a Court can find by reason of physical impossibility.

There is another matter in this connection which has to be considered. It is said that the assured is irretrievably deprived of the *Prince George* because the authorities charged with the management of these sea defences would not allow her to be moved or the works which are necessary for her removal to be undertaken. With regard to that, the position I find to be as follows. The management and direction of the works appears to be in the hands of the Diet, or Council, for North Holland, acting through their executive body or Governing Body of North Holland, who can only act through deputies or another board, a board whom I recently described by the name of the Dyke Reeve Board. I am satisfied that, so far as the Dyke Reeve Board is concerned, having seen the Engineer of that Board, and recognising the very strong view that the Engineer takes, and knowing how far that is likely to be influential with the Board, having regard to the obvious ability and sincerity of the gentleman, I think that the Dyke Reeve Board would have vetoed the works which would have been necessary, but I am satisfied that a decision such as that, in a matter affecting the legal rights of the owners of property, would have been subject to reconsideration or review in two ways, (1) by the Council of North Holland or its executive side or body, and if such reconsideration was unfavourable to the owner of the property, in that case it would have been subject to further review; (2) by the civil Courts of Holland.

I am satisfied, since both the Dutch advocate called by the plaintiffs, and the Dutch advocate called by the defendants agreed on it, that the decision of the Dyke Reeve Board, however influential it is, and however likely to strongly influence the Court, is not conclusive. I think I must assume for this purpose not matters of commercial consideration, but I must consider that somebody who would have been interested in applying for the recovery of the property would have been willing to spend the necessary money to guarantee the safety, or to satisfy a Court that they would ensure the safety, of the sea defences. Assuming that I am unable to say that either the executive body of the Provincial Diet or Council, or a Court, would have of necessity decided against the owners of the property, I am satisfied that, at an expense, the safety of the sea defences could have been ensured, although this groyne was interfered with. It seems to me almost impossible to hold that, although it might be commercially impossible to effect that safety in connection with the salving of this ship, having regard to its value and the other expenses, it could not be done. I am satisfied that it could; and, in those circumstances, I am not satisfied that there was such a certainty of deprivation as to amount to the deprivation being irretrievable. Accordingly, I decide that there is not actual total loss.

(9) CONSTRUCTIVE TOTAL LOSS

Irvin *v.* Hine

[1949] 2 All E.R. 1089

The definition of "constructive total loss" given in the Marine Insurance Act 1906, s. 60 is exhaustive.

During the Second World War a trawler was being towed to a dry dock. She stranded and was severely damaged. At all material times the assured would have been unlikely to obtain a licence to repair her or to place her in dry dock within a reasonable time. The assured claimed that she was a constructive total loss.

Held, by the King's Bench Division, that since the type of loss did not fall within any of the heads of loss stated in s. 60, there was no constructive total loss. The assured therefore was entitled to claim for a partial loss only.

DEVLIN, J. (at page 1091)

I have to consider whether on its true construction the Act expressly provides that s. 60 is a complete definition of constructive total loss. If it does, then any addition to the definition would not be admissible under s. 91(2).

Section 56(1) provides: ". . . Any loss other than a total loss, as hereinafter defined, is a partial loss". That seems, as LORD PORTER pointed out in *Robertson* v. *Nomikos*,[31] to mean that the definition of constructive total loss in s. 60 must be complete. If any loss outside s. 57 (which defines actual total loss) and s. 60 were to be held to be a total loss, it could not be a partial loss, as that would be inconsistent with the express provision of s. 56. I see no answer to this argument except possibly that it puts too literal a construction on the words of s. 56. That makes it material to consider whether such a construction is out of harmony with the object of s. 60, as shown in its marginal note, and with the general purpose of the Act. The marginal note is "Constructive total loss defined". This is in keeping with the words of s. 56 "total loss, as hereinafter defined" and shows that s. 60 is intended to contain a definition. I have used the words "complete definition", as LORD PORTER did, as a convenient and expressive term. I dare say it is not meticulously accurate, for, strictly speaking, a definition must be complete, else it is not a definition at all. The question really is whether s. 60 is a definition section, defining constructive total loss as a whole, and not merely categories of it, or whether, as Counsel for the plaintiff in terms argued, all it does is to lay down the main

---

[31] [1939] 2 All E.R. 723, at p. 734.

characteristics of a constructive total loss. This argument gives no weight to the word "defined", both in s. 56 and in the marginal note to s. 60. I think that that word shows conclusively that s. 60 is intended to *define* a constructive total loss, which is the same as saying that s. 60 circumscribes completely the conception of constructive total loss. As to the general purpose of the Act, it is described in its title as a codifying Act, and it would, I think, be surprising if its framers had not included in it a comprehensive definition of constructive total loss, or that, if they had intended only to define categories, they would not have made their intention clear.

Polurrian Steamship Co. *v.* Young

[1914–15] All E.R. Rep. 116

Under the Marine Insurance Act 1906, s. 60(2)(i) there is a constructive total loss of a vessel if it is "unlikely" that the assured can recover her.

The insured vessel was on a voyage from Newport to Istanbul. During it war broke out between Greece and Turkey. She was stopped by a Greek warship and escorted into a fresh port because she was carrying contraband. The authorities kept her, so the assured gave notice of abandonment and claimed for a constructive total loss. Six weeks later the vessel was released.

Held, by the Court of Appeal, that the assured could not recover for a constructive total loss because at the date of commencement of the action[32] the assured had not shown that it was "unlikely" that he would recover the vessel. To show that it was "uncertain" was insufficient.

WARRINGTON, J. (at page 123)

The section which governs the present case is s. 60(1) and (2). So far as it relates to a constructive loss by capture that section runs thus: "(1) Subject to any express provision in the policy, there is a constructive total loss where the subject-matter insured is reasonably abandoned on account of its actual total loss appearing to be unavoidable. . . . (2) In particular, there is a constructive total loss—(i) Where the assured is deprived of the possession of his ship . . . by a peril insured against, and (*a*) it is unlikely that he can recover the ship".

One may, I think, without disrespect, declare some regret that the two expressions "reasonably abandon on account of its actual total loss appearing to be unavoidable" and "unlikely that he can recover the ship" should be used apparently to describe the same position of things. For in my view, at any rate, it is one thing, to predicate that a total loss of a thing reasonably appears to be "unavoidable", and another to predicate that its recovery is "unlikely". Taking,

[32] The insurers had agreed to treat the date of the notice of abandonment as the date of the commencement of the action, and to put the assured in the same position as if a writ had then been issued.

however, the latter, and, as it seems to me, the less severe test of the right to treat a capture as constituting a constructive total loss, I think that the statute has modified the pre-existing law to the disadvantage of the assured. One is always properly afraid of incompleteness in attempting a definition, but I venture to say that the test of "unlikelihood of recovery" has now been substituted for "uncertainty of recovery". The assured must now show two things—the first, that he has been deprived of the possession of his ship: the second, that it is unlikely that he can recover it. Whence the statute derived the phrase "unlikely that he can recover" as expressing a necessary condition of the assured's right to recover for a constructive total loss by capture I do not know. I have referred to many of the reported capture cases and have been unable to find it used judicially in any of them. But there it stands in the section of the Act of Parliament; its meaning is quite clear.

(10) NOTICE OF ABANDONMENT

Associated Oil Carriers Ltd. *v.* Union Insurance Society of Canton Ltd.

(1917) 116 L.T. 503

By s. 57(2) of the Marine Insurance Act 1906: "In the case of an actual total loss no notice of abandonment need be given".

The assured had effected a freight policy including a war risk clause in respect of a vessel which was chartered to a German charterer for consecutive voyages for three years from January, 1913. War broke out in August, 1914. The insured instructed the master of the vessel to abandon the voyage and proceed to a port in the United States for orders. On the outbreak of war the charter-party became illegal, and the freight was lost to the assured.

Held, by the King's Bench Division, that there was an actual total loss of freight, and that no notice of abandonment was necessary.

ATKIN, J. (at page 505)

It was further contended that in any case the loss was a constructive total loss, so that notice of abandonment was necessary. Now, it appears to me that if a vessel, insured on freight generally, loses entirely from perils insured against the only freight in respect of which it has a contractual interest, and no other freight can be obtained on the insured voyage, the loss is an actual and not a constructive loss. If other freight can be obtained on the insured voyage, the question might arise whether it could be earned without an expenditure which would exceed its value when earned, and the loss might then be a constructive total loss or no loss at all. Here, as I have said, no freight could be obtained, and I think the loss an actual loss.

The question whether this was an actual or constructive total loss may be considered from another point of view. If this were a constructive total loss, what follows? By s. 61 of the Marine Insurance Act 1906 the assured may either treat the loss as a partial loss or abandon the subject-matter insured to the insurer, and treat the loss as if it were an actual total loss. The question of abandonment only arises where there has been, in fact, a loss of the subject-matter insured, and the issue is whether that loss shall be partial or actual. It involves the loss of something in which the assured has an insurable interest at the time of the loss. If a vessel is sailing with cargo on board, the owners have a right to earn freight by carrying the cargo to its destination by that vessel or a substituted vessel. That right is the subject of insurance, and, if vessel or cargo be injured, it may well be that the owner can abandon to the underwriters his rights so to carry the cargo as to enable them to earn freight. But when a vessel is sailing on an outward voyage to a loading port, intended to carry home cargo in respect of which a contractual obligation exists, and in the course of the outward voyage all the rights in respect of such cargo disappear by a peril insured against, what is there to abandon? The subject-matter in respect of which the loss is made has disappeared, and there is nothing left analogous to ship or cargo, or right to carry forward cargo, still in existence which can be made over to the underwriters. I cannot conceive that the ship has to be handed over to the underwriters to become a sinking ship. In such a case I do not think there can be either a constructive total loss or an abandonment. The only question that can arise is, was there an actual loss at all, either total or partial?

Captain J. A. Cates Tug and Wharfage Co. Ltd. *v.* Franklin Insurance Co.

(1927) 137 L.T. 709

By s. 62(5) of the Marine Insurance Act 1906: "The acceptance of an abandonment may be either express or implied from the conduct of the insurer".

A tug was sunk in a collision and notice of abandonment was given to the insurers. As a result of salvage operations which they instituted, the vessel was raised and towed inshore, and the abandonment was not accepted. Without the knowledge of the assured the salvors verbally made an offer to the insurers to purchase the vessel. The offer was later put into writing, but was withdrawn three weeks later. The assured contended that the negotiations between the insurers and the salvors constituted an acceptance of the abandonment.

Held, by the Judicial Committee of the Privy Council, that no acceptance of abandonment could be implied from the conduct of the insurers.

LORD SUMNER (at page 711)

While the surveys and estimates were being made, the salvors happened to ask the underwriters' representative whether, if the wreck were to be sold, they could be given a chance to purchase. A non-committal reply was given at the moment, but a little later an offer of $12,500 was made by word of mouth, to include the $6,500 salvage. In return a request was made that the offer should be put into writing, which was done, but after an interval of some three weeks this offer was withdrawn. The appellants knew nothing of this incident until after litigation had begun, so that, whatever else may be made of it, estoppel, on the basis of a representation available to the appellants and a consequent change of position on their part, is out of the question.

It was on this incident that the judgment turned, which the trial Judge gave in favour of the appellants for a total loss. He held that, by reason of these communications between the underwriters and a third party, there had been a binding acceptance of the abandonment, which had been tendered by the assured, in spite of their formal refusal of it. He held that they had done an act which could only be justified under a right derived from abandonment, "for", he said, "does not the solicitation and receipt of a *bona fide* bid to purchase necessarily imply power to make title should the bid be accepted?" Their Lordships can only say, as the Court of Appeal said, that it does not. The underwriters in this tentative negotiation did not act as owners of the tug or exercise dominion over it, and they did not purport to sell and convey or to make a title for that purpose. An agreement to sell, had it been concluded, would only have been an executory contract, which they would be able to perform if and when they chose to accept the abandonment, but in itself it could not be an act of ownership. As a matter of fact, this everyday proceeding was nothing more than a precaution, equally available in connection with proving a defence in case they should resist the claim or with preparing to make the best of the loss if they should give up the contest and elect to pay. The analogy of goods sold by sample, or delivered on approbation to a person, who thereupon sells them over to a third party, and so determines his right to elect whether he will take the goods or return them, is one which, though it was urged on their Lordships by Counsel at the bar, it is impossible to adopt.

(11) GENERAL AVERAGE

Watson (Joseph) & Son Ltd. *v.* Firemen's Fund Insurance Co. of San Francisco

(1922) 127 L.T. 754

By s. 66(2) of the Marine Insurance Act 1906: "There is a general average act where any extraordinary sacrifice or expenditure is voluntarily and reasonably made or incurred in time of peril for the purpose of preserving the property imperilled in the common adventure." But the insurer is not liable unless the peril concerned is a real one.

In the course of a voyage the master of a vessel saw something which appeared to be smoke coming from her hold, and thought that there was a fire there. He therefore caused high-pressure steam to be turned into the hold to put out the supposed fire. The insured cargo of rosin was damaged by the steam, but the master had been mistaken because there was, in fact, no fire in the hold. The assured claimed an indemnity from the insurance company on the ground that a general average loss had been incurred.

Held, by the King's Bench Division, that there was no general average loss, for the danger was not, in fact, a real one, but one merely imagined by the master to exist.

ROWLATT, J. (at page 755)

I do not think that the evidence establishes that there was a fire in the hold. I accept the theory that the vapour seen by the captain issuing from the hold was given off by the rosin which had become heated by steam escaping from a broken pipe. It has been argued that there is a "peril" within the meaning of s. 66 of the Marine Insurance Act 1906 in every case where the captain believes that a peril exists. I do not think so. Cases were cited which show that much depends upon the view taken at the time by the captain or person in authority as opposed to that taken by those who, after the event, may have had a better opportunity of forming a correct judgment. But it appears to me that there is an ambiguity in the contention which they were cited to support. It is one thing to say that where a peril, in fact, existed, we must take the view of the captain formed at the time with regard to what would be the outcome of that peril, and we must not say to him, "If you had held on, you would have found that all would have come right", or something of that kind. But it is another thing to say that we must take the captain's view as to whether the state of facts existed which are alleged to have constituted the peril.

The words of the Marine Insurance Act 1906 do not justify me in holding that there is a peril whenever it looks as if there was a peril. I do not think, therefore, that this was a general average loss.

But even if it was a general average loss, I do not think that the plaintiffs can recover, because they could only do so under their insurance against peril by fire. The underwriters insured against fire in fact, and if there had been a fire, they would have had to pay. But why should they pay if, in fact, there was no fire? They did not insure against an error of judgment on the part of the captain in deciding whether there was a peril or not. It has been argued that this was a loss incurred "for the purpose of avoiding, or in connection with the avoidance of, a peril insured against" within the meaning of s. 66, sub-s. 6, of the Act, but I do not think this was a loss of that kind. I am of opinion that the effect of that subsection is to include losses which are collateral to the main process of avoiding a peril insured against, and that it does not affect losses incurred in a mistaken attempt to avoid a peril which is in fact non-existent.

(12) MEASURE OF INDEMNITY

Helmville Ltd. *v.* Yorkshire Insurance Co. Ltd.: The "Medina Princess"

[1965] 1 Lloyd's Rep. 361[33]

In the case of a time policy the time at which the measure of indemnity under s. 69(3) of the Marine Insurance Act 1906 falls to be determined is the time when the policy expires.

ROSKILL, J. (at page 516)

Subsection (3) is silent as to the point of time at which the measure of indemnity is to be ascertained and quantified. But I think that help is to be derived from the opening words of the subsection namely: "Where the ship has not been repaired, and has not been sold in her damaged state during the risk . . .". The ship may be repaired at any time after the casualty and during the risk. If she is then wholly repaired, sub-s. (1) operates. If she is then partly repaired, sub-s. (2) operates. But if "during the risk", which I construe as meaning "during the period between the casualty and the expiry of the policy whether by effluxion of time or otherwise", she is neither repaired nor sold, then sub-s. (3) comes into operation. Until the moment when the risk expires, the ship might be repaired or indeed might be sold. The section is silent as to the position if the ship is sold unrepaired and I need not trouble with that contingency. But it is only when the risk is ended that it can be predicted for certain that neither repair nor sale will take place during the risk. That, in my judgment, is the moment at which sub-s. (3) operates and requires that the measure of indemnity shall be ascertained and quantified.

Helmville Ltd. *v.* Yorkshire Insurance Co. Ltd.: The "Medina Princess"

[1965] 1 Lloyd's Rep. 361[34]

Section 69(3) of the Marine Insurance Act 1906 requires the measure of indemnity to be quantified on the basis of what it would have cost to repair the vessel if the repairs had been carried out.

A vessel grounded at Djibouti and became a partial loss. The cost of towing her from there to Karachi where repairs could have been carried out would have been £14,560.

---

[33] The case also decided that the measure of indemnity under s. 69(3) is required to be quantified on the basis of what it would have cost to repair the vessel if the repairs had been carried out. As to this point, see *infra*.

[34] This case also concerned the question as to the time at which the measure of indemnity under s. 69(3) is to be quantified where a vessel is insured under a time policy. As to this point, see *supra*.

Held, by the Queen's Bench Division (Commercial Court), that this sum was recoverable as part of the partial loss claim, even though the cost of towing was not, in fact, incurred since the vessel was never repaired.

ROSKILL, J. (at page 521)

It follows that on my findings of fact, towage from Djibouti to Karachi would have been necessary in order to repair the ship. I accordingly hold that the sum of £14,560 which I have found to be the cost of towage is recoverable under the policy as part of the plaintiff's partial loss claim. That the plaintiffs have not incurred that expenditure is irrelevant. Section 69(3) requires the measure of indemnity to be quantified on the basis of what it would have cost to repair if the repairs had been carried out.

Wilson Bros. Bobbin Co. Ltd. *v*. Green

(1917) 116 L.T. 637

By s. 78(1) of the Marine Insurance Act 1906: "Where the policy contains a suing and labouring clause, the engagement thereby entered into is deemed to be supplementary to the contract of insurance, and the assured may recover from the insurer any expenses properly incurred pursuant to the clause, notwithstanding the insurer may have paid for a total loss . . .". Whether the expenses have been properly incurred is a matter of fact.

A cargo of birch wood was insured for a voyage from Rauma (Raumo, Finland) to Garston. The goods were loaded on a Norwegian vessel. The policy was against war risks only and contained a suing and labouring clause. The vessel sailed in November, 1914, and owing to the interference of German warships her master put in to Grimstad, a Norwegian port. The cargo was unloaded and stored there and afterwards re-shipped to Garston. The assured claimed under the suing and labouring clause the expenses incurred.

Held, by the King's Bench Division, that they were entitled to the cost of the storage until they could with reasonable diligence have secured facilities for re-shipment to Garston, and also to the proper cost of re-shipping and forwarding the cargo at that date.

BRAY, J. (at page 639)

The goods were at Grimstad, the port of destination was Garston, and the goods could not be safely got to Garston without incurring the expense of storage at Grimstad and the cost of reloading and forwarding, and therefore, in my opinion, these were expenses—I will leave out the word "proper" for the moment—incurred in endeavouring to avert that loss. The next question raised by [Counsel] was that the plaintiffs did not act reasonably; that if they had acted with reasonable diligence, the goods could have been re-shipped long before, at a much lower freight, and that they did not take reasonable steps to obtain tonnage as soon as they might have done. Now, I have carefully considered the case, and I am bound to say that I think [Counsel] is right on that point. On the evidence, I think that if the plaintiffs had acted with reasonable diligence, they could have had a ship ready to load the cargo at Grimstad by about the middle of April, 1915, at a lower rate of freight than they, in fact, paid.

In considering the question of the amount of the expenses, I think I must take it from the defendant's evidence that at that time the freight to London would be about 72*s*. for deal. But it was admitted by [the] defendant's witnesses that some additional freight would be required in respect of these birch squares, and I propose, therefore, to add 20*s*. to the 72*s*. which was named by the defendant, and to say that for 92*s*. a vessel could have been chartered by about Apr. 15, 1915, so that storage and re-shipping expenses must be calculated upon that footing.

British and Foreign Marine Insurance Co. *v*. Gaunt

[1921] All E.R. Rep. 447

Although s. 78(4) of the Marine Insurance Act 1906 states that "It is the duty of the assured and his agents, in all cases, to take such measures as may be reasonable for the purpose of averting or minimising a loss", this subsection relates only to suing and labouring, and does not qualify s. 55(2)(a) as to insurance against negligence or the misconduct of the master and crew.

LORD SUMNER (at page 458)

There remains an argument based on the reading of s. 78(4) of the Act which is very novel. It is one of the disadvantages of codification that new terms used or even unfamiliar sequences of propositions suggest that the law has been changed where those familiar with the old decisions would not have suspected it. The argument affords a striking instance of this. The section obviously refers to suing and labouring. It cannot possibly be read as meaning that, if the agents of the assured are not reasonably careful throughout the transit, he cannot recover for anything to which their want of care contributes. The point, therefore, fails.

(13) SUBROGATION

Yorkshire Insurance Co. Ltd. *v*. Nisbet Shipping Co. Ltd.

[1961] 2 All E.R. 487

Under the doctrine of subrogation embodied in the Marine Insurance Act 1906, s. 79, the insurer cannot recover from the assured anything more than he has paid to the assured.

A vessel was insured for £72,000. She became a total loss as a result of a collision with a Canadian Government ship. The insurers paid £72,000 to the assured, who then claimed damages from the Canadian Government. The action was successful, but meanwhile the pound sterling had been devalued in 1949, and the loss, when quantified and converted into English currency, came to nearly £127,000. This sum was paid to the assured. The assured then repaid the £72,000 to the insurers, and claimed that they were entitled to keep the excess sum of £55,000.

Held, by the Queen's Bench Division, that the assured were so entitled. The insurers could not recover from the assured under the doctrine of subrogation any more than they had paid, viz., £72,000.

DIPLOCK, J. (at page 494)

It follows that in my view the insurer's rights in this case were limited to recovering from the assured the amount overpaid, that is to say, £72,000. He is entitled to no more. The principle, I think, is a simple one. It renders irrelevant any consideration of the particular concatenation of circumstances which enable the assured to recover from the Canadian Government a sum in sterling in excess of the value of the ship at the time of the casualty. The fact that the policy was a valued policy, with, as it transpired, a policy value somewhat less than the real value is also irrelevant. The simple principle which I apply is that the insurer cannot recover under the doctrine of subrogation now embodied in s. 79 of the Marine Insurance Act 1906, anything more than he has paid.

(14) INSTITUTE CLAUSES

Scindia Steamships (London) Ltd. *v.* London Assurance

[1937] 3 All E.R. 895

It is only damage caused by the breakage of a shaft which is insured by the "Perils" clause. The breakage of a shaft itself is not covered.

A vessel was insured under a Lloyd's policy with the "Perils" clause attached. This clause stated: "This insurance also specially to cover . . . loss of or damage to hull or machinery caused by accidents in loading, discharging, or handling cargo, or . . . through explosions, bursting of boilers, breakage of shafts, or through any latent defect in the machinery or hull". While the vessel was in dry dock, her tailshaft broke owing to a latent defect in it. The end of the shaft broke, and the propeller fell into the dock and was damaged. The insurance company admitted liability for the damage to the propeller, but refused to pay for the provision of and fitting of a new tailshaft.

Held, by the King's Bench Division, that the insurance company was justified in its refusal to pay.

BRANSON, J. (at page 897)

The next point that is taken is that, if the words cannot be so isolated, then they may, at all events, be read in the following way: "This insurance also specially covers loss of or damage to hull or machinery through breakage of shafts". It is said that "shafts" are a portion of hull or machinery, being a portion of machinery, and that "loss of or damage to machinery caused by the breakage of the shafts" includes the actual breaking of the shaft itself. That, it seems to me, is a forced construction of the language, and not the ordinary meaning which, reading the clause as a bit of English prose, one would be inclined to put upon it. It follows other clauses in which, obviously, the loss or damage happens to something different from the thing by which the damage is said to be caused. The first group is "caused by accidents in loading", and so forth; "caused through the negligence of master, mariners", and so forth. Both of these groups obviously envisage, as it seems to me, a state of affairs in which the main cause produces damage which has an effect on something else: and I see no reason why, when one comes down, after these clauses, to the one with which I have particularly to deal, one should read it in any other way. It seems to me, therefore, that the proper reading is that the breakage of the shaft itself is not covered, nor can it properly be said that the breakage of the shaft is a loss of or damage to machinery caused by the breakage of the shaft. The breakage of the shaft is the breakage of the shaft, and, if, by reason of the breakage of the shaft, the machine is torn to pieces, then there would be damage caused by the breakage of the shaft. But, in this case, the only damage, beyond the damage to the propeller, which has been paid for, is the actual damage which happened to the shaft itself, to wit, the breakage of the shaft, and the breakage of the shaft is not caused by the breakage of the shaft. If that is damage to the machinery which the breakage of the shaft has caused, it seems to me that one gets a confusion both of thought and of language which I think should not be introduced into the construction of a clause of this kind.

I therefore think that the plaintiffs fail to establish a right to recover under that part of the clause which relates to breakage of shafts.

Prudent Tankers Ltd. S.A. *v.* Dominion Insurance Co. Ltd.: The "Caribbean Sea"

[1980] 1 Lloyd's Rep. 338

The "Perils" Clause covers loss of or damage to a vessel directly caused by "any latent defect in the machinery or hull". A "latent defect" is one which could not be discovered on such an examination as a reasonably careful skilled man would make.

A policy in respect of a vessel included the "Perils" clause, which covered damage to or loss of her directly caused by a "latent defect". She sank and was a total loss. The assured claimed an indemnity from the insurers on the ground that the loss was caused by a fatigue crack initiated at a weld joining a nozzle to the vessel's plate, with the result that sea water entered her through the main sea suction valve.

Held, by the Queen's Bench Division (Commercial Court), that there would be judgment for the assured because, on the evidence, the loss was caused by a latent defect, i.e. one which could not be discovered on such an examination as a reasonably careful skilled man would make.

ROBERT GOFF, J. (at page 347)

I am also satisfied that the defect in the present case, consisting as it did of the fatigue cracks in the wedge-shaped nozzle, constituted a latent defect. There was in fact no discussion before me of the meaning of the word "latent" in this context. In contracts of affreightment, a latent defect has been held to be a defect which could not be discovered on such an examination as a reasonably careful skilled man would make: see *Brown* v. *Nitrate Producers S.S. Co.*[35] In the American cases cited to me a latent defect has been said to be one which cannot be discovered by any known and customary test: see the dictum from *Parente* v. *Bayville Marine Inc. and General Insurance Co. of America*,[36] which I have already quoted. I prefer the former of these two tests, which appears to me to be more in accordance with commercial sense, taking into account as it does the possibility that a ship may be properly and carefully maintained and yet a defect may not be discovered although a more meticulous examination would have revealed its existence: a casualty caused by such a defect is surely covered by the ["Perils"] clause. I therefore conclude, on that test, that the loss of the ship in the present case was directly caused by a latent defect in the hull, within the cover provided by the ["Perils"] clause, and it follows that the owners are entitled to recover.

Furness Withy & Co. Ltd. *v.* Duder

[1936] 2 All E.R. 119

The "Collision Liability" clause covers only collision damages payable in respect of a tort. It does not cover liability arising in contract.

A marine insurance policy included the "Collision Liability" clause by which the insurer agreed to indemnify the assured "if the ship hereby insured shall come into collision with any other ship or vessel and the assured shall in consequence thereof become liable to pay and shall pay by way of damages to any other person any sum . . .". An Admiralty tug was engaged by the assured to tow the insured ship. The towage contract contained a clause under which the assured agreed "to make good to the Admiralty all damage suffered by the Admiralty through injury to Admiralty

[35] (1937) 58 Ll.L.Rep. 188.

[36] [1975] 1 Lloyd's Rep. 333. Supreme Court of New York, Appellate Division, at p. 333 (*per* HOPKINS, J.).

property . . . by reason of or arising out of . . . the service [of the tug]". The insured ship collided with the tug owing to the negligent navigation of the tug. The assured paid the amount of the damage to the Admiralty, and claimed an indemnity from the insurer under the "Collision Liability" clause.

Held, by the King's Bench Division, that the action failed. The clause only applied to liability arising in tort, and not to liability arising out of a towage contract.

BRANSON, J. (at page 120)

The question here is whether the £119 12*s*. 8*d*. which the plaintiffs have paid to the Admiralty is a sum which they became liable to pay in consequence of the ship having come into collision with another ship, and became liable to pay by way of damages. [Counsel] urges that the collision was the proximate cause of the liability on the part of the plaintiffs to pay, and therefore that it can correctly be described as the cause in consequence of which the plaintiffs became liable to pay. But my view is that the running-down clause must be read as one sentence. It does not help to divide it into two and to ask oneself whether payment arose in consequence of the collision, and was it, if it did so arise, a payment in consequence of damage. It leads to a clearer view of the meaning of the clause to read it as it was written in one sentence and to ask oneself, "What did the parties mean? What are the circumstances that the parties contemplated?" It may be that this is not more than a case of first impression. Looking at it from that point of view, I think that the sentence means that where, as a result of the collision, there arises a legal liability upon the shipowners to pay something which may be described as damages, then the underwriters will indemnify. The expression "become liable to pay and shall pay by way of damages" indicates a method of liability arising by way of tort and not by way of contract. There is no such liability here.

I need only add that if this language in the running-down clause was sufficient to cover any sort of liability which a shipowner might pay by way of contract, the prospect for the underwriters would only be limited by the pity which the shipowners might be expected to extend.

(15) PROCEDURE

Palamisto General Enterprises S.A. *v.* Ocean Marine Insurance Co. Ltd.: The "Dias"

[1972] 2 All E.R. 1112

Where the insurers allege that a vessel has been scuttled, R.S.C. Order 18, r. 12(1) and Order 72, r. 7(2) and fair treatment require that so far as practicable the matter should be pleaded with particularity so that the assured may know what case he has to meet.

The insured vessel sustained a fire in her boiler room and sank about 2½ hours later. The assured claimed under the policy, but the insurers put them to strict proof that the loss was due to a peril insured against, and also contended that the vessel had been scuttled. The assured applied for particulars of the scuttling. But the insurers maintained that it was sufficient for them to put the assured to strict proof of the claim, and that particulars of the scuttling need not be given.

Held, by the Court of Appeal, that an order for particulars would be made.

BUCKLEY, L.J. (at page 1125)

I agree with EDMUND DAVIES, L.J., in thinking that, where a party asserts his opponents' complicity in fraudulent conduct amounting, as in a case of scuttling, to criminal misconduct, the case is pre-eminently one in which not only the rules of court (R.S.C. Order 18, r. 12(1) and Order 72, r. 7(2)) but also fair treatment require that, so far as practicable, the matter shall be pleaded with particulars, so that the party accused may know what case he has to meet. This does not mean that he is entitled to know what evidence will be adduced against him. Nor, I think, should he at any rate normally, be entitled to particulars of circumstantial matters from which inferences will be sought to be drawn. He ought, in my judgment, to have the best particulars available of those circumstances which his opponents will, whether by direct evidence or by inference, attempt to establish as constituting the scuttling of the ship. To put it concisely, he should be told, not why his opponent will say that the ship should be found to have been scuttled, but how his opponent will say that the ship was scuttled, if the circumstances are such that it is realistic to suppose that his opponents can furnish such particulars. Moreover, it seems to me that, where the issues can be defined or narrowed by particulars in such a case, this is very desirable, not only because of the gravity of the charge but also because the evidence of members of the crew may be relevant and seamen are likely to be difficult witnesses to produce at short notice.

Where insurers have secured information from which either they actually know how the ship was scuttled, or they have formed a clear theory (or maybe alternative theories) about it, it seems to me that it would be right that their opponents should know how they will say that the ship was scuttled. Moreover, I consider that this would be so even if the insurers have good reason for wanting to keep open the possibility of investigating other ways in which the ship may have been cast away. I am not at present satisfied that, (a) having put the owners to strict proof that the ship was lost by a peril of the sea, and (b) having alleged that the ship was scuttled in a particular manner, the insurer would be debarred from investigating by cross-examination the possibility of the ship having been lost in some way involving a method of scuttling other than the particular method pleaded. The plea of scuttling might, I am inclined to think, be regarded as a separate and alternative plea, distinct from the putting of the shipowners to strict proof of their perils-of-the-sea allegation. As such, the former should not, it seems to me, be allowed to inhibit the freedom of action of the insurers on the latter.

But if I were wrong about this, the point is one which, I think, could be satisfactorily dealt with under R.S.C. Order 18, r. 12(3), which enables the Court to order particulars on such terms as the Court thinks just. If the Court were to consider that the insurers should not be ordered to give particulars of a scuttling plea except on condition that the giving of particulars should not restrict their right to investigate by cross-examination or otherwise the validity of a shipowner's plea that his ship was lost by perils of the sea, it could so order. This would not, I think, by any means necessarily render the giving of the particulars useless. Where insurers are able to give particulars of a scuttling plea, even if such particulars are, in fact, no more than deductions based on inferences from surrounding circumstances, I can see no valid reason for treating them as being in a particularly privileged position justifying them in withholding such particulars contrary to the rules of court. That the facts are better known to the applicant for particulars than to his opponent has never been regarded as a sufficient ground for excusing the latter from particularising any allegations of a general nature in his pleading.

In no case, however, can a party exact better particulars from his opponent than the latter is capable of giving, nor, in my judgment, should the Court order particulars in any case where it is satisfied that the best particulars that the party can or will be at all likely to be able to give will not contribute to the fair conduct of the trial and the avoidance of unfair surprises or of unnecessary expense or waste of time. If, for example, the information presently available to insurers is no more than enough to lead them to believe that at the trial they will be able to satisfy the Court that the only credible explanation of the loss of the ship is that it was scuttled in some way, the particulars of which are unknown, the insurers will be incapable of giving before trial any particulars of the scuttling allegation, or at any rate particulars in any useful form. In such circumstances the Court might, in the exercise of its discretion, refuse to order any particulars, or it might order the insurers to give the best particulars that they are able to give.

Probatina Shipping Co. Ltd. *v.* Sun Insurance Office Ltd.

[1974] 2 All E.R. 478

An order for ship's papers should not be made automatically.

The owners of a vessel insured her for £75,000. On Apr. 29, 1972, she was stranded on a rocky island off Crete and became a total loss. In August, 1972, the assured disclosed to the insurers all immediately available and apparently relevant documents including the chart referred to in the master's statement. In October and November, 1972, further documents including the crew list were disclosed. On Apr. 5, 1973, the assured issued a writ claiming an indemnity under the policy. On July 5, 1973, the insurers applied for (i) an order for ship's papers under R.S.C. Order 72, r. 10(1); and (ii) a stay of the action under R.S.C. Order 72, r. 10(2) pending compliance with the order for ship's papers. At the same time they stated that a plea of scuttling was going to be made.

Held, by the Court of Appeal, that an order for ship's papers should not be made automatically, and that no order would be made in the present case. Further, it was in the discretion of the Court whether to order a stay pending compliance with an order for ship's papers.

LORD DENNING, M.R. (at page 494)

The singular feature about an order for ship's papers is that it is an order on the plaintiff to give discovery of documents before the defendant delivers his defence. This feature should be retained. In scuttling cases it may still serve a useful purpose. When a shipowner claims on a policy for loss by perils of the sea, he will be anxious that the underwriters should admit his claim as soon as may be. He will, therefore, or at any rate should, produce all papers that are relevant to his claim, and, in addition, all other papers that the underwriters reasonably ask to see. If he does not do so, but instead goes ahead with his action, it will be open to the defendants to apply for an order for ship's papers before defence. But the order could not be made automatically. The Judge should see whether or not it is a proper case for it. For this purpose Counsel should put before the Judge the reasons for it. Counsel will not, of course, disclose any material which would be privileged or which it would be inadvisable to mention. But he should give such reasons as he can properly disclose without embarrassment or giving away too much of this client's case.

BUCKLEY, L.J. (at page 495)

An order for ship's papers is an order for discovery which is exceptional in at least two respects: first, it is not confined to documents which are or have been in the possession or control of the plaintiff, but extends or, as we were told, is treated by practitioners as extending to almost any document capable of throwing the smallest light on the possible fate of the ship, the production of which the plaintiff might be able to procure in whomsoever possession or control the document may be; and secondly, it is customarily made before delivery of defence. The genesis of this type of order was clearly the difficulty under which defendant insurers were in days when means of communication were very limited and it was consequently very hard for them to obtain reliable information about the relevant facts. Nowadays circumstances are very different. The telephone and the aeroplane have to a great extent contracted distances and abbreviated time. In these days the need for such discovery as is procured by means of an order for ship's papers seems to me to be much less than in the past. But there may well be cases in which the order will serve a useful purpose, and it should not be forgotten that in scuttling cases the physical evidence may be at the bottom of the sea and therefore inaccessible.

In my judgment it is the duty of a Judge, who is asked to make an order for ship's papers, to weigh the advantages which may result in the search for truth against the disadvantages of delay and expense involved in discovery of this kind. That delay and expense may be very substantial. If the Judge considers that the advantages outweigh the disadvantages, he will make an order for ship's papers; but otherwise, in my opinion, he should not, notwithstanding that the defendants indicate that they intend to plead scuttling. It goes without saying that the Judge should not make such an order if he has reason to suppose that it is being sought as a means of extorting a settlement.

Whether on an application for ship's papers Counsel should disclose to the Court the grounds on which a plea of scuttling is proposed to be put forward must, in my opinion, be a question for Counsel to decide. The circumstances of the case may be such that the Judge is unlikely to make an order for ship's papers without some indication of the kind of suspicions entertained by the defendants. In such a case Counsel may consider it desirable to tell the Court the nature of his client's suspicions. If he chooses to disclose any evidence that may be known to his client, that is a matter for him. If by the words "Counsel for the insurers should always give some sufficient indication to the Court of the justifiability of the plea before any question of a *prima facie* entitlement to an order for ship's papers can arise" the learned Judge meant something more than this, I venture to think that he went too far. It cannot, I think, be right to require Counsel to disclose his client's case at an interlocutory stage in the action and more particularly before pleadings are closed, but Counsel may very possibly feel able to indicate the nature of the defendants' belief or suspicions without making any undesirable disclosure and he may think that to do so will assist him in his application for an order for ship's papers. The Court should not, I think, readily suppose that an experienced and responsible Counsel would associate himself with an allegation of scuttling—a grave charge of fraud—without sufficient reason; but some indication of the basis of the allegation may well be necessary for deciding what kind of discovery of documents would fit the case.

PART VI

POLLUTION BY OIL

Federal Steam Navigation Co. Ltd. *v.* Department of Trade and Industry: The "Huntingdon"

[1974] 1 Lloyd's Rep. 520

Both the owner and the master of a vessel can be charged with an offence under the Prevention of Oil Pollution Act 1971, s. 1(1).

The *Huntingdon*, a British vessel registered in the United Kingdom, discharged oil into a prohibited area off Nova Scotia. The owner and the master were both charged with contravening the Oil in Navigable Waters Act 1955, s. 1(1), which stated: "If any oil to which this section applies is discharged from a British ship registered in the United Kingdom into a part of the sea which is a prohibited area, . . . the owner or master of the ship shall . . . be guilty of an offence".[1] They were convicted and appealed against conviction on the ground that the word "or" should be read disjunctively, and that there could only be a conviction of one or the other but not both.

Held, by the House of Lords, that the appeal would be dismissed. The word "or" must be read conjunctively, and both the owner and the master could be guilty of an offence under s. 1(1).

LORD SALMON (at page 532)

Section 1 deals with pollution of the sea in a prohibited area by oil from a British ship registered in the United Kingdom. Section 3 deals (amongst other things) with the pollution by oil of United Kingdom waters from any ship. Section 5 provides for regulations being made by the Minister requiring British ships registered in the United Kingdom to be fitted with certain equipment for the prevention or reduction of pollution of the sea by oil. These sections all create offences. If a ship pollutes the sea with oil under ss. 1 or 3 or puts to sea without the equipment prescribed by regulations made under s. 5, then the "owner or master of the vessel shall be guilty of an offence". These offences are absolute in the sense that they are committed without any *mens rea* being necessary, if the events postulated in the sections occur. Section 4 provides for

[1] Now Prevention of Oil Pollution Act 1971, s. 1(1).

certain special defences under ss. 1 and 3 which are available alike to the owner and the master.

If "or" in those sections is to be treated as disjunctive, it is, in my view, quite impossible to give the sections any intelligible meaning. The sections would be unintelligible and absurd for they would be providing that the owner or the master is guilty, but not both, without giving any indication to show which is guilty. If either or both were prosecuted, neither could, in any circumstances, be convicted. Each, to my mind, would have the unanswerable defence "It is true that on the facts which have been proved, one or other of us must be guilty but both of us cannot be guilty. Since the Act does not give any indication as to which of us is guilty, the prosecution has embarked upon the impossible task of attempting to prove beyond reasonable doubt that it is I who am guilty". The appellants seek to escape from this insuperable difficulty by arguing that the Act gives an option to the prosecutor to elect which of the two is guilty. This argument is, however, impossible to accept unless words can be read into the relevant sections which are not there. It would be necessary to insert after the words "the owner or master of the vessel" some such words as "at the option of the prosecutor". This might make the sections intelligible but they would remain absurd and also become otherwise objectionable. It is conceded that no offence has ever before been created, the existence of which depends upon the exercise of such an option or indeed of any option. It would be repugnant to our law that the question as to whether A or B is guilty of an offence should depend upon the whim of the prosecutor. It is only very rarely that words can be read into a statute, and then only if it is necessary to do so for the purpose of making the statute comply with the obvious intention of Parliament. There is no precedent for implying words into a statute in order to give it the bizarre meaning for which the appellants contend and which, in my view, Parliament cannot possibly have intended. On the other hand, there are ample precedents of the highest authority for reading the word "or" for "and" or substituting the word "and" for "or" when otherwise, as here, the statute would be unintelligible and absurd.

It has always been the invariable constitutional practice of Parliament to enact who shall be guilty of the offences which it creates. It would be a sad day for this country were Parliament to abdicate those functions by writing words into a statute giving a Minister, or anyone else, the power to choose who is to be guilty of a statutory offence.

Parliament has written no such words into the Act of 1955. The learned trial Judge and the Court of Appeal have not done so. The Courts have interpreted the language of the Act by giving it an intelligible and sensible meaning in accordance with authority. The niceties of grammar are no doubt of great importance. But there are things of even greater importance—as our Courts have always recognised.

My Lords, it would surely be a catastrophe if this House were to compel the Courts to read words into the statute which are not there in order to confer upon the Minister a power which he expressly disclaims and which would be offensive both to long established constitutional practice and the whole spirit of the common law. This is what, in my view, lends a real importance to this appeal which otherwise would turn solely on a narrow point of construction.

The fact that the words "owner or master", used disjunctively, make sense, and indeed if used conjunctively, would not make sense in a different context in other sections of the statute, does not seem to me to be significant of anything except of an indifferent standard of draftsmanship. Nor am I impressed by the argument on behalf of the appellants founded on s. 6 which provides that an offence shall not be punishable on summary conviction by a fine exceeding £1,000. It does not surprise me that if, in the events postulated in ss. 1, 3 and 5, the owner and the master is each, as I think, guilty of an offence, each should be liable to the maximum fine. This, of course, does not mean that the maximum fine would always be imposed.

I recognise that a prosecutor is sometimes in possession of evidence which, if accepted, shows that A and B are each guilty of an offence. He could prosecute them both but he is not bound necessarily to do so. He has a discretion which, in certain circumstances, he might properly exercise, to prosecute A and not B. This discretion is, however, fundamentally different from the power of deciding whether, given certain facts, the statute means that A and not B is guilty of an offence.

The Legislature rightly regarded pollution of the sea as one of the serious evils of modern times. That, in my view, is why it considered that the owner and the master should each, irrespective of *mens rea*, be guilty of an offence in the circumstances referred to in ss. 1, 3 and 5 of the Act. What I am quite certain Parliament could not have intended is to have provided that either the master or the owner should be guilty of an offence—but not both—without giving any clues as to which was to be guilty.

PART VII

ADMIRALTY JURISDICTION AND PRACTICE

The "Jupiter"

[1925] All E.R. Rep. 203

By s. 20(2)(a) of the Supreme Court Act 1981, the Admiralty jurisdiction of the High Court includes the jurisdiction to determine "any claim to the possession or ownership of a ship . . .". The Court can entertain an action for the possession of a foreign vessel, but may in its discretion refuse to do so.

The plaintiffs, a company incorporated in Russia before the Russian Revolution, were the owners of the S.S. *Jupiter*. All private property in shipping was abolished by Government decree in 1918. The plaintiffs moved their business to France. In 1924 an English company acting as agents for the Soviet Government purported to sell the vessel to the defendants, an Italian company. The plaintiffs brought an action *in rem* against the vessel claiming possession. The defendants applied for the writ to be set aside on the ground that the court had no jurisdiction.

Held, by the Court of Appeal, that the Court had jurisdiction to entertain the action for possession, even though the parties were foreigners.

ATKIN, L.J. (at page 207)

The first question is as to the jurisdiction of the Court to entertain this claim for possession by one foreigner against another foreigner in respect of a ship that is within the territorial jurisdiction. It appears to me now reasonably plain that there is jurisdiction in the Court to entertain such claim. I think there was jurisdiction before the Admiralty Court Act 1840, and, in my opinion, there is statutory jurisdiction by that Act.

The only question that is left is whether or not there is a discretion in the Court to decline to exercise jurisdiction in such cases, and, if so, whether that jurisdiction ought to be so exercised in this case. As to that, the law seems to me still to obtain that the Court, in such a case, has a discretion whether it will exercise its jurisdiction or not, and in cases where the parties both belonging to a foreign State have merely taken the occasion of the ship being temporarily here to get a question of title, which depends on the municipal laws of another country, determined by the Courts of this country, the Court may, in the exercise of its discretion, decline to do so. But, on the facts of this case, there seems to me to be no reason why the Court should not exercise its discretion and entertain the suit. The vessel has been in this country for a period of years, and the question arises in respect of her disposition by a contract entered into in this country by a limited company of this country—the Arcos Shipping Co. Ltd.—and, although questions may arise as to the right of title of the vendors to the defendants, yet it appears to me to be a case which can properly be tried in this country, and I see no reason for interfering with the discretion of the learned President in that respect.

The "Standard Austria S.H. 1964"

[1965] 2 Lloyd's Rep. 189

Although s. 20(7) of the Supreme Court Act 1981 states that the preceding provisions of the section apply in relation to "all ships or aircraft", this does not give the Queen's Bench Division (Admiralty Court) jurisdiction to determine a claim to the possession of an aircraft under s. 20(2)(a), which states that it has jurisdiction to determine a "claim to the possession of a ship".

The plaintiffs applied for a warrant of arrest to issue against a glider for which the defendants had not paid.

Held, by the Probate, Divorce and Admiralty Division, that it could not allow the arrest, for it had jurisdiction over aircraft only in relation to claims in the nature of salvage, towage and pilotage.

HEWSON, J. (at page 190)

In support of her argument [Counsel] has asked me to look at sub-s. 4 of s. 1 of the Administration of Justice Act 1956 [now s. 20(7) of the Supreme Court Act 1981], the material part of which is as follows:

> The preceding provisions of this section apply—
> (*a*) in relation to all ships or aircraft, whether British or not and whether registered or not and wherever the residence or domicile of their owners may be . . .

Now, the preceding provisions of this section define in considerable detail the Admiralty jurisdiction of this Court. They are put under a number of headings in s. 1(1) of the Act [now s. 20(2) of the Supreme Court Act 1981]. They run from (*a*) to (*s*). In all of those subsections the word "ship" is either mentioned or necessarily implied. In only three of those subsections does the word "aircraft" appear, namely, in (*j*), (*k*) and (*l*). These are respectively in relation to claims in the nature of salvage, towage and pilotage. In subsections (*k*) and (*l*) they are in relation to claims in the nature of towage and pilotage respectively in respect of a ship or an aircraft. The aircraft referred to in s. 1(4) [now s. 20(7) of the Supreme Court Act 1981] are, in my view, the aircraft which are referred to in s. 1(1)(*j*), (*k*) and (*l*) [now s. 20(2)(*j*), (*k*) and (*l*) of the Supreme Court Act 1981], to which I have just referred, and to them alone.

The "Acrux"

[1965] 1 Lloyd's Rep. 565

By s. 20(2)(c) of the Supreme Court Act 1981 the Admiralty jurisdiction of the High Court includes the determination of "any claim in respect of a mortgage or a charge on any ship or any share therein". The word "charge" means a charge in the nature of a mortgage and does not cover a charge or lien for wages.

An Italian corporation to whom by Italian law social insurance contributions in respect of seamen on board their vessels were payable by Italian shipowners, brought an action *in rem* against the proceeds of sale of the *Acrux*, which was registered in Italy, in respect of unpaid contributions. It was proved that under Italian law the plaintiffs had a right to arrest a vessel registered in Italy where such contributions were unpaid, and that contributions were part of the seamen's wages.

Held, by the Probate, Divorce and Admiralty Division, that the Court had no jurisdiction under s. 1(1)(*c*) of the Administration of Justice Act 1956 [now s. 20(2)(*c*) of the Supreme Court Act 1981] for the word "charge" meant a charge in the nature of a mortgage, and not a charge or lien for wages.

HEWSON, J. (at page 572)

Is this a charge upon the ship and has this Court jurisdiction over it, either under s. 1(1)(*c*) of the Administration of Justice Act 1956 [now s. 20(2)(*c*) of the Supreme Court Act 1981], or under s. 3(3) of the same Act [now s. 21(3) of the Supreme Court Act 1981]?

As to s. 1(1)(*c*) [now s. 20(2)(*c*) of the Supreme Court Act 1981]—I do not think I need read it—this particular subsection, together with sub-paras. (*a*) and (*b*) of the same subsection, relates solely, in my view, to a right in the property of a ship, and, as I held in *The St. Merriel*,[1] "charge" in (*c*) relates to a charge in the nature of a mortgage, and it would not, in my view, cover a charge or lien for wages.

As to s. 3(3), that was considered in *The St. Merriel*,[2] and there I found that "other charge" was meant to refer to something which, though not within the restricted definition of a maritime lien, was, nevertheless, not as wide as any claim arising in connection with the ship. In that case, the Court was dealing with the right of the holder of a possessory lien under English law and it was not necessary to look at foreign law. Obviously s. 3(3) does not refer to charges in the nature of a mortgage because they are already dealt with under s. 3(2). "Other charge", in my view, means any charge on a vessel given under the law of any nation to secure claims similar to those recognised by this Court as carrying a maritime lien such as wages, damage, salvage and bottomry. The categories of maritime lien as recognised by this Court cannot, in my view, be extended except by the Legislature.

---

[1] [1963] P. 247; [1963] 1 Lloyd's Rep. 63.
[2] *Supra*.

Section 3(3) is procedural and it only applies to cases within the jurisdiction of this Court, that is, the Admiralty jurisdiction as defined in s. 1 of the Administration of Justice Act 1956, or which, under foreign law, are equivalent or akin thereto, or come within such inherent or residual jurisdiction as lay in this Court before 1873. If s. 3(3) were not procedural, I should have expected to have found it not in s. 3 but in s. 1. This Court had no original jurisdiction to entertain claims *in rem* for insurance contributions, or anything like them, because they were not thought of.

United Africa Co. Ltd. *v.* Owners of m.v. "Tolten"

[1946] 2 All E.R. 372

By s. 20(2)(e) of the Supreme Court Act 1981 the Admiralty jurisdiction of the High Court includes jurisdiction to "hear and determine . . . any claim for damage done by a ship". This jurisdiction includes the right to hear a claim in rem *for damage done to foreign land.*

A British vessel caused damage to a wharf in Lagos, Nigeria. Her owners contended that the Probate, Divorce and Admiralty Division of the (English) High Court had no jurisdiction to hear the claim brought in respect of the damage, since it related to a trespass to foreign land, and the House of Lords had decided in *British South Africa Co.* v. *Companhia de Mocambique*[3] that the English Courts could not entertain such an action.

Held, by the Court of Appeal, that the Court had jurisdiction, for the claim was for the enforcement of a maritime lien by proceedings *in rem* and the rule in *British South Africa Co.* v. *Companhia de Mocambique*[4] did not apply.

COHEN, L.J. (at page 389)

Two alternative grounds for the decision in *British South Africa Co.* v. *Companhia de Mocambique*[5] have been suggested (1) that the Court will not make an order which it cannot make effective, and (2) that the comity of nations requires that our Courts shall not adjudicate in cases where the title to foreign land might be an issue. In my opinion, neither of these grounds precludes us from upholding the decision of BUCKNILL, L.J. On the facts of the present case it could not be said that a judgment if given would be ineffective, and if the Court is to refuse to exercise jurisdiction, it must, I think, be on the ground that to do so would be against the comity of nations. Can it be against the comity of nations that the Admiralty Court should entertain an action at the instance of a person claiming to be the owner of foreign land for damage done to that land by a ship? Such jurisdiction is based on the presence within

---

[3] [1983] A.C. 602.
[4] *Supra.*
[5] *Supra.*

the jurisdiction of the offending ship. The accident (subject to an exception to which I will refer later) creates a right of property known as a maritime lien in favour of the owners of the property, be it a ship as in *The Bold Buccleugh*[6] or a wharf in England as in *The Veritas*.[7] Maritime liens are recognised in the legal systems of most countries, and I can see nothing inconsistent with the comity of nations in the Admiralty Division of this Court holding that a maritime lien arises in favour of the owner of land situate outside the jurisdiction.

Counsel for the appellants says that such a conclusion is inconsistent with the principle of the decision of this Court in *The Tervaete*,[8] which, he says, shows that there can be no maritime lien in favour of the owner of land situate out of the jurisdiction. In that case it was held that damage occasioned by collision with a foreign State-owned vessel does not impose a maritime lien upon the vessel, and if the vessel be subsequently sold into private ownership, she is not then liable to arrest in an action *in rem*. The basis of that decision seems to me to be that the recognition of a maritime lien would affect the property of a foreign sovereign: see *per* BANKES, L.J.[9] and *per* SCRUTTON, L.J.[10] I can see nothing in that decision to justify us in holding that a lien cannot be created in favour of the owner of foreign land by the action of a ship not the property of a foreign sovereign.

On the whole I think the comity of nations requires that the Admiralty Division of this Court should recognise and enforce a maritime lien in favour of the owner of land situate abroad, for if not and the ship were arrested here, the owner of the foreign land might find himself postponed to the owner of an English ship injured in the same accident or to claims enforceable *in rem* but not protected by a maritime lien.

Corps and Corps *v.* The "Queen of the South"

[1968] 1 Lloyd's Rep. 182

By s. 20(2)(h) of the Supreme Court Act 1981, the Admiralty jurisdiction of the High Court includes the determination of "any claim arising out of any agreement relating to . . . the use or hire of a ship".

The plaintiffs were watermen, who claimed £290 3*s*. 0*d*. for services rendered to the defendants' paddle steamer in that they had moored and unmoored her through the use of the plaintiffs' motor boats.

Held, by the Probate, Divorce and Admiralty Division, that the Court had

---

6 (1851) 7 Moo. P.C. 267.
7 [1900–3] All E.R. Rep. 501. See p. 15, *ante*.
8 [1922] P. 259.
9 *Ibid.*, at p. 266.
10 *Ibid.*, at p. 272.

jurisdiction under s. (1)(*h*) of the Administration of Justice Act 1956 [now s. 20(2)(*h*) of the Supreme Court Act 1981] to entertain the claim.

BRANDON, J. (at page 188)

I will deal with para (*h*) first. Counsel for the plaintiffs argued that the agreement between the plaintiffs and the ship's managers, under which the services claimed for were rendered, was "an agreement relating to the use or hire of a ship" within the meaning of the paragraph. He said that the plaintiffs' services were rendered by the use of their motor boats suitably manned for the work to be done; that by s. 8(1) of the Act[11] the expression "ship" included a motor boat; and by s. 1 of the Interpretation Act 1889,[12] the singular included the plural. Therefore, he said, the agreement came within the paragraph.

Counsel for the interveners, in disputing these arguments, sought to draw a distinction between an agreement relating to the use of a ship, and an agreement relating to the rendering of services in the course of which a ship was used. He said that the former was within para. (*h*), but the latter was not. He further said that the agreement in the present case was in the second category.

I did not think that his argument based on this distinction was convincing. I can see that there might be an agreement for services, in the course of which there was only some incidental and minor use of a ship, which it might be inappropriate to describe as an agreement relating to the use of a ship. In the present case, however, it seems to me clear, on the written and oral evidence before me, that the whole of the services rendered by the plaintiffs were based on the use of motor boats owned and operated by them. It is true that in some cases the men engaged in mooring and unmooring did their work on a quay or on a buoy. But they were landed on the quay or on the buoy from a motor boat, and taken off again by the same means.

In these circumstances I have come to the conclusion that the argument of Counsel for the plaintiffs that the claim comes within para. (*h*) is well founded, and I hold that the Court has jurisdiction to entertain it on that ground.

The "Conoco Britannia": J. H. Pigott & Son Ltd. *v.* Owners of the ships "Conoco Britannia", "Conoco Espana" and "Conoco Libya"

[1972] 2 All E.R. 238

By s. 20(2)(h) of the Supreme Court Act 1981 the Admiralty jurisdiction of the High Court includes jurisdiction to determine "any claim arising out of any

[11] Now Supreme Court Act 1981, s. 24(1).
[12] Now Interpretation Act 1978, s. 6.

agreement relating to the carriage of goods in a ship or to the use or hire of a ship". These words are wide enough to cover damage sustained by a tug supplied under a towage contract.

The plaintiffs supplied the defendant owners of the *Conoco Arrow* with the tug *Hullman* under a towage contract under which the defendants agreed to indemnify the plaintiffs against any loss of or damage to the tug. The tug was sunk in a collision with the *Conoco Arrow*. The tug owners brought an action *in rem* against three other vessels owned by the defendants. The defendants applied for the writ to be set aside on the ground that the Court had no jurisdiction *in rem* under the Administration of Justice Act 1956, s. 3(4) [now s. 21(4) of the Supreme Court Act 1981], since the writ disclosed no claim under s. 1(1)(*h*) [now s. 20(2)(*h*) of the Supreme Court Act 1981].

Held, by the Queen's Bench Division (Admiralty Court) that the Court had jurisdiction because the words of s. 1(1)(*h*) were wide enough to cover a towage contract.

BRANDON, J. (at page 242)

I consider, first, the question whether the claims endorsed on the amended writ come within any of the paragraphs of s. 1(1) which I have cited. For the plaintiffs it was argued that all three claims came within para. (*h*). It was said that they were claims arising out of an agreement relating to the use or hire of a ship, namely, the tug *Hullman*. For the defendants it was argued that the words "relating . . . to the use or hire of a ship" should be construed *ejusdem generis* with the preceding words in para (*h*), namely, "relating to the carriage of goods in a ship", and should accordingly be given a narrow construction which would not cover the case of a towage contract under which a tug is hired to attend on and assist a ship. I am of the opinion that there is no reason for giving a restricted meaning to the words "relating to the use or hire of a ship". It seems to me that the words in their ordinary and natural meaning are amply wide enough to cover the case of the hire of a tug under a towage contract, and, even if this Act stood alone without any history behind it, I should be of that opinion. The point is, however, to my mind, put always beyond doubt when one does consider the history of the jurisdiction in this matter. The jurisdiction, so far as I understand it, was first conferred by the Administration of Justice Act 1920 and then re-conferred by the Supreme Court of Judicature (Consolidation) Act 1925. And, although the arrangement of the words is different in the relevant provisions of those Acts, the substance of the jurisdiction conferred seems to me to be very much the same.

By s. 22(1)(*a*) of the 1925 Act, the Court was given jurisdiction in relation to Admiralty matters to hear and determine any of the following questions or claims:

> . . . (xii) Any claim—(1) arising out of an agreement relating to the use or hire of a ship; or (2) relating to the carriage of goods in a ship; or (3) in tort in respect of goods carried in a ship . . .

and then there is a qualification with regard to the domicil of the shipowner that is not relevant for this purpose. Now, when one looks at that provision, it is impossible, as Counsel for the defendants himself conceded, to argue that item (1) should be construed as *ejusdem generis* with item (2) and it seems to me that, in that Act at any rate, it would be almost impossible to argue that a restricted meaning should be given to the expression "agreement relating to the use or hire of a ship". It was suggested that, by rearranging the wording in the 1956 Act, Parliament was cutting down the jurisdiction. I cannot accept that argument.

I have, therefore, no hesitation in holding that the first ground relied on by Counsel for the defendants is bad.

The "Goring"

[1986] 1 Lloyd's Rep. 129

By s. 20(2)(j) of the Supreme Court Act 1981 the Admiralty jurisdiction of the High Court includes jurisdiction to determine "any claim in the nature of salvage". The Court has jurisdiction even though the salvage takes place in non-tidal waters.

Salvage services were rendered by a ferry boat to the passenger vessel *Goring* on the River Thames near Reading. When a salvage award was claimed the owners of the vessel applied for the writ to be set aside on the ground that the Court had no jurisdiction under the Supreme Court Act 1981, s. 20(2)(*j*) to entertain the claim because the services had been rendered in non-tidal waters.

Held, by the Queen's Bench Division (Admiralty court), that the application would be dismissed for the Court had jurisdiction under that subsection.

SHEEN, J. (at page 127)

The Admiralty jurisdiction of the High Court is prescribed by s. 20 of the Supreme Court Act 1981. That jurisdiction can be invoked by a writ *in rem* in respect of salvage services occurring anywhere in the world provided that a writ *in rem* can be served upon a ship liable to pay salvage. I say "a ship" and not "the ship" because in the case of a claim in the nature of salvage an action *in rem* may be brought in the High Court against a "sister ship" by virtue of s. 21(4) of that Act.

The world-wide jurisdiction which may thus be exercised by this Court and also by Admiralty Courts in other parts of the world, within whose jurisdiction a British ship may be served with a writ *in rem* and arrested, makes it important that so far as possible that jurisdiction be exercised upon the same principles.

I have no doubt that it was with this aim in mind that on Sept. 23, 1910, there was signed at Brussels a Convention for the unification of certain rules of law respecting assistance and salvage at sea. Great Britain was a signatory of that Convention and ratified the Convention of Feb. 1, 1913. Article 1 of that Convention provides:—

> Assistance and salvage of sea-going vessels in danger, of any things on board, of freight and passage money, and also services of the same nature rendered by sea going vessels to vessels of inland navigation or vice versa, are subject to the following provisions, without any distinction being drawn between these two kinds of service (viz., assistance and salvage), and in whatever waters the services have been rendered.

It was recognised that assistance to vessels of inland navigation in whatever waters the services have been rendered may be salvage services. It would have been anomalous if that had not been recognised. My reason for saying that can best be given by a few examples, taken at random, of places at which services may be rendered to ships in danger in non-tidal waters. There spring to mind the Great Lakes of North America, the waters of which can be very rough, the rivers Mississippi and Amazon many miles above that part of the river in which the tide ebbs and flows, and the very large docks in Rotterdam or Antwerp and other major ports.

. . . The vast majority of salvage services are rendered at sea. But . . . many Courts have made salvage awards for voluntary services rendered to ships in harbours and in docks and any navigable waters. I can see no justification for an artificial rule which would differentiate between services rendered to a ship in tidal waters and identical services rendered to a ship in non-tidal waters. To take a very simple illustration, if a ship at anchor in tidal waters is in danger by reason of a fire and that fire is extinguished by jets of water from a tug, it could not be disputed that the tug-owners would have a valid claim for a salvage reward. Is it to be said that no such reward would be made for identical services if the ship were in non-tidal waters of a river or dock? In my judgment—the answer must be "No".

If a ship or her cargo is in danger in non-tidal waters it is highly desirable as a matter of public policy that other ships should be encouraged to go to their assistance without hesitation. The fact that waters are non-tidal may greatly affect the degree of danger from which a ship is salved. But that goes to the amount of the salvage reward and not to the question whether the services attract any reward.

The "Fairport" (No. 5)

[1967] 2 Lloyd's Rep. 162

By s. 20(2)(m) of the Supreme Court Act 1981, the Admiralty jurisdiction of the High Court includes the determination of "any claim in respect of goods supplied to a ship for her operation or maintenance". Moneys provided for necessaries are deemed to be "necessaries" for this purpose.

The plaintiffs were ships' chandlers, who made two advances of £100 each to the vessel for the payment of wages. They now claimed repayment.

Held, by the Probate, Divorce and Admiralty Division, that the Court had jurisdiction under s. 1(1)(*m*) of the Administration of Justice Act 1956 [now s. 20(2)(*m*) of the Supreme Court Act 1981] to entertain the action.

BRANDON, J. (at page 163)

In my judgment, the claims described in s. 1(1)(*m*) of the Administration of Justice Act 1956, are certainly no narrower than the claims which were formerly described as claims for necessaries in the Supreme Court of Judicature (Consolidation) Act 1925, and since there is authority that the word "necessaries" covers payments made by way of advances to enable necessaries to be purchased, then I consider that a similar construction should be given to sub-para. (*m*).

The "D'Vora"

[1952] 2 Lloyd's Rep. 404

By s. 20(2)(n) of the Supreme Court Act 1981, the Admiralty jurisdiction of the High Court includes jurisdiction to determine "any claim in respect of the construction, repair or equipment of a ship". The word "equipment" does not include the supply of fuel oil.

The plaintiffs supplied fuel oil to a vessel at Haifa, and issued a writ claiming the price.

Held, by the Probate, Divorce and Admiralty Division, that the Court had no jurisdiction to entertain the action because the claim was not one in respect of the "equipment" of a ship.

WILLMER, J. (at page 405)

In my judgment, there is an important difference between "equip" and "supply", "supply" being a word which is appropriate for use in connection with consumable stores, such as fuel oil whereas "equip", to my mind, connotes something of a more permanent nature than consumable stores. I can well understand that anchors, cables, hawsers, sails, ropes, and such things, may be said to be part of a ship's equipment, and that, none the less, although they may have to be renewed from time to time; but such things as fuel oil, coal, boiler water and food—consumable stores—seem to me to be in quite a different category. [Counsel] conceded that he can find no authority in support of his proposition that the word "equipment" is wide enough to cover such supplies, or that the word "equipping" is wide enough to cover the supplying of consumable stores such as fuel oil.

I cannot help reflecting on what consequences might follow from a decision of mine that the word "equipment" is wide enough to cover the supply of consumable stores. If I were to lay that down as a matter of law in this context, I can well image that it might have wide repercussions in quite different fields of the law. Had it been the intention of the Legislature that the supply of consumable stores should be included in the jurisdiction conferred under para. (x) of s. 22(1)(a) of the Act, it would have been the easiest possible thing for the draftsman to say so in unambiguous terms; but, as I have already pointed out, he has not done so. Unless consumable stores can be included under the word "equipping", they are not within the ambit of para. (x) of s. 22(1)(a) of the Act.[13]

The "St. Merriel"

[1963] 1 All E.R. 537

By s. 21(3) of the Supreme Court Act 1981 the Admiralty jurisdiction may be invoked by an action in rem *"in any case in which there is a maritime lien or other charge on any ship". A ship repairer's possessory lien is not an "other charge".*

The motor vessel *St. Merriel*, which was owned by the defendants, was chartered to British Car Carriers, Ltd., under a charter-party by demise. Various repairs were carried out to the vessel by the plaintiffs, who were ship repairers. The plaintiffs brought an action *in rem* against the defendants claiming the cost of the owners' repairs. The defendants applied for the writ to be set aside on the ground that the plaintiffs could not proceed by an action *in rem*.

Held, by the Probate, Divorce and Admiralty Division, that the writ would be set aside for although the plaintiffs had a possessory lien on the vessel by reason of the repairs, this did not amount to an "other charge" within the meaning of the Administration of Justice Act 1956, s. 3(3) [now s. 21(3) of the Supreme Court Act 1981].

HEWSON, J. (at page 541)

There is no doubt that a maritime lien is a charge upon a ship and if, argues Counsel for the plaintiffs, "other charge" in sub-s. (3) does not include such a tie or burden as is imposed by a possessory lien, then what does it mean? Counsel for the defendants has gone far to assist me in that matter. He has referred me to three instances in the Merchant Shipping Acts, to which I must now refer. The first one is s. 513(2) of the Merchant Shipping Act 1894 which reads as follows:

> Any damage sustained by an owner or occupier in consequence of the exercise of the rights given by this section shall be a charge on the vessel, cargo, or articles in respect of or by which the damage is occasioned, and the amount payable in respect of the

[13] I.e., the Supreme Court of Judicature (Consolidation) Act 1925, which was a predecessor of the Supreme Court Act 1981.

> damage shall, in case of dispute, be determined and shall, in default of payment, be recoverable in the same manner as the amount of salvage is under this Part of this Act determined or recoverable.

There are various ways in which charges may be recovered under the Merchant Shipping Act 1894 but ultimately, if the amount exceeds £200, the claimant may proceed by arrest and ultimate sale of the property. That seems to me to be giving to the owner of land in certain circumstances at least the same rights as the holder of a lien. I have been referred also to s. 35(2) of the Merchant Shipping Act 1906, which deals with the recovery of expenses from any owner, that is, expenses attendant on the illness, hurt or injury of a seaman. I quote sub-s. (2):

> If the expenses are not so repaid, the amount thereof shall with costs be a charge upon the ship, and be recoverable from the master or from the owner of the ship for the time being [and so on] either by ordinary process of law or in the Court and in the manner in which wages may be recovered by seamen.

A seaman has, of course, a maritime lien for his wages. Section 42(1) and (2) of the Act of 1906 also provide for the recovery of expenses of relief of distressed seamen. "Those expenses", so the section provides, "(1) . . . shall be a charge upon the ship", recoverable "(2) . . . either by ordinary process of law or in the court and manner in which wages may be recovered by seamen".

It will be seen, therefore, that, although "charge" is not defined in the Administration of Justice Act 1956 [now the Supreme Court Act 1981], there exist in shipping statutes the very words "a charge upon the ship". In the absence of any direct words by the Legislature which enlarge the meaning of "other charge", I am not disposed to extend its meaning beyond the words which I find in the Merchant Shipping Acts to which I have been referred. Though I have much sympathy with the argument put forward so powerfully by Counsel for the plaintiffs, I am not satisfied that the holder of a possessory lien has been put by this statute into such a position that his rights and his remedies amount to a charge on the ship for the amount claimed. They certainly amount to an inconvenience, but, as I say, in the absence of express words such as "other charge or right to possess by the holder of a possessory lien", or some such words, I am not disposed to extend the meaning further than I have indicated. "Other charge" seems to me to have some meaning based on statutes dealing with merchant shipping.

The "St. Elefterio": Schwarz & Co. (Grain) Ltd. *v.* "St. Elefterio" ex "Arion" (Owners)

[1957] 2 All E.R. 374

By s. 21(4) of the Supreme Court Act 1981 there is a right to arrest a ship in respect of which the cause of action is alleged to have arisen or another ship in the same ownership. The right can be asserted in rem *without it being first established that there is a cause of action* in personam *sustainable in law.*

The owners of a cargo, which had been carried on the *St. Elefterio*, caused a warrant to be issued for her arrest on the ground that the cargo had been damaged. Her owners moved to set aside the warrant of arrest on the ground that the Court had no jurisdiction under s. 3(4) of the Administration of Justice Act 1956 [now s. 21(4) of the Supreme Court Act 1981] to entertain the action *in rem*, since the cargo owners had not first established that they had a cause of action *in personam* sustainable in law.

Held, by the Probate, Divorce and Admiralty Division, that the Court had jurisdiction to entertain the action, and the warrant of arrest would not be set aside.

WILLMER, J. (at page 376)

The defendants' argument is founded on the proposition that s. 3(4) of the Act of 1956 [now s. 21(4) of the Supreme Court Act 1981] introduces a new restriction on the right to proceed *in rem*, and that a plaintiff cannot arrest a ship under that subsection unless he can prove at the outset that he has a cause of action sustainable in law. In my judgment that proposition rests on a misconception of the purpose and meaning of s. 3(4). As it appears to me, that subsection, so far from being a restrictive provision, is a subsection introduced for the purpose of enlarging the Admiralty jurisdiction of the Court. As I view it, its purpose is to confer for the first time in England the right to arrest either the ship in respect of which the cause of action is alleged to have arisen or any other ship in the same ownership. That is an entirely new right so far as the law of England is concerned, although it previously existed in other countries including Scotland. The reason for conferring that right now is for the purpose of bringing this country into line with other countries as a result of an international convention. In my judgment the purpose of the words relied on by Counsel for the defendants, that is to say the words, "the person who would be liable on the claim in an action *in personam*", is to identify the person or persons whose ship or ships may be arrested in relation to this new right (if I may so express it) of arresting a sister ship. The words used, it will be observed, are "the person who would be liable" not "the person who is liable", and it seems to me, bearing in mind the purpose of the Act, that the natural construction of those quite simple words is, "the person who would be liable on the assumption that the action succeeds". This action might or might not succeed if it were brought *in personam*. That would depend on the view which the Court ultimately took of the various contentions raised by Counsel for the defendants. But clearly, if the action did succeed, the person or persons who would be liable would be the owner or owners of the steamship *St. Elefterio*. In such circumstances, in the absence of any suggestion that the action is frivolous or vexatious, I am satisfied that the plaintiffs are entitled to bring it and to have it tried, and that, whether or not their claim turns out to be a good one, they are entitled to assert that claim by proceeding *in rem*.

The "Banco": Owners of the motor vessel "Monte Ulia" *v.* Owners of the ships "Banco" and others

[1971] 1 All E.R. 524

By s. 21(4) of the Supreme Court Act 1981 the Admiralty jurisdiction can be invoked by an action in rem *against a ship or against any other ship beneficially owned by the same person. But this does not mean that a plaintiff can arrest more than one vessel belonging to the defendant.*

The plaintiff owners of the *Monte Ulia* which had collided with a jetty claimed that the collision was due to the negligent navigation of the defendants' vessel *Banco*. The plaintiffs served a writ and warrant of arrest on six other ships owned by the defendants. The defendants applied for the service of the writ and warrants of arrest to be set aside except in the case of the *Banco*.

Held, by the Court of Appeal, that the application would be granted because, by reason of the Administration of Justice Act 1956, s. 3(4) [now s.21(4) of the Supreme Court Act 1981] the plaintiffs were entitled to arrest one vessel only.

LORD DENNING, M.R. (at page 532)

In 1952 there was an international convention[14] held at Brussels. It was held because of the different rules of law of different countries about the arrest of sea-going ships. Some countries, like England, did not permit the arrest of any ship except the offending ship herself; whereas many continental countries permitted the arrest, not only of the offending ship, but also of any other ship belonging to the same owner. In the result a middle way was found. It was agreed that *one* ship might be arrested, but only *one*. It might *either* be the offending ship herself *or* any other ship belonging to the same owner; but not more. This was an advantage to plaintiffs in England because it often happened previously that, after a collision, the offending ship sank or did not come to these shores. So there was nothing to arrest. Under the convention the plaintiff could arrest any other ship belonging to the same owner whenever it happened to come to England.

I need not set out all the articles of the convention. I need only set out those which are particularly apposite.

Article 1(1) defines a Martime Claim. It includes "damage caused by a ship either in collision or otherwise". Then: "1(2) 'Arrest' means the detention of a ship by judicial process to secure a maritime claim, but does not include the seizure of a ship in execution or satisfaction of a judgment". Article 3 provides:

(1) . . . a claimant may arrest *either* the particular ship in respect of which the maritime claim arose, *or* any other ship which is owned by the person who was, at the time when the maritime claim arose, the owner of the particular ship . . .

(2) Ships shall be deemed to be in the same ownership when all the shares therein are owned by the same person or persons.

---

[14] International Convention relating to the Arrest of Sea-going Ships (Cmd. 8954).

> (3) . . . if a ship has been arrested in any one of such jurisdictions, or bail or other security has been given in such jurisdiction . . . *any subsequent arrest of the ship or of any ship in the same ownership* by the same claimant for the same maritime claim *shall be set aside*, and the ship released . . .

That convention makes it clear that only *one* ship of the same owner may be arrested. It has been ratified by the United Kingdom, Belgium, France, Greece, Portugal, Spain, Egypt and some others. But not, apparently, by the United States, the Netherlands, Norway, Sweden, Japan and others. So it is not comprehensive. But, nevertheless, it does represent a considerable body of agreement. At any rate, Parliament in this country in 1956 did pass an Act to give effect to the convention. It is the statute which we have to construe. It is the Administration of Justice Act 1956. Section 3(3) [now s. 21(3) of the Supreme Court Act 1981] states that, in any case in which there is a maritime lien on any ship for the amount claimed, the Admiralty jurisdiction may be invoked by an action *in rem* against *that* ship.

Section 3(4) [now s. 21(4) of the Supreme Court Act 1981] is the important one for our purpose. It provides, so far as material, that in the case of any claim (*inter alia*) for damage done by a ship, the Admiralty jurisdiction:

> . . . may (whether the claim gives rise to a maritime lien on the ship or not) be invoked by an action *in rem* against—(*a*) that ship, if at the time when the action is brought it is beneficially owned as respects all the shares therein by that person; or (*b*) any other ship which, at the time the action is brought, is beneficially owned as aforesaid.

The important word in that subsection is the word "or". It is used to express an alternative as in the phrase "one *or* the other". It means that the Admiralty jurisdiction *in rem* may be invoked *either* against the offending ship *or* against any other ship in the same ownership, but not against both. This is the natural meaning of the word "or" in this context. It is the meaning which carries into effect the international convention. It is the meaning which on high authority we ought to give to it. In *Morgan* v. *Thomas*[15] SIR GEORGE JESSEL, M.R., said: "You will find it said in some cases that 'or' means 'and'; but 'or' never does mean 'and'; unless there is a context which shews that it is used for 'and' by mistake". So also in *Re Diplock, Wintle* v. *Diplock*,[16] SIR WILFRID GREENE, M.R., said: "The word 'or' is *prima facie*, and in the absence of some restraining context, to be read as disjunctive . . ."

Shortly after the Act was passed, WILLMER, J., in *The St Elefterio*,[17] said that the purpose of the Act is to confer: ". . . the right to arrest *either* the ship in respect of which the cause of action is alleged to have arisen *or* any other ship in the same ownership."

That is clearly right. There is no doubt about it. I would add that the word

---

[15] (1822) 9 Q.B.D. 643, at pp. 645, 646.
[16] [1941] 1 All E.R. 193, at p. 200; [1941] Ch. 253, at p. 260.
[17] [1957] 2 All E.R. 374, at p. 377; [1957] P. 179, at p. 185.

"ship" in the phrase "any other ship", means "ship" and not "ships". Although the Interpretation Act 1889 states that words in the singular include the plural, that does not apply when the contrary intention appears. The contrary intention does appear here. The jurisdiction may be invoked against *either* the offending ship *or* any other ship in the same ownership, but not more than one.

The "Prins Bernhard"

[1963] 2 Lloyd's Rep. 236

By Order 75, r. 11(1) of the Rules of the Supreme Court service of a warrant of arrest or writ in an action in rem *against a ship, freight or cargo must be effected by "(a) affixing the warrant or writ for a short time on any mast of the ship, or on the outside of any suitable part of the ship's superstructure, and (b) on removing the warrant or writ, leaving a copy of the [warrant] affixed in its place or a copy of the [writ] on a sheltered, conspicuous part of the ship".*

A vessel arrived in the River Thames. On the same day her master was shown the writ and given a carbon copy of it.

Held, by the Probate, Divorce and Admiralty Division, that the service of the writ must be set aside, for the degree of irregularity in the service could not be overlooked.

HEWSON, J. (at page 247)

This method prescribed by Order 9, r. 12,[18] of giving notice to all interested parties is a rule of the Court. It has been established firmly by many, many years of usage. It may not be a perfect way of informing all interested parties that an action *in rem* is laid against the ship; but no other method has yet been suggested or devised. As I say, this method is based on many, many years' experience and is well known throughout the maritime countries of the world. It is a method which is based upon experience for the protection of all interested parties. It seems to me that in the circumstances of this case it would be an undue departure from the practice to save the writ, so far as it is addressed to the owner, and start anew with the other parties interested by giving to them public notice of the past service of the writ. It seems to me that is too great a departure from the recognised and long-established practice.

---

[18] Now R.S.C. Order 75, r. 11.

The "Beaverford"

[1960] 2 Lloyd's Rep. 216

By Order 75, r. 18(1) of the Rules of the Supreme Court: "In an action to enforce a claim for damage the plaintiff must lodge in the Registry a document [called] a Preliminary Act". The words of the Order do not restrict the filing of Preliminary Acts to vessels, provided there is a collision between two vessels.

A collision occurred between the plaintiffs' barge and a steamship belonging to the first defendants in a cutting in the London Docks. The second defendants were the Port of London Authority and were concerned with the movement of vessels.

Held, by the Probate, Divorce and Admiralty Division, that the Court could order the second defendants to file a Preliminary Act, for their employee had been directing or taking an active part in the movement of one or other of the colliding vessels.

HEWSON, J. (at page 219)

I know of no case where preliminary acts have been ordered in respect of parties other than vessels, but the fact that there is no reported case does not, in my opinion, bind me to restrict the application of preliminary acts to vessels in some way or another interested in or connected with the collision. The words of Order 19, r. 28(1)[19] are plain: "In actions in any Division for damage by collision between vessels, unless the Court or a Judge otherwise orders . . ." the plaintiff and the defendant shall file preliminary acts. I feel in no way constrained by those words to restrict the filing of preliminary acts to vessels, provided there is a collision between two vessels.

The matter is then left as one of discretion of the Court, and in exercising discretion the Court must be informed fully enough to weigh up the contentions of the parties and the position in which each party was at the material time in order to observe those facts which go to the making up of a preliminary act. [Counsel] has strongly pressed upon me that one of the main questions in the preliminary act is: "What measures were taken, and when, to avoid the collision". In this case, so far as I am aware, we have the second defendants, the Port of London Authority, with employees actively engaged at the time in both the movement of the barge and the direction of the ship. I have in mind that for, I think, over a hundred years now it has been the practice in this Division for vessels in collision to file preliminary acts so that there may be on record admissions binding on the parties, but not upon the Court, which are set down at the earliest possible moment after the collision. It is a practice which should not be departed from except in very exceptional circumstances.

I have already referred to the particular and peculiar facts of this case. It seems to me that, when you have a port official directing or taking an active part in the movement of one or other of the vessels which came into collision,

[19] Now R.S.C. Order 75, r. 18.

a preliminary act should be filed by the colliding vessels and should also be filed by that directing authority.

The "Merdeka"

[1982] 1 Lloyd's Rep. 401

Where a person breaks the arrest of a vessel, proceedings for contempt of Court may be instituted against him.

The *Merdeka* was arrested at Milford Haven on a claim by the crew for unpaid wages. The next day the master, who knew that she had been arrested, broke the arrest and took her out of the jurisdiction.

Held, by the Queen's Bench Division (Admiralty Court), that he was guilty of a contempt of Court and would be fined £350.

SHEEN, J. (at page 403)

Captain Verhey is 28 years old and he is the owner of this small ship. It was his first command. He is a man who comes from a seafaring family. His grandfather was master of a ship; his father and mother lived on a ship and he grew up on one. His livelihood has always been earned through working in ships in a number of different capacities, both in the engineroom and on deck, and he has recently obtained a certificate which enabled him to command coastal vessels. As I say, he is the owner of *Merdeka*. He tells me, and I have no reasons to doubt it, that earlier this year he was not making a great profit out of the vessel. He employed these four Ghanaian seamen at an agreed wage and paid certain bonuses. His ship was arrested once by cargo claimants and then the arrest was lifted. He then found on the following day that his ship was arrested again on a claim by these four seamen for over £10,000 unpaid wages. He was greatly distressed by that. I think it would be wrong for me to make any comment on the size of the claim because it may be dealt with in another jurisdiction. There is no doubt that he became somewhat inflamed and, as [Counsel] has said on his behalf, not really himself because of the distress which he felt.

That may explain, but it does not excuse, his very foolish conduct. He broke the arrest and sailed in the circumstances which I have recounted. It was made easier for him to do so by what appears to me to be a complete dereliction of duty by two watchmen, namely A. D. Ayers and his son, L. A. Ayers. I have not heard their oral evidence; I have read their affidavits. But, having been told to keep a watch on the vessel—and they only had to keep a close watch for two hours—they thought that looking out once every 20 minutes was adequate. Clearly it was not. As I have said, not long after Captain Verhey sailed he realised the foolishness of his action and it is to his credit that he has come back to this country voluntarily, not in the course of trading but at his own expense. He has come back to this Court to face these proceedings and he has apologised.

It must not be thought that this Court will not commit a master to prison. In a proper case the Court will certainly do so. Were it not for the extenuating circumstances which I have outlined, this case is one in which I might well have decided to make a committal order because it was a flagrant and deliberate contempt. I regard it as important that the Court should be moved on behalf of the Admiralty Marshal whenever the orders of the Court are not obeyed.

Proceedings of this nature are necessary in order to impress on others the consequences of flouting the orders of this Court. Having decided that I can properly deal with this case by imposing a fine, the question arises as to how much that fine should be. I must make my sense of the seriousness of the offence, but I take into account three matters: firstly, Captain Verhey's contrition, which I believe to be genuine; secondly, that he has incurred expenses himself in instructing solicitors and Counsel (and in the weeks ahead he may think that that was money well spent because the case has been extremely attractively presented on his behalf); and thirdly, that he must pay the costs of the Treasury Solicitor, which I assess in the sum of £2000. For these reasons, and bearing in mind the other expenses which I have already mentioned, I think that justice can be done in this case by imposing a fine of £350.

The "Silia"

[1981] 2 Lloyd's Rep. 534

In the contest of an action in rem *the word "ship" includes all property aboard her except that which is owned by someone other than the shipowner.*

An order was made for the vessel *Silia* to be sold. She had a quantity of fuel oil on board. A question arose as to whether the proceeds of sale of the oil were part of the *res* and as such available to the judgment creditors *in rem* only.

Held, by the Queen's Bench Division (Admiralty Court), that the word "ship" in an action *in rem* included all property aboard her other than that which was owned by someone other than the shipowner. The proceeds of sale of the oil were available for distribution among the judgment creditors *in rem* only and not among all creditors generally.

SHEEN, J. (at page 537)

I have no doubt that in the context of an action *in rem* the word "ship" includes all property aboard the ship other than that which is owned by someone other than the owner of the ship. I will set out the reasons which have led me to this conclusion.

If one goes back to the days before ships were driven by power derived from coal or oil, a warrant served on a ship covered everything that belonged to it as part of its equipment even to sails and rigging which are detached from it. (See *The Alexander.*[20]) The personal property of the captain and crew were exempt. For many years before the [Administration of Justice Act 1956] was enacted it was the practice of the Admiralty Court to treat bunkers as part of the ship, unless they were shown to be the property of charterers. If Parliament intended that an action *in rem* should be brought against the hull and machinery, and not against oil in the tanks, Parliament would have used language which made that clear. The language of the 1956 Act suggests that for this purpose no definition of "ship" was needed, and that the practice prevailing immediately before the 1956 Act should continue. The advantage of an Admiralty action *in rem* is that it enables the plaintiff to detain property of the shipowner which has come within the territorial jurisdiction of the Court in order to secure a maritime claim. That advantage would be reduced if part of the property of the shipowner were exempt from attachment. In the majority of cases the threat of arrest of a ship persuades the shipowner to give security to meet a claim. If a ship has been arrested, security is frequently given in order that the ship will be released. Usually it is only when the shipowner is unable to pay his debts that it becomes necessary to sell the ship. One asks why in those circumstances any property of the shipowner which is on board for the prosecution of the maritime adventure should be exempt from arrest, and not made available to pay the creditors. It would obviously be absurd if oil in drums, which were part of the ship's stores, could be sold as part of the *res* and oil in the tanks could not. Ship's stores have always been sold by the Admiralty Marshal for the benefit of claimants *in rem*.

[Counsel] advanced an argument that in principle the bunkers cannot be part of the ship. He submitted that if bunkers are part of the ship, then a maritime lien would attach to the bunkers whenever the circumstances gave rise to such a lien. That argument imports a logical nicety which is inappropriate to the nature of a maritime lien. The inchoate right which attaches to a ship in favour of the lienor (e.g., the owner of another ship damaged in collision) is not perfected until the moment of arrest. A ship which is damaged in collision is frequently repaired before there is an opportunity to arrest her. She is then more valuable than when the lien attached. On the other hand, she may have had to engage salvage tugs to enable her to reach port. The salvors would have a lien taking priority over the lien for collision damage. The claimant with a maritime lien takes the vessel as he finds her at the moment when he is able to exercise his lien.

I have considered the submissions made by [Counsel] from another angle. If [Counsel] were right in his submission that bunker oil is not part of the ship for the purposes of an action *in rem*, the question would arise as to what is to happen to the proceeds of sale of that oil. [Counsel] submitted that those

[20] (1811) 1 Dods. 292.

proceeds must be paid into a separate fund in Court, which would be available for attachment by anyone who can get a judgment *in personam* against the owners of the ship. But shipowners have their registered offices in many different cities all over the world. Not every creditor is able to obtain a judgment *in personam* against a foreign company. Thus, for example, many Admiralty actions arise out of collisions on the high seas. An action to enforce a claim for damage arising out of a collision between ships is specifically excluded from the cases covered by R.S.C. Order 11, r. 1(1). Therefore if a ship is arrested in such an action and "the ship" does not include bunker oil (or other property of her owner), there would be no way of attaching that property even if the judgment remained unsatisfied.

Finally, I consider the practical realities. If the proceeds of sale of the oil are not part of the *res*, it would follow that in every case in which a ship is sold by the Court there would be money in Court which would not be available to judgment creditors *in rem*.

Accordingly, in my judgment the proceeds of sale of the oil are part of the *res* and, as such, available to judgment creditors *in rem*.

INDEX